**Organisation and Management
in the Public Sector**

Organisation and Management in the Public Sector

SECOND EDITION

Alan Lawton · Aidan G. Rose

PITMAN
PUBLISHING

PITMAN PUBLISHING
128 Long Acre, London WC2E 9AN

A Division of Longman Group Limited

First published in 1991
Second edition 1994

© A Lawton and A G Rose 1991, 1994
A CIP catalogue record for this book can be obtained from the British Library.
ISBN 0 273 60191 1

Transferred to digital print on demand, 2002

Printed & Bound by Antony Rowe Ltd, Eastbourne

The Publishers' policy is to use paper manufactured from sustainable forests.

We dedicate this book to the memory of
our friend and colleague Alan Parker, and to Vicky,
Dominic and Freya.

CONTENTS

14 Conclusion   **212**

Introduction • The changing environment • A change in culture • The sceptic's response • Round and round again? • The quality orientation • The European dimension • Summary

PREFACE

Public sector organisations carry out their activities in a constantly changing environment. As new legislation is passed, as new ideas gain prominence or as new politicians gain power then changes in the size, scope and functions of the public sector can be anticipated. This second edition brings the reader up to date on some of these changes and how they have impacted upon the management of public sector organisations. Some of the changes that we highlighted in the first edition have also worked their way through the public sector more fully and three years on it is easier to assess their impact. Purchaser–provider splits are now common, quality is being pursued vigorously, and market principles are being applied to many activities.

We have increased the length of the book allowing a more in-depth treatment of many of the issues. We have also added an extra chapter that focuses upon the role of the manager. As public sector organisations strive to become more responsive to the customer, client or user of services then this has implications for the management task. The implementation of changes is achieved through middle and junior managers and through front-line staff. In order for implementation to be successful then managers need to be involved in, and consulted about, decisions concerning organisational changes and attention needs to be paid to their needs as well as the needs of those who receive services.

The student on a course studying public sector organisations is faced with a bewildering range of literature. In recent years the volume of books, articles, journals and papers that feature on reading lists seems to have grown exponentially. In adding to this we seek to provide a book which, firstly, introduces the reader to the theoretical literature on organisations, and secondly, applies that literature to the modern British public sector. The book is intended for teachers and students on undergraduate degree courses, BTEC Higher National programmes, and on professional courses such as the Institute of Chartered Secretaries and Administrators (ICSA).

Chapter 1 examines the development of the modern public sector and explores some of the features which distinguish the public sector from the private sector. It also introduces the concept of public sector management.

Chapter 2 explores a number of values and concepts that are of particular importance in the public sector, in particular, the distinction between policy and administration, and the notion of accountability.

Chapter 3 examines the idea of bureaucracy, its features and how it has been used in modern public sector organisations. The literature on the dysfunctions of bureaucracy is also considered.

In Chapter 4 we look at formal approaches to organisations. The chapter includes discussion of the work of the classical school of management, and systems and contingency theories of organisations, and goes on to examine the formal expression of organisational structures in terms of organisational charts.

Following this, Chapter 5 examines the informal side of organisations, the importance of the individual, groups, culture and discretion.

Chapter 6 discusses power and conflict. Theories of power within society are examined alongside power within organisations. Power in the context of decision making is analysed as is the notion of conflict characterising organisations.

Chapter 7 examines the leadership factor, theories of leadership and what is expected of a leader in the public sector.

In Chapter 8 theories of motivation are linked to psychological explanations of individual behaviour examined in Chapter 5.

Chapter 9 looks at planning and decision making. It examines prescriptions as to how organisations should plan and decide and also looks at how they behave in practice.

Chapter 10 is concerned with resourcing the public sector. It includes three case studies on central government, local government, and the National Health Service.

Chapter 11 brings together a number of themes which can collectively be called the 'new agenda' for the public sector. It examines the idea of how organisations respond to change in theory and returns to the theme of public management that was introduced in the first chapter.

Chapter 12 examines how public sector organisations have responded to the new agenda through the commitment to a number of themes such as consumerism. It also looks at the proposition that a new orientation has taken place within public sector organisations.

Chapter 13 focuses on the management task in the public sector. It examines the relevance of generic management competences and highlights some of the challenges that are facing public sector managers.

Chapter 14 examines some current themes which seem likely to be of continuing importance in the 1990s. It also raises doubts concerning the scope of, and commitment to, the changes that we examine in Chapters 11 and 12.

At the end of the book we provide a section that, we hope, will be of particular help to the reader. In Appendix A we provide a guide for further study. This is intended to supplement the guides to further reading provided at the end of each chapter by listing potential sources of information which are likely to help the reader regarding current and future developments. Secondly, Appendix B offers some exercises which will enable the reader to apply the material covered in the book.

We owe a debt to numerous people. In particular we wish to mention students on public administration courses at Teesside Polytechnic between 1982 and 1988; those at the University of Northumbria at Newcastle (formerly Newcastle Polytechnic) since 1987; and those at the University of Glamorgan since 1988. A number of colleagues at those institutions have also provided valuable assistance and comment on drafts: they include Eileen Gill, Paul Griffiths, Paul McGregor (now at North Tyneside College) and Anthea West. We have also benefited from the assistance of some first-class librarians, including Austin McCarthy, and the staff in the Government Publications Centre at the University of Northumbria. We are also indebted to the many anonymous civil servants and local government officers who have provided useful material. Although we could not have completed the book without the help of all these people, as well as the assistance and persistence of Penelope Woolf at Pitman Publishing, we remain responsible for any inaccuracies, errors and omissions.

Finally we wish to thank Gillian who suffered our disruptions for longer than she ought to have done.

CHAPTER 1

The public sector

INTRODUCTION

This book is about organisation and management in public sector organisations. It is about how such organisations are structured, what people do in them, why people do what they do and how all of these things have changed over the years. How do we find out about such organisations? Approaches to the study of public administration reflect different academic disciplines including economics, sociology, psychology and politics. Any examination of organisation theory and its application will make extensive use of a variety of academic disciplines. These different disciplines will offer differing and often competing ideas which need to be examined, analysed and criticised.

The study of public sector organisations is made all the more complex and thought-provoking because of the competition of ideas between different academic and political standpoints. Added to this is the input from those who actually practise administration or management, giving us a 'real world' perspective. This essential input often gives us insider accounts of a world which, in a system where much work of government is conducted away from the public gaze, we are not normally privileged to see. Diaries and essays, such as Richard Crossman's political diaries (1979) or the work of Sir Geoffrey Vickers (1965), have made substantial contributions to the literature on public sector organisations. However, the reader must be prepared to treat some insider accounts with a certain amount of scepticism. Authors may be bitter because of personal experience, they may be members of a sectional interest group, or may simply be biased or malicious. Perhaps it is better to ask a few simple questions about anything that is written: Who wrote it? What is their background? Why did they write it? What did they seek to achieve? Who published it and why?

In recent years there has been a vigorous and often heated debate about how public administration courses should be taught. One school of thought has maintained that courses should place a strong emphasis on scholarship, academic training and a liberal education. Thus, many degree level courses in public administration begin with a year studying the disciplines of the social and political sciences, typically politics, economics, sociology, psychology and research methodology. This is then followed by courses in administrative structures, organisation theory and policy making which integrate and apply much of the literature from the disciplines introduced in the first year.

The alternative approach is to suggest that courses should equip the student with the skills and techniques of administration. Such courses would stress communication skills, problem solving and the mastery of techniques such as cost-benefit analysis and project planning. The major proponent of such an approach has been the Business and Technology Education Council which set out detailed guidelines for public administration courses based on providing the student with the knowledge and skills to make a contribution to the world of work.

Within the former approach, the study of public sector organisations has been underpinned by a concern with a number of approaches. Firstly, as Butcher (1984) points out, it has been approached through the study of public institutions such as the civil service, the National Health Service and local government. The concern has been with how they are structured and what people do in these organisations. This method, known as the public administration approach, was dominated by respect for the importance of the Westminster model of government and the role of administrative and constitutional law. Though few texts reflect this approach today, Greenwood and Wilson (1989) provide a review of many of the major issues. We assume that the reader has a basic knowledge of the structures of the institutions we discuss in this book.

Secondly, the study of public sector organisations has focused on the structure of organisations, how people behave in them, what motivates employees in these organisations and so on. It is this approach that we examine in the early chapters of this book.

Thirdly, such organisations have been studied from the perspective of decision making. Consideration is given to how public policies are made and put into action. This approach examines how policy is influenced, how decisions came to be made, how they are put into effect and how they are reviewed. The public policy approach is considered in such texts as Burch and Wood (1990), Hogwood (1987) and Hogwood and Gunn (1984).

Sources of information on public sector organisations are nothing if not diverse and the unfamiliar reader is likely to be bewildered by the range of sources available. In Appendix A we provide guidance on gathering information about current and future developments in and about public sector organisations.

PROBLEMS OF DEFINITION

So far we have assumed that there is something called the public sector that is waiting to be studied. However, defining public sector organisations is not always easy. Certain organisations, for example government departments and local authorities, are obviously part of the public sector while others are not. We would not consider McDonald's or the local newsagent as part of the public sector. But the language that we use in describing the public sector sometimes only serves to confuse. We have public schools that are private schools and which are subsidised. In the civil service we find administrators who now call themselves managers who are accountable to senior officials known as secretaries who may not know one end of a typewriter keyboard from the other.

The careless use of language can also serve to confuse. The term 'opting out' when used in relation to hospitals or schools misleadingly implies to many that there is the possibility of transfer from the public sector to the private sector. What is actually meant is opting out from an existing form of administration rather than a complete transfer from one sector to the other.

More importantly, there is a grey area where organisations may not obviously belong to one sector or another. For example, is an industry in the public sector if the government owns 51 per cent of the shares and in the private sector if the government owns 49 per cent of the shares? If a local authority provides 100 per cent funding for, say, a law centre, is it a public sector organisation or a voluntary body if it relies, in part, on voluntary workers? Is a committee consisting of civil servants and representatives from industry a public sector committee or not? The examples will continue to multiply as long as public sector organisations, however defined, continue to engage in partnership and joint ventures with the private sector.

Increasingly, public sector organisations have been encouraged to change their role from the provider of services to the monitoring of other organisations that actually deliver those services. This is particularly true of local authorities which are encouraged by central government to deliver services through the voluntary or private sector. Public sector managers are acquiring the role of monitoring other organisations and developing skills in managing contracts. The development of such arrangements is blurring the boundary between the public and other sectors.

Not only is it the case that the distinction between the public sector and other sectors is becoming increasingly blurred, it is also becoming increasingly difficult to define who exactly is the recipient of the products and services of the public sector. Is there a difference between the citizen, client, customer, consumer or user? There is a tendency to use these terms indiscriminately, and yet is the customer of social services the same as the customer of the local supermarket? Can the customer of social services exercise consumer choice and go elsewhere?

Such definitional and conceptual problems are compounded when we consider who public services are provided for. This appears to be relatively straightforward; for example, it might be argued that education is provided for pupils. But we might want to consider the views of parents who have a vested interest in their child's education; the views of the business community which may desire a better-educated workforce; the views of citizens generally who desire to live in a society where education is deemed to be important in developing social and communal obligations. A major feature of the public sector is that many individuals or groups may have a stake in what it does. These will include the users of services, those who pay for them through taxation, politicians, managers, local communities and so on. The public sector is characterised by a multiplicity of different stakeholders, all of whom may have a legitimate interest in its performance.

It is clear that we are more concerned with certain organisations such as government departments, local authorities and the National Health Service.

However, we do not seek to provide a hard and fast definition. Rather, we ask the reader to consider the influence of a number of themes that we consider in the book such as the impact of the political process and the role of politicians, public accountability, bureaucratic organisation, finance and so on.

THE SIZE AND SCOPE OF THE PUBLIC SECTOR

Before the industrial revolution the family, a private sector organisation, was both a unit of production and of consumption. The family as a unit produced food, clothes and shelter prior to the consumption of those goods. The family provided social services such as care for the elderly and education. The mass move to the Victorian cities resulted in pressure for services to be provided on a collective basis. The period from the late nineteenth century until 1945 saw the state take on and develop new functions. From 1945 until the mid-1970s there was perceived by many to be a broad consensus that the overall balance between the public and private sectors was about right. Since the mid-1970s there has been a vigorous debate about the proper size and role of the public sector. In no small way we may have come full circle when the then Prime Minister, Mrs Thatcher, urged families to care for the elderly instead of relying on the state to provide homes for the elderly.

The size, scope and operation of the public sector are at the heart of the debate about the success of the economy, the nature of community relations, the state of law and order and defence, the cultural climate and the freedom of the individual. If schools are unable to recruit teachers it may affect the quality of the workforce in the future. The values of the police officer may affect the relationship between minority groups and the penal system. Investment in the arts can serve to improve our broader cultural education. Remote bureaucracies may mean that individuals are unable to get access to, or influence, services.

The scope of government activity is extensive. In the United Kingdom central government departments are concerned with overseas affairs and defence, welfare functions, economic affairs including trade and industry, the environment, transport, employment and agriculture. Most western developed nations will have similar functions as part of central government remit. Local government will have responsibility for welfare, including social services, parts of education, the local environment, economy and leisure, public health and local planning. Of course, the exact responsibilities of central and local government will vary from country to country but all of the above activities will be the responsibility of one tier of government or another. In different countries the relationship between central and local government will vary and the amount of power that each has will not be the same. The United Kingdom is an example of strong central control in central government.

Apart from the scope of government activities the scale will also be significant. In the United Kingdom, for example, approximately one in five of those employed actually work in the public sector. There are some half a million civil servants, nearly a million working in the National Health Service and some 2,250,000 in local government. If those working in public corporations, the armed forces and nationalised industries are added, over five million people work in the public sector. Government is big business.

Writers concerned about the growth of the state have attempted to measure that growth. Different measures have been constructed including changes in revenues to the government, changes in the expenditure of the government, the number of people employed by the government, the extent of service provision and counts of the numbers of laws passed (see Taylor, 1983). While all measures are ultimately unsatisfactory, Schmidt concludes that 'The role of government in most advanced industrial democracies increased dramatically in the three decades following World War II', and that: 'The major component of this expansion was growth in welfare expenditure' (Schmidt, 1983, p. 261).

Various explanations have been offered as to why this is the case. These include:

- the public sector expands in direct relation to the expansion in the economy as a whole;
- tax systems which rely on indirect taxation and insurance contributions encourage growth;
- politicians try to maximise votes and promise spending at election time, and frequent elections, therefore, encourage growth;
- bureaucrats have a vested self-interest in expanding the size of the agencies they work in;
- economies unable to maintain full employment tend to have large public sectors because of the need for income support programmes (see Schmidt, 1983).

Although it is not our intention or our purpose to engage in a critical examination of the growth of public sectors throughout the industrialised world, it is worth making a number of points which arise from the literature that will be examined in later chapters. Firstly, we cannot consider the public sector in isolation. We must view it in the context of the economic environment and economic performance of the country. As we shall see, the economic problems precipitated by the oil crises of the 1970s were to have a dramatic impact upon public sector management in the 1980s. Secondly, the nature and extent of the democratisation of the political system will be reflected in the organisation and extent of the public sector. Perceived inadequacies in the system of representative government have resulted in alternative forms of citizen representation such as the ombudsman, consumer councils and the customer evaluation of performance. Thirdly, the behaviour of politicians and officials can determine whether or not organisations grow. Politicians may promise higher levels of service provision in return for votes, and the internal structures and processes of public sector organisations may encourage officials to fight to increase their share of budgets rather than be interested in saving money.

PUBLIC AND PRIVATE ORGANISATIONS

The year 1979 saw the election of a Prime Minister and a government that was committed to 'rolling back the frontiers of the state'. This was to take a number of forms:

- reduced expenditure on the public services allowing income tax to be reduced;
- taking out of state control companies and industries that it was felt ought to be in the private sector;
- the sale of assets such as council houses;
- exposing services to competition.

There were both political and economic reasons for this commitment to limit the role of the state. The Conservative Party believes in the pursuit of individualism and the freedom of choice rather than state provision or collectivism. At the same time an increase in the number of people owning their own homes or shares would do the Party no harm at the ballot box. From an economic point of view, reducing the burden of state ownership would, it was felt, allow cuts in income tax. There was also the belief that exposing nationalised industries or local authorities to the competitive marketplace would increase their efficiency. The culture of the private sector would, it was felt, lead to a more efficient and effective public sector. As we shall see later, this belief translates into attempts to introduce the practices and techniques of private sector managers into the public sector. To what extent, though, is the public sector like the private sector? Opinion seems to be divided between those who argue that the public sector is unique and operates under different conditions than the private sector. More recently this conventional wisdom has been questioned, with writers stressing similarities and arguing that increasingly any differences between the two sectors are becoming blurred.

The public sector is unique

A range of arguments have been advanced to indicate the uniqueness of the public sector:

- public sector organisations are not exposed to the competitive world of the market and hence have no incentives to reduce costs or operate efficiently;
- objectives are usually ill-defined and expressed in vague terms such as serving the public, maintaining law and order, reducing inequality, reducing poverty or improving health;
- strategic planning is more difficult because of the short-term considerations of politicians;
- the public sector organisation is susceptible to greater and more open accountability with politicians, pressure groups, taxpayers and voters all having an interest in the performance of the public sector;
- the functions of the public sector are limited by statute;

- the public sector is funded by taxation and not by charging for its services;
- certain goods have to be provided by the state. Defence, law and order and street lighting are consumed collectively and are, in theory, equally available to all. The provision of such 'public goods' cannot be left to the vagaries of the market.

The public and private sectors are converging

Critics of the above view hold that increasingly such distinctions are becoming blurred and we should recognise the similarities:

- increasingly the public sector charges for some of its services, for example through increased prescription charges or charges for leisure facilities;
- the private sector also operates within a political environment as decisions made by politicians to. for example, keep interest rates high will have a profound effect upon the very existence of some firms faced with high borrowing costs and reduced sales;
- the activities of the private sector are also constrained by statute as firms are regulated over unfair trading practices, health and safety at work or environmental pollution;
- public and private partnerships have developed over urban redevelopment where groups such as *Business in the Community* have promoted private sector involvement at local levels.

Thus, it is often difficult to distinguish clearly between the two sectors and it may be more fruitful to examine organisational differences in terms of size, decision-making processes, structure and management style rather than concentrate upon which sector the organisation is in (see Howells, 1981).

A management study of the service offered by government departments to the public undertaken by the Cabinet Office also included research on private sector organisations. It concluded that:

> Comparison with the private sector has to be treated with caution. In the private sector there is a direct relationship between commercial success – as measured by profitability and market share – and the standard of customer service. The public sector position is more complicated and in many instances distinctly different. In general the reasons for providing a service in the first place, the nature of that service and the manner in which it is delivered, are not dictated by markets. In these circumstances the balance between public expectations and the level of service to be provided is decided on the basis of political judgements about economic and social priorities. All that said, those who execute public service functions have a professional responsibility to do so to the highest standards of service possible, within the given level of resources, and this is what civil servants want to achieve. (Cabinet Office, 1988, para 1.5, p. 2.)

Such sentiments could be applied to any part of the public sector and the issues that the quote raises are issues that we address throughout this book.

FROM PUBLIC ADMINISTRATION TO PUBLIC MANAGEMENT

In recent years many writers and practitioners have considered the changes in the organisation and the management of public services and have sought to reflect those changes by using the term 'public management'. Evidence of this can be seen by the change in the name of organisations such as the Institute of Health Service Administrators to the Institute of Health Service Managers. Many courses taught at colleges and universities which were referred to by titles such as Public Administration, Public Sector Studies or Public Policy Studies now find that the word management is creeping into the title. Whether this reflects profound changes in the syllabus or is a marketing ploy is open to debate.

A typical definition of an administrator might include the following of rules and regulations, the carrying out of decisions that are taken by others, following routines, bureaucratic, risk-avoiding and so on. In contrast management is seen as dynamic, entrepreneurial, innovative, flexible and so on. In reality those working in the public sector will, depending upon the organisation, their role and responsibilities within it, combine a number of the above characteristics. We examine such characteristics in Chapter 13.

Although our primary focus is the United Kingdom. we note that many of the issues concerning public sector management are not UK specific. For example, the Organisation for Economic Co-operation and Development (OECD, 1992) carried out a survey of twelve of its members including Finland, Greece, Turkey, the USA, New Zealand and the UK and noted a number of general themes emerging:

- a move away from central government to more localised forms of government;
- an increasing role for the not-for-profit sector in the provision of services;
- increase in the use of the private sector for delivering services;
- central government taking on a more strategic role;
- increasing awareness of costs and the need to examine alternatives to central taxation as the main revenue.

These themes are being translated into greater openness in how government works, greater involvement for clients and users, increasing flexibility to meet the needs of individual clients, improved physical access to government, and more information about government (see Ormond, 1993). We examine the UK response to these developments in Chapters 11, 12 and 13.

CONCLUSION

The focus of this book is on the organisation and management of public sector organisations rather than on the environment within which such organisations operate. Any organisation has to cope with its external environment and to changes within that environment. Managers have to respond to such changes as do organisations if they are to survive and prosper. Whether the changes in the environment are caused by commercial or legislative pressures, managers have to adapt and to operate with uncertainty.

Managers working in the public sector in the UK have, in recent years, experienced changes in the structures of their organisations, in organisational processes and in working practices. Perhaps the biggest challenge has come from sceptical politicians and members of the public who have a perception of inefficient bureaucrats unresponsive to their needs. The manager in the public services operates within the goldfish bowl of public scrutiny and accountability.

Whatever the changes in structure, operating environment, processes, functions and so on a more fundamental change is required in the values and beliefs that managers hold. To move from an administrator to a manager involves more than a change of title. It is to these values that we now turn our attention.

FURTHER READING

Greenwood and Wilson (1989) set the context of public administration in Britain in Chapter 1. Many of the issues concerning the differences and similarities between the public and private sectors are to be found in the collection of essays edited by Perry and Kraemer (1983). A commentary on the different approaches is to be found in Gunn (1987). A short synopsis of some of the issues is to be found in Dopson and Stewart (1990). Fuller treatment of the arguments surrounding the size of the public sector are to be found in Taylor (1983).

CHAPTER 2

Values and concepts

INTRODUCTION

The aim of this chapter is to introduce a number of concepts essential to the study of public sector organisations. In particular, we are concerned with the values of the administrator and with the impact of political values on the public sector. Implicit in such a discussion is that there is a division between politics and administration and that one activity is performed by politicians and the other by officials. We need to examine whether this demarcation exists in practice or whether the roles of politicians and officials are more complex than this contention implies.

VALUES IN ADMINISTRATION

It is important to understand the idea of values. Values can underpin the thinking of those involved in the provision of services and dictate the nature of what they provide, how they provide it and to whom they provide the services. It is expected that politicians will bring political values to the process. For example, Labour politicians have traditionally emphasised ideas such as a more equal distribution of wealth, democracy and participation, while Conservative politicians have tended to emphasise ideas such as market freedom, enterprise and self-help. These will, of course, change from time to time and from place to place. Equally, we can identify administrative values which will be generated by administrative cultures and will also be subject to change.

Accountability can ensure legal and financial rectitude and expresses the need for public bodies to reflect the demands which society makes on it for honesty and freedom from corruption. In certain societies levels of political and administrative corruption exist and are often tolerated. As we shall see, British administration prides itself on its honesty and lack of corruption.

It is argued by Stanyer and Smith (1976, p. 31) that 'public services are generally provided under the imperative of equality; that is, public bodies are expected to treat everyone equally'. However, it is difficult to establish what this means on a case by case basis: they cite the example of payments of cash benefits where everyone should be treated on an equal basis. Other examples reveal that equality may not always be easy to define. For instance, over recent years it has become clear that different police forces have adopted different policies with regard to the possession of small quantities of cannabis for personal use – some caution offenders while others refer for prosecution. Equally, health service statistics reveal that waiting lists for particular operations in some areas are considerably longer than in other areas. Thus because of the decentralisation of administration, people in similar circumstances in different areas can expect to receive a different service.

With the benefit of hindsight – and in the light of the debates of the 1980s – the term *equality* or making people equal or uniform might be better substituted by the term *equity*, a term which relates more closely to fairness in the application of rules. A problem arises with officers who are in a position to exercise discretion or make judgements in order to arrive at a decision. We have to consider what guidance these officers need in order to arrive at those decisions – should general rules be established or should they be allowed to use discretion?

Consider the example of the housing allocations officer who has to make a decision about the allocation of housing for three families, one black and two white, only one of which, in the opinion of social services, urgently needs long-term accommodation. There are two permanent allocations available. Let us assume that the allocations officer is prejudiced and actively dislikes black people and allocates the two white families. Clearly this is not the sort of conduct that society expects of our public servants. This requires us to consider how this problem can be countered. Perhaps the answer lies in the values of the organisation: if individuals who are able to exercise discretion identify with the values of the organisation rather than their personal motives then we will achieve not only organisational effectiveness but also, in this extreme case, fairness and equity (see Simon, 1976, Chapter 10).

It is impossible to make broad generalisations because of the diversity of public sector organisations in terms of the number of decision-making or rule-making bodies and the range of activities carried out. Law is often specific to particular types of organisations, for example local government or the health service, and can only be applied to those bodies. Organisational rules are made by individual bodies and will, of course, vary from body to body: with more than 400 local authorities in England alone we can expect up to 400 different sets of rules about how to go about doing business. Organisations and groups in organisations develop their own cultures, norms and values and these will influence the eventual products or outputs of the organisation. The diversity of the public sector means that there will be extensive variations in practice and it is therefore impossible to formulate general rules. Values in the public sector can be seen, in part, as a function of the values of society in general such as they can be defined.

Christopher Hood (1991) presents the view that there are different 'families' of values associated with the public services. He identifies three sets of values in particular:

- *Sigma-type values* characterised as 'keep it lean and purposeful'. This set of values is concerned with economy and efficiency, matching resources to

narrowly defined tasks. The criterion of success is based on limiting the resources required to achieve given goals.
- *Theta-type values* which are concerned with 'keeping it honest and fair'. These values may be appropriate in maintaining the tradition of a public service ethos. Openness and independent scrutiny are key principles.
- *Lambda-type values* characterised as 'keeping it robust and resilient'. The concern is with the ability of the organisation to service catastrophes and breakdowns, to develop as a learning organisation and avoid paralysis in the face of challenge or threat.

However, it is possible to identify certain ideas that have underpinned administrative thinking in Britain.

Trust

A feature of the British system of government is the relationship between the official and the politician. As we shall see in a later section of this chapter, the convention is that of the official serving the politician and offering information and advice. In return the politician defends the official. For example, in central government the convention of ministerial responsibility protects the official from the public eye.

Another aspect of trust is that between the officials themselves. Heclo and Wildavsky's (1981) study of the Treasury suggests that Whitehall is one big village where everybody knows everybody else and trust is the currency which the inhabitants of the village deal in. Trust is something that builds up over time and is based upon the expectations that individuals have of each other. Newly elected politicians may have to take their officials 'on trust' as they have had little opportunity to build up relationships with them. Officials will have their expectations of politicians which may include providing strategic direction, supporting officials in dealings with other departments or the media, or not interfering in day-to-day operations. Politicians will expect appropriate advice and information. Trust is not written down in official documents describing the roles and responsibilities of politicians and officials; it has to be earned and can be easily forfeited.

Neutrality

The tradition is that of the official not taking sides but offering impartial advice. Personal beliefs are suspended in order that the official can deal with any political master. Later we discuss the impact of thinking about human relations which could lead us to question whether the idea of neutrality ever existed in practice.

Neutrality can be linked to trust. Where the official is perceived to be offering partial advice or submitting misleading information the politicians may wonder to what extent they are receiving bias-free advice.

Probity

The tradition is that of officials serving the public as guardians of the public purse, charged with acting in the public interest rather than reflecting private interests. In Britain the official is deemed to be relatively incorruptible compared to counterparts elsewhere in the world where corruption amongst officials is common. Occasionally, we have cause to question the level of probity. The Poulson scandal which affected both local and central government in the early 1970s, the Wardale enquiry in 1983 into allegations of misconduct in the Property Services Agency, and allegations of corruption in the sale of cemeteries by Westminster Council (see the *Guardian*, 17 February 1990) serve as examples.

Professional honour

Unwritten codes of conduct for public officials include virtues such as loyalty, impartiality and pride in a job well done. Cricketing metaphors are used in Whitehall circles so that an individual who has a 'safe pair of hands' is approved of, as is somebody who 'is a team player' and 'goes into bat for the department'.

In a classic statement of the professional ethic of the administrator, Wilding includes: '. . . two spoonfuls each of honesty, tenacity and obedience; and one spoonful of humility' as part of the ingredients that go to make up this ethic (1979, p. 185).

The public official is expected to conform to the highest principles of the public service ethic and to put these principles above personal gain.

Permanence

A difference between senior officials in the United Kingdom and those, for example, in the United States of America, is that UK officials are non-elected and enter the organisation as a career. Thus there is a tradition of serving government rather than seeking short-term political gain.

Secrecy

It is impossible to leave our consideration of values without mentioning secrecy. While some of the former communist states of eastern Europe are opening personal files and military installations it is ironic that in Britain we have what is considered to be one of the most secretive systems of central government amongst Western democracies. It is dominated by the Official Secrets Act and the 'thirty-year rule' which prevents the release of certain government papers, such as minutes of Cabinet meetings, until at least thirty years have elapsed. Officials are constrained by the requirements of secrecy and the lack of openness of the organisation itself. Proponents of open government argue that as government becomes more open it will be more difficult to hide incompetence and error behind the cloak of secrecy. Government would thus become more accountable and the 'faceless bureaucrat' would become a thing of the past. In Sweden there is a right of public access, with certain constraints, to official documents. Similarly, in the United States of America, freedom of information legislation gives the individual the right to inspect certain files.

Local government is, in theory, more open since the Local Government (Access to Information) Act of 1985. The influence of the Prime Minister's Committee on Local Government Rules of Conduct (Redcliffe-Maud, 1974) and the Royal Commission on Standards of Conduct in Public Life (Salmon, 1976) led to local authorities refining procedures on conflict of interest. the receiving of gifts and hospitality from clients and so on (see Parker *et al.*, 1986).

Organisational values

The values that we have described as typically associated with administrative behaviour by individuals will be complemented by the values expressed by the organisation as a whole. Many organisations will have their own 'mission statements' which purport to characterise what kind of organisation they are, what their goals are, how they operate and what values underpin their activities. For example, Sandwell Metropolitan Borough Council is committed to the following values:

- The Council will always act legally.
- The Council will always act in a caring manner, and will be equally caring towards all of the people of Sandwell.
- The Council will be responsive to the needs, ideas and decisions of the people of Sandwell and will encourage their active participation.
- The Council will deliver its services in an effective and efficient manner and will ensure value for money. (Sandwell MBC 'Aims and Values'.)

Values will act different levels:

- at the political level – depending on the political, social and economic beliefs of the ruling party, these will provide a general context;
- some values may be suppressed by the organisation:
- the individual values of officials represent commitment to the prevailing principles of professional behaviour.

All of these will change over time, and some will be in conflict with each other. In the 1980s some Labour Party controlled local authorities refused to implement central government policies because such policies were incompatible with their own beliefs and values.

POLITICS AND THE POLICY/ADMINISTRATION DICHOTOMY

As we noted in the previous chapter, a distinguishing feature of the public sector is the existence of the political dimension. Politicians will bring political demands to the process just as consumers make economic demands in the market-place. These will reflect the values and policies of the politicians which we discussed in the previous section. For example, Labour politicians commonly emphasise the provision of welfare services and equity in the provision of those services, while Conservative politicians may place emphasis on law and order and the control of overall public expenditure as a political priority. As Peter Self has argued, one of the problems that the public sector faces is trying to limit demand for services where there is potentially infinite demand such as with health care:

> An imperative of business efficiency – some would say its first rule – is market *innovation*. New products must be developed which consumers want sufficiently to yield a profit. But in government the problem is more one of market *compression*. Administrative controllers must somehow weed out the surplus of political demands for expenditure as best they may. (Self, 1977, p. 267.)

It should be noted that certain policy areas and activities are often exposed to close political scrutiny, for example schools or social services, while others – such as the security services – are relatively insulated from scrutiny by politicians.

In the section on accountability below we will discuss the significance of this in terms of the demands that politicians make. Then we will look at the potential conflict between the policies of politicians which reflect convictions and values and possibly enhance their electoral prospects, and the administrative and management mechanisms that exist to further rational and efficient government. We need first to consider the roles that politicians and administrators play. In doing so, we are concerned with what actually happens in practice rather than making any normative statements about what politicians and administrators should do.

Orthodox views of the way in which public sector bodies work tell us that it is the role of politicians to make policy. They will do this with the help and advice of officials and a knowledge of the views of their constituents and pressure groups. Although the constitutional position is that Parliament is a sovereign body, the literature on the subject informs us that, in practice, the powers of Parliament have declined over the last hundred years to a point where one writer on the subject, Philip Norton (1985), terms it as 'policy peripheral'. While this may be the case when a government has a small majority, if Parliament is at the margins of policy making then we need to look further to establish the locus of decision making. The politicians who form the government of the day are assisted by a body of permanent officials – civil servants. We need to examine the relationship between the elected politicians and the appointed civil servants. To do this, it is helpful to look at a set of models developed by Aberach *et al.* (1981). Table 2.1 indicates the four basic images of administrators that the models identify. Image 1 administrators reflect the view that firstly there is a clear distinction between policy and administration, and secondly that it is established practice that politicians have exclusive control over the making of policy and that administrators have exclusive control over administration. Such a distinction may have been applicable at one time, but with the complexities of modern government this simplistic distinction no longer applies. Politicians will often take a detailed interest in the implementation of policy, so in addition to setting the broad parameters for education or transport policy, ministers may pay particular attention to, for example, an application by a school to opt out of local authority control or an application for a bypass round a rural village.

Table 2.1 Types of administrative actors

Image	Typology	Example
Image 1	Policy/administration dichotomy is an ideal and an empirical reality	Northcote Trevelyan blueprint for the civil service in the 1850s. Discredited view of contemporary patterns of policy making
Image 2	Career officials involved in policy, but restrict themselves to imparting relevant facts and knowledge	Orthodox description of minister–civil servant relations
Image 3	Any participation in policy making requires some level of political calculation and manipulation, but administrators eschew passionate commitment	Official identifies with policy but respects constitutional position
Image 4.1	Officials involved in defensive bureaucratic obstruction	'Yes Minister' civil servant
Image 4.2a	Officials involved in positive executive – bureaucratic government, have detailed policy knowledge. Proactive policy commitment	Professionally qualified officials, e.g. social workers, planners, architects, housing professionals
Image 4.2b	Officials identify with fortunes of specific political party	Downing Street Policy Unit members; advisers, politicians, etc.

Source: Adapted from Campbell and Guy Peters (1988).

Image 2 concedes that administrators will be involved in policy, but argues that their role will be restricted to providing politicians with the relevant facts and information. While there may be administrators that conform to this image, there is ample evidence available to suggest that administrators may identify with policies either on an individual or departmental basis.

Image 3 proposes that administrators are required to make political calculations either when dealing with politicians or when putting policies into practice. For example, when civil servants are drafting answers to parliamentary questions or providing advice to ministers, they take into account the likely response that ministers will make to that advice. The Clive Ponting case, when he alleged that civil servants were drafting misleading parliamentary answers relating to the sinking of the *General Belgrano* in the Falklands War, brings this point out clearly (Ponting, 1985).

However, this may not be a complete description of reality. There is evidence to suggest that officials may be more active in the role that they play. This brings us to Image 4. This model has been developed by Campbell and Guy Peters (1988) to distinguish between different types of administrators all of whom are active in policy making.

Many politicians have been highly critical of the way in which civil servants can obstruct the will of politicians. Accounts by (usually left wing) politicians with ambitions to reform government illustrate how their policies were frustrated by the unofficial policies of their departments (see Benn, 1980). The familiar process of the frustration of the will of the politician as satirised in *Yes Minister* and *Yes Prime Minister* illustrates Image 4.1. This is essentially a situation where administrators will receive a proposal from a minister and proceed to engage in defensive obstruction in order to maintain their interests. They are not initiating but reacting in a way that will attempt to preserve the status quo and the interests of the bureaucracy.

Image 4.2a is one where administrators are proactively engaged in policy making. Here, the expertise of officials and the situation in which they find themselves will allow them to play crucial roles in the development and execution of policy. An extreme example of this will be the security services who, according to the accounts of journalists such as Duncan Campbell and former security officials such as Peter Wright (1987) and Colin Wallace, are unaccountable and therefore make policy without reference to politicians. In local government, professional officers will have substantial expertise in their area of policy. As such they will play an important role in the shaping of policy before it is presented to local politicians.

In recent years we have seen a proliferation of policy advisers being recruited to central government and local government to provide advice direct to politicians. The Image 4.2b administrator will identify with the fortunes of the politician or party whom he or she serves. These officials have often been appointed by politicians frustrated by the obstruction of the administrative machine as an attempt to gain control over the process of policy making and administration (see Carvel, 1984, for Ken Livingstone's prescriptions from a left-wing point of view and Hoskyns, 1984, for a view from the right).

The four images of administrative actors are helpful in analysing what role the actors are playing. It is important to understand that different images will apply at different times and that the same person may play several roles depending on the situation. What the model does tell us is that the simple distinction between policy and administration is unrealistic. Although most detailed decisions do not become political matters, politicians can and do become involved in small and detailed administrative matters.

This serves to add to the complexity of our system of public administration. According to the orthodoxy, politics is a world normally inhabited by politicians with the values that they bring to the process typified by uncertainty and indeterminacy, whereas administration is a world inhabited by the administrator typified by rationality, routine and stability. Experience tells us that the reality is not as simple as that, and that in practice the two worlds are closely integrated and the possibility of distinguishing the ends which politicians want to reach from the means to achieve those ends is a remote one (see Self, 1977, Chapter 5).

ACCOUNTABILITY

Accountability is, of course, not exclusive to the public sector. Private sector organisations attach great importance to accountability as a method of examining how people discharge responsibility and the financial performance of the organisation. However, it has been argued that the concept of accountability takes on greater importance in the public sector for a number of reasons:

- Public sector organisations are the guardians of monies collected through taxation and policies approved through the democratic processes, and the public demand that those responsible for public monies and public policies present a public account of their activities.
- Because of the responsibilities entrusted to public servants, we expect high standards of conduct from them. These standards will cover the way in which they spend money, the way in which policy is determined and put into practice, and sometimes even the way in which they conduct their private lives.
- The goals of private sector organisations may be much more precise and more widely understood than those in the public sector. A characteristic of public sector organisations is that they often have multiple goals which may conflict with each other. For example, the prison system has as two of its main tasks: 'to keep in custody, with such degree of security as is appropriate, having regard to the nature of the individual prisoner and his offence, sentenced prisoners for the duration of their offence . . .' and 'to provide for prisoners as full a life as is consistent with the facts of custody, in particular making

available the physical necessities of life; care for physical and mental health; advice and help with personal problems; work, education, training, physical exercise and recreation; and opportunity to practise their religion'. (Home Office, 1989b, p. 3.) There is potential for conflict between the first and second objective. The first is aimed at punishing the offender and protecting the rest of society from dangerous people, while the second is aimed at enhancing the quality of life for the offender with a view to effective rehabilitation.

Other reasons for understanding the concept of accountability are:

- The diversity of public sector organisations and the huge variations in the activities that they undertake mean that differing methods of accountability will apply in different situations. It is therefore difficult to generalise about the process of accountability in the public sector. The mechanisms of accountability in local authorities are different from those in central government, which in turn vary from those in the National Health Service. It is, however, possible to detect certain trends such as the increasing importance that is being attached to management accountability in all parts of the public sector.
- The scale of the public sector organisations, which are frequently large organisations with long chains of command, often present logistical problems in controlling the activities of those charged with putting policies into practice.

Accountability defined

Accountability is a process where a person or groups of people are required to present an account of their activities and the way in which they have or have not discharged their duties. They are required to present this account to a nominated person or agency. The way in which they present the account may be governed by a set of rules – written or unwritten – which may vary in sophistication. As we shall see, accountability is a complex phenomenon and operates in different ways in different circumstances.

To understand the concept of accountability we need to appreciate its different dimensions and the way in which these dimensions are applied to public sector organisations.

As members of the public, we *expect* our public servants, whether they are politicians or officials, to be accountable for the way in which they discharge the duties of their office. However, there are occasions when people are not held to account, or the scrutiny to which they are subjected is found wanting. For example, during recent years there has been much criticism about the lack of accountability of the security services such as MI5 which is responsible for internal security in this country. This is because Parliament has been unable effectively to scrutinise its work.

A Home Office scrutiny of the management and resourcing systems for the magistrates' courts pulled no punches:

There is no coherent management system for the service. At the national level, the role of the Home Office is so uncertain, and its powers so limited, that it might be truer to say that there are 105 local services, each run by a committee of magistrates. But the local structure is just as confused, with 285 justices' clerks enjoying a semi-autonomous status, under committees which are fundamentally ill-suited to the task of management. It is impossible to locate clear management responsibility or accountability anywhere in the structure. (Home Office, 1989a, para 4.)

Accountability can be linked to the concept of responsibility. As Day and Klein remind us: 'One cannot be accountable to anyone, unless one also has responsibility for doing something' (1987, p. 5). Simon *et al.* (1950) state that responsibility can be viewed in three ways:

- responsibility as legal authority – for example having responsibility for a job;
- responsibility as a moral obligation – the irresponsible parent may not fulfil his or her obligations to their children;
- responsibility as responsiveness to values – where a public servant is charged with carrying out the wishes of others with particular reference to the values that are held by those charging the servant with carrying out the function.

Taking the third of these approaches, accountability can be defined as 'those methods, procedures and forces that determine what values will be reflected in administrative decisions. Accountability is the enforcement of responsibility'. (Simon *et al.*, 1950, p. 513.)

In other words, when studying public sector organisations, we are concerned about accountability as a method of achieving responsive government and administration. As we know, accountability works in different ways in different situations. However, we can develop our understanding of the concept by following a framework set out by Gray and Jenkins (1985). They maintain that in any accountability relationship there are two actors or sets of actors: the *steward* and the *accountees*. The steward entrusts an actor or a set of actors with responsibility for resources or responsibilities or both. Those charged with that responsibility are known as the accountees who, usually in return for a reward, will be required to present an account of the way in which they have discharged their responsibilities.

The nature of the account will depend on the *code of accountability*. The code, which is a set of guidelines for the conduct of stewardship, will vary from one situation to another. For example, accountants have a rigid code (Financial Reporting Standards) governing the way in which accounts are presented and financial information is used, while the code by which the public holds local government councillors to account is imprecise and subject to definition by individual electors. Indeed the evidence available to us through empirical studies shows that voters in local elections 'tell us very little indeed, if anything at all, about citizen preferences on specifically local matters' (Newton, 1976, p. 29) and that '80 per cent of voters at local elections vote in accord with their national party choice' (Miller, 1986, p. 172).

When an account is presented, the steward should have the power to pass judgement on the way in which the duties have been discharged. As we have pointed out above, accountability is normally seen as a positive exercise attempting to secure responsive administration, yet the process could ultimately result in the accountee being discharged of the responsibility.

Early forms of accountability concentrated on the way in which monies were spent and the question of whether the activities of organisations were within the law. There was concern about the misuse of public funds and bribery and thus rules were made to ensure the probity of organisations. Although, as we shall see, this concern has been a continuing one, the concept of accountability was to be refined.

Political accountability

More recent forms of accountability have concentrated on the political dimension. This manifested itself, for example, in the method of accountability that we expect to find in central government. The senior civil servant in the department – the Permanent Secretary – would be accountable to his or her minister. The minister, as a member of the Cabinet, will be accountable to Parliament for the discharge of office. This is known as the doctrine of Ministerial Responsibility, one of the conventions upon which our system of central government depends. The model assumes that powers are vested in the appropriate minister, with civil servants taking decisions in the name of the minister.

Such a system of accountability may have been appropriate in a time when the scale of the public sector was much smaller than today. In the twentieth century the growth of the state has meant that this model of accountability is no longer sufficient. Large government departments will make thousands of operational decisions and it is unrealistic to assume that ministers can be held responsible for, for example, the loss of a benefit claim form.

Therefore we have a much more complex system of accountability which has a number of dimensions. Under the model of Ministerial Responsibility, civil servants have traditionally been protected from public scrutiny. However, in recent years the faces of senior civil servants have become increasingly more visible with appearances before the departmental select committees to answer questions on behalf of their ministers and appearances in front of the Committee of Public Accounts as accounting officers of their departments.

As we have mentioned above, the criteria by which local electors hold local government councillors accountable is imprecise. This is not to state that the process is a static one – indeed it is subject to change over time. The Thatcher governments sought to make local authorities more accountable to their electorates through the implementation of the Community Charge or Poll Tax. Critics responded that charge payers were not fully made aware of the different charges set by counties and districts, and that Poll Tax capping was not necessary if enhanced local accountability was the overriding criterion for its implementation.

Managerial accountability

Perhaps the simplest way to distinguish between political accountability and managerial accountability is to see political accountability as involving an account being presented to an external and public audience while managerial accountability is concerned with the internal processes. This may involve a shift in the nature of the account from a potentially more global set of considerations to a more restricted set of considerations about how things are done with particular reference to organisational objectives and resource considerations. For example, the values that politicians possess have been superimposed on the process, the overall priorities set, and policy decisions made. The process moves on to issues such as how the policy should be put into practice, how this can be done within the available resources, and how the implementation of the policy is to be reviewed.

Managerial accountability is concerned with issues such as cost effectiveness, efficiency, budgetary control, monitoring performance and policy effectiveness. Systems of accountable management may be introduced to delegate responsibility to those nearest the point of service delivery, for example area office managers. This takes place on the assumption that those close to the point of delivery are best able to make decisions about service delivery. It involves making decisions including, for example, delegating powers such as viring money from one budget heading to another, promotion of staff, making of local rules and so on, further down the hierarchy.

It is unrealistic to pretend that policies are simply passed over to administrators who unproblematically put them into practice in strict accordance with the wishes of the politician. Instead the public sector contains large departments and agencies which play an important role in shaping the policies that are delivered at the end of the day. It is important that these agencies and the individuals and groups that make them up are held accountable for the tasks for which they are responsible.

As we have already noted, people working in public sector organisations are not neutral and do not blindly follow the wishes of their managers and political masters. The idea that administrators leave their political views, moral codes and values at home each morning is a view which is widely discredited. Instead, as human behaviourists argue, people and groups in organisations develop their own goals which may be incompatible with the goals of the organisation.

With the growth of the size of the public sector, there have been demands for greater managerial accountability in public sector organisations. This derives from the concern that in periods of budgetary growth new money allowed new activities to be undertaken without any questioning of whether existing activities were being performed as efficiently as possible or, indeed, if they were any longer necessary. In relation to the civil service, the Fulton Report (1968) argued that the service suffered from a lack of managerial accountability, with little awareness of the need to question activities or justify expenditure. Since Fulton, government has responded with a number of initiatives with varying degrees of success. These initiatives, which include Programme Analysis and Review (1970–1979), the Management Information System for Ministers (1980 and ongoing with different names in different departments), the Financial Management Initiative (1982 and ongoing), and most recently, the Next Steps (1988 and ongoing), are considered later in the book, especially Chapters 10, 11 and 12.

There is an inevitable tension between the demands for political accountability where control is exercised from the top down, often with layers of administration exercising supervisory functions, and managerial accountability where decisions are often delegated down the hierarchy as close as possible to the point of delivery. Decentralisation of decision making conflicts with the traditional requirement for control through hierarchical chains of command. A continuing tension exists between the need for control and the need for organisations to be responsive to their external environments. Where central government, for example, is concerned that local authorities should be more accountable for what they do and imposes charge-capping, national curricula and compulsory competitive tendering, then the ability of local authorities to respond to local citizens' requests may be reduced. Local accountability may be in tension with central accountability.

Added to this, managerial accountability may involve decisions based on assumptions about so-called rational management techniques based on a scientific study of work which may come into conflict with the demands of political accountability which involve the incorporation of values, party political considerations, convictions and prejudices which lack any rational foundation. For example, one of the most sensitive planning decisions in recent years has been the proposed location of the rail route from London to the Channel Tunnel. Rational techniques developed to aid decision making, in particular cost-benefit analysis, advanced the case for certain routes. However, the environmental impact of noise, redevelopment and disturbance to local communities led to the mobilisation of interest groups campaigning against those proposed routes. Members of Parliament, with constituencies in the affected areas, sensitive to the wishes of their local constituents (and their majorities in Parliament), were also articulate in their objections to the proposed routes.

A further problem needs to be considered when we look at nationalised industries. If the public sector engages in commercial operations such as producing motor cars or steel, there is a tension between the demands for public accountability and the needs for commercial confidentiality. If a state-owned car company is to compete on equal terms with car companies in the private sector, it will need to adopt the same principles of commercial confidentiality as its rivals. It will therefore wish to keep secret information on, for example, new product design and investment programmes if its competitors are not to gain an advantage. On the other hand, if government is subsidising the operation for economic or social reasons, politicians may demand an account of the performance of the company (see Curwen, 1986).

Accountability to the law

The actions of public sector organisations are subject to challenge in the courts of law. Many critics of our system of public administration believe that its actions are not subject to sufficient scrutiny and that the public need greater safeguards against the actions of the administration.

Since the end of World War II we have seen the development of judicial reviews of the decisions of government bodies. Central to this is the doctrine of *ultra vires* which limits the powers of public bodies to that which the law empowers them to do. Here the decisions of local authorities, ministers and so on can be challenged in the courts on the grounds that, for example, they have exceeded their powers.

Government is also subject to scrutiny over its proper discharge of public funds. The National Audit Office for central government and the Audit Commission for local authorities and the National Health Service in England and Wales carry out audits and value-for-money exercises. Public officials thus operate within a framework of controls.

However, these controls are sometimes not clear. There are areas of uncertainty. At the time of writing it is not clear how European law applies to the privatisation of public services. The European Acquired Rights Directive (1977) sets down rules to safeguard employees' rights when a new employer takes over the organisation they work for as in privatisation. When a Directive has been issued member states frame their own legislation to implement it. In the UK this was the Transfer of Undertakings (Protection of Employment) Regulations (TUPE) in 1981. Ministers have argued that the EU Directive does not apply to contracting out so that, for example, a private contractor could undercut a local council tender by employing people on less favourable terms and conditions. Local authorities and trade unions have argued that employee rights should be protected under the EU Directive. Confusion reigns, throwing into doubt market testing of central government services and contracting out.

Accountability to the consumer or client

As stated above, the doctrine of Ministerial Responsibility has been shown to be an unsatisfactory mechanism to question detailed administrative decisions. In response to demands for a more accountable administration, there has been a development in machinery through which individuals who feel aggrieved at the decisions of the administration can attempt to gain redress. In many cases there is the opportunity to appeal against an administrative decision to a tribunal. This opportunity exists if, for example, a planning application is refused or where an application for a social security benefit is denied.

During the 1960s there was sustained pressure for a mechanism which would allow members of the public with grievances relating to administrative decisions to pursue those complaints through ombudsmen. This was because of the sheer volume of administrative decisions taken by public sector organisations and the unsuitability of Parliament, the courts and tribunals as mechanisms for resolving those disputes. This pressure resulted in the creation of the Parliamentary Commissioner for Administration in 1967 and the Commissioners for Local Administration in 1974 who were given limited sets of powers to investigate complaints made by the public of maladministration by central and local government respectively. Similar machinery exists for the National Health Service.

Throughout the 1980s, public sector organisations were under attack for being unresponsive to the needs of consumers. Many critics argued that such organisations grew in size to serve their own interests rather than concentrating on financial control and meeting the needs of those to whom they are supposed to be providing a service. This criticism led many organisations to reconsider the way in which they organise and deliver the services they provide in order to be more accountable and responsive to their customers. Local authorities may be more responsive by adopting clear methods for the receipt and investigation of complaints by local people. Public housing organisations may become more responsive to tenants by ensuring more effective delivery of the service with decentralised local offices in easy reach of tenants or, to use the current language, customers. They can also make contracts with customers which include undertakings to complete repairs within a stated period or develop consultative networks to establish the needs and wants of customers and respond to them.

However, some critics argue that market accountability and accountability through contracts weakens public accountability generally. John Stewart (1992) has argued that increasing choice for customers and clients is, in practice, limited: parents can choose, within certain limits, a school for their child but what is studied is largely determined by central government. Similarly, Stewart argues that attempts to improve accountability through the use of contracts may be problematic where the contract is not legally enforceable or where responsibility is not clearly specified between the contractor and the client.

Professional accountability

The public sector employs many types of professionals for their expertise in specific areas of work. Professionals spend many years studying for qualifications in, for example, accountancy, law, architecture, engineering or social work. Sociologists have argued that this process of professional training together with the fact that they spend much of their working lives surrounded by people with similar qualifications means that they will absorb the values of the profession and see their reference group as their peers rather than their political masters. This may lead to distortions in policy, particularly in local government where professionals tend to assume dominant positions and can exercise considerable influence. It is quite possible that the wishes of political masters may be for one set of policy preferences while the professional group tend to prefer another. The resolution of this conflict may be in favour of the trends of the profession rather than those policies of the politicians – particularly when professional advancement and career development may be decided by fellow professionals in the broad professional community rather than by local politicians.

There are areas of work in the public sector where politicians may not wish to exercise direct political control, for example areas where professionals make scientific judgement about a particular issue such as safe levels of radiation for the public. Politicians may decline to question or comment on the appropriateness of such levels as this is seen as a matter of scientific rather than political judgement. Supporters of this view will maintain that there are matters which should be left to those who have the appropriate qualifications (an argument used to support the clinical judgement of doctors) whilst critics argue that such judgements involve moral judgements which should be subject to public accountability. For example, decisions on whether to deploy resources in the direction of one form of medical care rather than another should be subjected to political accountability.

An alternative view is advanced by health economists who have argued that the allocation of National Health Service resources should be determined by the rational criteria that economists use to allocate resources elsewhere. Hence the concept of the quality adjusted life year, the idea being to allocate health resources in such a way as to maximise the number of years that patients will live with an adjustment for the actual quality of those years.

Accountability summarised

As we have seen, accountability is a complex phenomenon. In public sector organisations it is not restricted to hierarchical accountability to politicians at either the local or national level. Accountability of public sector organisations has a number of dimensions:

- political accountability;
- managerial accountability;
- legal accountability;
- consumer accountability;
- professional accountability.

It is important to recall that the mechanisms of accountability may not provide for full and effective scrutiny of the actions of public sector organisations. For example, if professionals see their fellow professionals as points of reference for accountability then this may be at the expense of public accountability. Efficient and prompt delivery of services may occur at the expense of detailed and time-consuming scrutiny by political masters. Also, there remain parts of the public sector over which there exists little or no accountability. We are well aware of the arguments of the critics of the secret services who argue that they lack any effective accountability. Similarly, critics of recent initiatives, such as the creation of urban development corporations, have argued that these have assumed wide-ranging powers in relation to planning with the ability to make decisions without reference to the interests of the local communities and thus serve the interests of those who seek to develop property rather than the interests of long-standing residents of the area.

John Stewart (1992) has argued that the accountability of local authorities to their electorate for activities within the locale is being undermined as responsibilities are increasingly being transferred to non-elected bodies. According to Stewart:

> A new magistracy is being created in the sense that a non-elected élite are assuming responsibility for a large part of local governance. They are found on the boards of health authorities and hospital trusts, Training and Enterprise Councils, the board of governors of grant-maintained schools, the governing bodies of colleges of further education and Housing Action Trusts. (1992, p. 7.)

A primary consideration for Stewart is that often the membership of these bodies is not known locally and the meetings of such bodies are not subject to the same openness and public scrutiny as local authorities.

Accountability is thus an ongoing issue in the public sector. As we have seen, mechanisms of accountability change over time and reflect cultural, political and social demands. This will continue to be the case as accountability will be only one of many considerations in the organisation and management of the public sector.

CONCLUSION

In this chapter we have introduced a number of concepts which are ongoing themes in the public sector in Britain. So far we have made no attempt to draw any conclusions as to whether the public sector is intrinsically different from the private sector; we have merely pointed to those themes which will be referred to and developed in later chapters. We acknowledge that accountability is a concern for most large organisations irrespective of whether they are in the public or private sectors. Equally, many organisations will experience the problem of making a distinction between policy making and administration and how and who is involved in these activities. Further, all organisations will have cultures and sets of values which influence the way they work and relate to the outside world. At this stage we are merely setting the ground for debate.

What is obvious is that these values will change over time as the external and internal environments of organisations change. In Chapter 13 we examine in detail how public sector officials are encouraged to be more managerial in their behaviour. A consequence of this impetus is whether the traditional administrative values that we have outlined above are still relevant. Giving evidence to the Treasury and Civil Service Committee (1993), the head of the civil service Sir Robin Butler indicated that impartiality and objectivity, integrity, selection and promotion on merit, and a notion of accountability to ministers through Parliament remained central civil service values. Other witnesses to the Committee wondered if such values were still appropriate, could be applied to all civil service functions and represented a unified and coherent set of values.

Later chapters will consider how people behave in public sector organisations and cope with recent developments in the organisation and operation in those organisations, which will assist the reader to draw more informed conclusions.

FURTHER READING

Day and Klein (1987) provide a very useful review of accountability in five public services. Gray and Jenkins (1985) discuss the mechanics of the process in detail and its application in central government. Metcalfe and Richards (1987) provide the same. Accountability is a consistent theme in Savage and Robins (1990) and Flynn (1990). On secrecy. see Jones *et al.* (1990). Hennessy (1989b) reassesses the need for a professional ethic in the civil service and attempts to indicate what such an ethic might consist of. Wass (1983) examines the traditional values of the civil servant in modern times.

CHAPTER 3

Bureaucracy: idea and operation

INTRODUCTION

In this chapter we will examine what is meant by the term 'bureaucracy' and the way in which the concept is used in the public sector. As we shall see, bureaucracy is an idea which has made a major contribution to the structure and functioning of large organisations including those in the public sector in the twentieth century. Therefore we need to understand the principles which underpin the idea of bureaucracy. In addition to this, we need to understand how it has operated in practice and to consider criticisms of the idea and alternative ways of organising public sector organisations.

Bureaucracy has been defined in many ways (see Albrow, 1970, or Smith, 1988). Albrow identified three major concepts of bureaucracy. Firstly, bureaucracy can be conceptualised as a form of government which could be distinguished from other forms such as monarchy or democracy. Under such a system, bureaucrats are employees of the state. Secondly, bureaucracy can be seen as a system of administrative efficiency. As Jackson (1982) observes, this approach sees bureaucracies as complex organisations with hierarchies which can be found in both the public and private sectors. Finally, the word is commonly used as a pejorative term of abuse by the public when they come up against red tape and obstruction in the system of public administration. People use the term to refer to an inefficient system of public administration that misuses public money.

Although there is no agreed definition of the term, when studying public sector organisations, the term is more properly used to refer to a particular method of determining how organisations are structured and the methods by which the tasks of the organisation are achieved.

ORIGINS OF THE TERM

For students of public sector organisations, the study of bureaucracy inevitably starts with Max Weber (1864–1920), a German sociologist, who saw it as a method of rational organisation. Weber was an academic whose concern was to examine organisations and offer a detached analysis. He was concerned about the nature of authority systems in organisations and why people followed orders without coercion. If those in a subordinate position follow orders of those in a superior position they are conferring legitimacy on the authority system.

He identified three types of legitimate authority systems:

1 **Charismatic authority** – 'resting on the devotion to specific and exceptional sanctity, heroism or exemplary character of an individual person.'
2 **Traditional authority** – 'resting on an established belief in the sanctity of immemorial traditions and the legitimacy of status of those exercising authority.'
3 **Rational/legal authority** – 'resting on the belief in the "legality" of patterns of normative rules and the right of those elevated to authority under such rules to issue commands.' (All quotes from Weber, 1971, p. 15.)

These three classifications are known as 'ideal types'. This is not to imply that they are ideals to which organisations should aspire. Rather, Weber states that we are unlikely to find them existing in the real world; instead he merely formulated the three concepts 'in the sharpest possible form'. He constructed them hypothetically for the purpose of comparison.

Under a system of rational/legal authority, 'obedience is owed to the legally established impersonal order' or in other words to a legal system where orders are issued and obeyed because of the authority that the office holder has. Bureaucracy is the purest form of the rational/legal authority system.

WHAT ARE THE FEATURES OF BUREAUCRATIC ADMINISTRATION?

Beetham summarises Weber's basic features of a bureaucratic system as:

> *hierarchy*: each official has a clearly defined competence within a hierarchical division of labour, and is answerable for its performance to a superior;
> *continuity*: the office constitutes a full-time salaried occupation, with a career structure which offers the prospect of regular advancement;
> *impersonality*: the work is conducted according to prescribed rules, without arbitrariness or favouritism, and a written record is kept of each transaction;
> *expertise*: officials are selected according to merit, are trained for their function, and control access to the knowledge stored in the files. (Beetham, 1987, pp. 11–12.)

WHO ARE THE BUREAUCRATS?

In Box 3.1 we can see an extract from Weber which identifies the main criteria against which bureaucrats are appointed. As Beetham points out, at its simplest, administration can be understood as 'the coordination and execution of policy', and a system of administration as 'an arrangement of offices concerned with translating policy into directives to be executed at the front line of the organisation (shop floor, coal face, battlefield, etc.)' (Beetham, 1987, p. 13.)

Box 3.1 Weber's criteria for the appointment of bureaucrats

---

1 They are personally free and subject to authority only with respect to their impersonal official obligations.
2 They are organised in a clearly defined hierarchy of offices.
3 Each office has a clearly defined sphere of competence in the legal sense.
4 The office is filled by a free contractual relationship.
5 Candidates are selected on the basis of technical qualifications. In the most rational cases, this is tested by examination or guaranteed by diplomas certifying technical training, or both. They are appointed, not elected.
6 They are remunerated by fixed salaries in money, for the most part with a right to pension . . . The salary scale is primarily graded according to rank in the hierarchy . . .
7 The office is treated as the sole, or at least the primary, occupation of the incumbent.
8 It constitutes a career. There is a system of 'promotion' according to seniority or to achievement or both. Promotion is dependent on the judgement of superiors.
9 The official works entirely separated from ownership of the means of administration and without appropriation of his position.
10 He is subject to strict and systematic discipline and control in the conduct of the office.

(From Weber, 1971, pp. 21–2.)

Therefore, not everyone involved in a bureaucratic organisation is a bureaucrat. We need to distinguish the administrative staff from the corporate group that employs them. For example, in a local authority, the administrative staff could be a bureaucracy whilst the corporate group that employs them – the council – is certainly not. They are normally part time, elected and involved, at least notionally, in policy making. We also need to distinguish between those who are charged with the process of administration and exercise authority within the organisation and those who assist that process. Whereas typists are essential to the administrative process, they are not bureaucrats as they do not exercise authority in the Weberian sense (Beetham, 1987, pp. 11–12). Thus it does not necessarily follow that those at the top and bottom of organisations are bureaucrats. In local government, approximately one-third of the labour force are manual workers, one-third are teachers or fire-fighters, which leaves one-third as non-manual workers (see Fowler, 1988a, p. 13). Therefore if we follow this approach to defining bureaucracy, we are only concerned with a part of the organisation.

We now need to examine why Weber attached so much importance to the idea of bureaucracy. He argued that bureaucracy was potentially superior to systems based on charismatic authority or traditional authority. Smith cites Weber's claims for the bureaucratic system. Weber argued that it is technically:

capable of attaining the highest degree of efficiency and is in this sense formally the most rational known means of carrying out imperative control over human beings. It is superior to any other form in precision, in stability, in the stringency of its discipline and its reliability. It thus makes possible a particularly high degree of calculability of results . . . It is the scope of its operation, and is formally capable of application to all kinds of administrative task. (Weber, cited by Smith, 1988, p. 4.)

In other words, bureaucracy has the potential to be 'more efficient (with respect to the goals of the formal hierarchy) than are alternative forms of organisation . . .' (March and Simon, 1971, p. 30). It must be recognised at this point that this potential may not be realised and that so-called dysfunctions which undermine the efficiency and operation of the organisation may manifest themselves.

Crucial to the success of the bureaucratic form is the existence of formal rules. Hood summarises the features of a rule structure that would conform to the wishes of the 'rule and rote' school of thought:

● the rules are known by all;
● the purpose of the rules is clear and based on a valid theory of cause and effect;
● rules are consistent with each other;
● it is clear when rules are to apply;
● the scope for subjective interpretation is limited;
● where rules involve the categorisation, they are robust and unambiguous. (Hood, 1986, pp. 21–2.)

IS BUREAUCRACY SUITABLE FOR PUBLIC SECTOR ORGANISATIONS?

Weber's ideal type may appear attractive to those seeking to organise public administration. As Brown and Steel put it: 'Clients of large (and particularly public) organisations expect fair, and therefore uniform, treatment which can best be secured by a system of centralised authority implemented according to rules.' (Brown and Steel, 1979, p. 160.)

Parts of the public sector, such as the benefits service, the Inland Revenue and the immigration service, can be expected to conform to this set of criteria since the public have every right to expect that different people in similar circumstances will be treated in a similar way. Yet, as Brown and Steel (1979, p. 162) note, even in these cases, there is a substantial amount of discretion involved in the way the service is run. As they go on to point out, there are many areas of the public service where the Weberian ideal type is hard to find. For example, in the National Health Service, government scientific establishments, or social service departments of local government, the professionals (be they practising doctors, scientists or social workers) will exercise a considerable degree of influence in the decisions that are made rather than being controlled by some hierarchy above them.

Because bureaucrats, at least in theory, work without arbitrariness or favouritism, they are able to deal with successive governments of different political beliefs. Indeed it is the detachment of the public servant that is cited as a virtue of the civil service by Sisson – himself a former civil servant:

> The most serious responsibility of the administrator is to lay aside his preferences in favour of an objective assessment of the situation, not in terms of anything he may hold to be good, but in terms of the game as it is played in Whitehall. (Sisson, 1959, p. 152.)

ARE PUBLIC SECTOR ORGANISATIONS BUREAUCRACIES?

So far we have worked on the assumption that public sector organisations in Britain do in many cases approximate to the ideal type. In order to verify this assumption, we need to look at the evidence. We know from the very idea of an ideal type such as Weber's rational/legal ideal type, that it will never be found to exist in reality. We can, however, examine how closely certain public sector organisations approximate to the theoretical construct.

In his study of Birmingham City Council (1980) Haynes argues that local government has long been organised along the lines of classical bureaucratic design. This has happened for very good reasons. Classical bureaucratic design has allowed local government to cope with the increase in the number of tasks and the growth of the complexity of the system. It also assisted the local authorities to provide impartial and accountable administration (Haynes, 1980, p. 10). As evidence of this, Haynes cites the creation of strong functional specialisation (or departmentalism); the principle of vertical hierarchy for control, authority and communication; the emphasis on rights, duties, technical qualifications; and the rigid grading structures and standardised procedures (Haynes, 1980, p. 12). He argues that the pressures to continue managing the plethora of legislation and provide services took priority over organisational reforms. Indeed, it was not until the late 1960s that organisational reform came on the agenda. As we shall see later, considerable changes have taken place during the last twenty years in the way that local government is organised.

The civil service of the mid-eighteenth century was characterised by a spoils system of nepotism and jobbery. Hennessy's major work on the service (1989a) documents the ongoing emphasis placed on the need for efficiency. The Northcote–Trevelyan Report on the civil service (1854) recommended a system of administration based on a clear division of work, entry to the service through competitive examinations, and promotion on the basis of merit. These recommendations were adopted in the period up to the end of the century by a service that was steadily accumulating a wider range of functions. During the twentieth century, the service has grown from a relatively small service to an employer of over 700,000 people in the late 1970s. Even today, despite the Thatcher cuts in the service, it remains a major employer with about 570,000 employees. We still have to ask the question: is the civil service a bureaucracy in the Weberian sense?

In his analysis of the systems of administration in four countries, Page argues that British and French senior civil servants can 'relatively accurately be described as career officials' (Page, 1985, p. 33). Members of the French 'grand corps' have much in common with our senior officials. However, Mrs Thatcher made significant interventions in the appointments of a number of Permanent Secretaries in an attempt to create a service which would serve her more effectively. Ridley (1983) suggests that this selection takes place on a non-party political basis – the criteria is the ability to be forceful in policy implementation. Recruits to the service are selected through a process of competitive examination though there are major criticisms of the method of selection of the so-called 'high-fliers' which tends to favour those from particular educational backgrounds.

The ideal type places an emphasis on control in order to ensure that the wishes of those at the top of the hierarchy are carried out by those at the bottom of the hierarchy. This is not always the case in practice. Many workers at comparatively low positions in the hierarchy in public sector organisations will be relatively isolated from direct supervision. Lipsky (1979) cites the examples of teachers, policemen and women and social workers who, because of the nature of the work, have the opportunity to exercise considerable personal initiative in the exercise of their duties. However, it is important to note that such work is subject to increasing control from above: teachers through the imposition of the national curriculum and performance appraisal; policemen and women through technological advances, including the two-way radio; and social workers through organisational responses to cases such as the Cleveland child abuse crisis and the Jasmine Beckford case in the 1980s.

BUREAUCRACY ASSESSED

A cursory examination of many modern public sector organisations may lead one to conclude that they often approximate to the Weberian ideal type. Not only in Britain either. Ministries in Germany are structured on a hierarchical basis and rigid departmentalism, and task allocation exists (Peters, 1990). However, we need to remember that Weber stressed that the rational/legal bureaucracy was only potentially the most efficient form of administration. He did concede that this would not necessarily be the case. Much of the writing on public sector organisations has been written with the ghost of Weber in the background. Watson argues that every organisation is faced with a basic paradox:

> The means used by the controlling management of the organisation to achieve whatever goals they choose or are required to pursue in an efficient way (i.e. at the lowest feasible cost – short and long term) do not necessarily facilitate the effective achievement of these goals since these 'means' involve human beings who have goals of their own, which may not be congruent with those of the people managing them (1987, p. 174).

In other words, we are introducing an organisation's most dynamic variable:

people. People will identify with an organisation's objectives to varying degrees; some will be loyal to the *n*th degree, others will identify very closely with the success of the organisation. Still others may be motivated by economic reward alone and seek personal satisfaction elsewhere, for example from family and friends.

Because of this paradox, many writers have examined the so-called dysfunctions of bureaucracy and the possibility that in addition to the intended consequences of rational and efficient administration, bureaucracies produce unintended consequences which may conflict with the goals of those in authority and inhibit the efficient and effective operation of the organisation.

At this point it is appropriate to examine a number of classical studies of organisations which illustrate examples of these unintended consequences. Although by their very nature these case studies relate to specific organisations at particular points in time, it is possible to look at other organisations and identify the same or similar traits and patterns of behaviour. These studies show the following dysfunctions:

- rules can become ends in themselves;
- problems of close supervision and vicious circles;
- rules can be adapted to increase the effectiveness of the organisation;
- the dictatorship of the official.

Rules can become ends in themselves

All organisations have certain objectives that those in positions of authority choose or are required to achieve. A system of rules is thus intended as a means to achieve those objectives. These rules are set by those in authority as a method of achieving control over the organisation and achieving reliable and uniform behaviour by those holding office in the organisation. Merton's study (1940) shows how rules become internalised by those working for the organisation and therefore it becomes possible for people to lose sight of the objectives behind the rules. A particular feature is rigidity of behaviour. The consequences are that demands for reliability are satisfied, individual cases are decided by the use of simple categories and that there are increased difficulties in dealing with clients.

The problems of close supervision and vicious circles

A study of a gypsum plant by Alvin Gouldner (1954) revealed that if workers are perceived by supervisors to have a lack of motivation then one response is to supervise their work more closely. This response by the supervisor raises two possible problems. Firstly, if workers are motivated they may do the job better without close supervision. Secondly, workers associate close supervision with strictness and punishment. Gouldner observes:

> . . . close supervision enmeshed management in a vicious circle: the supervisor perceived the worker as unmotivated; he then carefully watched and directed him; this aroused the

worker's ire and accentuated his apathy, and now the supervisor was back where he began. Close supervision did not solve his problem. In fact, it might make the worker's performance in the super's absence, even less reliable than it had been. (Gouldner, 1954, pp. 160–1.)

The effect is that impersonal rules are formulated in order to reduce the tensions which are brought about by subordination and control, but the result (illustrated in Figure 3.1) is that the rules serve to perpetuate the tensions they are designed to eliminate by reinforcing the low motivation of the workers.

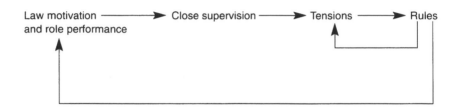

Fig. 3.1 The vicious circle of close supervision and rules
(*Source* : Gouldner, 1954, p. 178.)

Following Gouldner, Michel Crozier's (1964) study of two parts of the French public service reveals the development of impersonal rules which prescribe behaviour to be followed for all possible circumstances. For example, promotion from one level in the hierarchy to another is by open competitive examination. Therefore, a person's personal attributes and career achievements are not taken into consideration. Similarly, when a person moves within a level in the hierarchy, this is governed by the seniority principle again without reference to other factors. The result of this is that there is no scope for individuals to exercise initiative – all workers are protected from their superiors and subordinates by a set of rules imposed from outside.

Crozier also cites further means by which the exercise of discretionary power is reduced. For example, decision making tends to be centralised. The power to make decisions or rules or to change or interpret rules moves further and further away from the point where the rules are carried out. The consequence of this is that the organisation becomes increasingly rigid, that innovation is stifled and that those making decisions – those at the top of the organisation – concentrate on ensuring internal issues such as fairness and the elimination of favouritism rather than adjusting the organisation to fit better with its environment. The very people with the knowledge and facts at their fingertips, those at the operational level, are excluded from the decision- and rule-making process.

Crozier's study reveals that the goals of the organisation are displaced by the goals of the various groups at different levels of the hierarchy. Each group wishes to protect itself against other groups in the organisation. Each group will assert its own uniqueness and importance to the organisation as a whole. Also, those with expertise in a particular area will have power because their task cannot be subjected to detailed prescription and regulation. This can lead, paradoxically, to a situation where the tighter the regulation of the organisation, the greater the independence and power of the experts because, as Crozier argues, in a bureaucratic organisation 'power increases in direct ratio to its rarity' (1964, p. 192).

Following from this analysis, Crozier argues that the system of vicious circle of displacement of goals identified by Merton and Gouldner which was outlined above can be elaborated. The displacement of goals leads to difficulties in dealing with customers, poor communication with the outside world, lower productivity and difficulty in completing the tasks of the organisation. Those seeking to control the organisation use impersonal rules, close supervision and centralisation which lead to increased frustration at all levels because decisions are not discussed. The consequence of this is that those at the top of the hierarchy then move decision making further up the hierarchy, which only serves to aggravate the problems that they seek to solve. The problem is compounded by the fact that those lower in the hierarchy seek rules to govern relationships between subordinates and superiors in order to protect themselves from arbitrary or unpredictable decisions by the manager.

Rules can be adapted to increase the effectiveness of the organisation

Until now the criticisms of bureaucratic organisations have illustrated how systems of control can break down and reduce the effectiveness of the organisation. Although we are still concerned with the importance of control in the organisation, the point that Blau (1963) makes is that rules can be adapted to increase the effectiveness of the organisation. He conducted a study of two American public sector organisations – a law enforcement organisation and a careers service – which illustrate this point. In the law enforcement agency a major rule of the organisation was that all bribes must be reported and acted on. However, the group who were likely to be offered bribes had developed an informal rule that nobody reports the offering of a bribe. The rule was enforced by the groups through the threat of ostracism from the group if a bribe was reported. This led to increased organisational effectiveness because, firstly, it eliminated the need for time to be taken up in reporting the bribe and the subsequent investigation that would take place, and secondly, the officer then gained the upper hand in the investigation because the 'client', unaware of the informal rule, would co-operate with the officer conscious of the ramifications if the bribe was reported.

In his study of the careers service, Blau observed that senior management sought to introduce a culture of competition amongst officers charged with the task of placing people in jobs. The procedure was to compare the performance of each officer. Blau found that the statistical evaluation of performance interfered with operating efficiency and there was an organisational need for mechanisms to combat competition. This was done in one section by developing co-operative norms (1963, pp. 80–1).

We are all aware that trade unions can impose a sanction known as 'working to rule' in order to stifle the effectiveness of the organisation. The lesson we learn from Blau is that organisations involve people and that if they are motivated towards the objectives of the organisation, they can increase the effectiveness of the organisation by breaking or ignoring rules.

The dictatorship of the official

Weber understood the possibility that the actions of the bureaucracy could be in conflict with the democratic process:

> The pure interest of the bureaucracy in power, however, is efficacious far beyond those areas where purely functional interests make for secrecy. The concept of the 'official secret' is the specific invention of the bureaucracy, and nothing is so fanatically defended by the bureaucracy as this attitude which cannot be substantially justified beyond these specifically qualified areas. In facing a parliament, the bureaucracy, out of a sure power instinct, fights every attempt of the parliament to gain knowledge by means of its own experts or from interest groups . . . Bureaucracy naturally welcomes a poorly informed and hence powerless parliament. (Cited in Hennessy, 1989a, p. 347.)

The fear of an overpowerful bureaucracy is thus not a new one. It has been a concern for politicians such as Tony Benn who points to the power of the civil service to manage and absorb the Labour Party's policies (see for example Benn, 1980). Brian Sedgemore (1980), a former civil servant and Labour politician, points to the difficulties that politicians face in breaking out from the established values and thinking of government departments. Thompson argues that the two systems that find themselves working so closely together have sharply conflicting value systems. Democracy emphasises equality, participation and individuality while efficiency of bureaucracy is based on hierarchy, specialisation and impersonality (Thompson, 1983, p. 235). In later chapters we will consider strategies which have been mounted to resolve this conflict.

THE NEW RIGHT CRITIQUE OF BUREAUCRACY

One of the most important critiques of bureaucracy, primarily because of the political currency that it enjoyed on both sides of the Atlantic in the 1980s, is the critique offered by authors on the New Right. Many of these writers sought to apply economic thinking to public sector organisations. Therefore just as business people can be seen as profit maximisers, politicians can be seen as vote maximisers and bureaucrats as bureau maximisers.

In particular, Niskanen (1971, 1973) argues that bureaucrats have a personal interest in the growth of the bureau as they have a vested interest in large budgets and rewards in terms of salary, status, public reputation and so on. This is compounded by a system in the United States which provided weak Congressional control over state spending, thus allowing high budgets to go through. He argues that these budgets may be up to twice the size of a comparable budget prepared by a private sector organisation operating in a competitive environment. Although it is debatable to what extent this argument applies in Britain, the acceptability of Niskanen's thesis by Mrs Thatcher's government led to active consideration of alternatives to bureaucracy.

Niskanen advances alternative forms of service provision in an Institute of Economic Affairs (Niskanen, 1973) paper. Firstly, he points to bureaucratic alternatives such as competitive bureaucracy. Under this system, bureaux would compete to provide services and in doing so they would drive prices down and reduce the over-supply which monopoly providers of services are allegedly guilty of. Also, incentives could be offered to maximise the profit of a bureau. These could take the form of reward systems such as performance-related pay and deferred prizes for managers who reduce costs. The introduction of performance-related pay in the civil service and incentives for National Health Service managers demonstrate the influence of these ideas.

Secondly, Niskanen points to market alternatives such as the provision of services by non-governmental agencies financed by per-unit subsidies or vouchers for, for example, education, or private supply of services such as tele-communications.

Thirdly, he argues that there are political alternatives such as the regular re-allocation of posts on committees which review the work of bureaux. The intended effect of this could be to stop politicians 'going native' or identifying with the service providers and high levels of service provision. Also, a two-thirds voting rule could be introduced to prevent legislatures passing high budgets on a simple majority, or the taxation system could be made more progressive so that those in low-income groups who demand high levels of service provision would be less inclined to articulate their demands.

FROM BUREAUCRACY TO ADHOCRACY

While bureaucracy may ensure consistency, uniformity and fairness and seek to allocate responsibility, critics argue that adherence to such principles do not allow for the flexibility, innovation and responsiveness that enable organisations to adapt to a turbulent environment. This argument has been applied to private sector as well as public sector bureaucracies. R. Moss Kanter (1990) has argued that, in order to be competitive, larger corporations have to evolve flatter and leaner organisations with fewer management levels, to be more responsive to change and to develop strategic alliances with other companies.

> The new corporate ideal involves a smaller fixed core but a larger set of partnerlike ties. There is less 'inside' that is sacred – permanent, untouchable, unchangeable people, departments, business units, or practices – but more 'outside' that is respected, representing opportunities for deal-making or leverage via alliances. (1990, p. 352.)

Moss Kanter argues that vast size can produce sluggishness and lack of flexibility. Similar themes have been observed by Osborne and Gaebler (1992) in their analysis of government in the USA and developed in their call to 'reinvent government'. They argue that the adoption of ten principles can transform a bureaucratic government into an innovative one.

1 Government should seek to act as a catalyst to allow other organisations to provide services. It should seek to steer rather than to row.
2 Citizens should be empowered by transferring control from bureaucracies to the community.
3 Government should promote competition between service providers.
4 Government should be driven by its mission – what it is there to do – rather than by rules and regulations.
5 The performance of government should be judged by the outcomes – what it achieves – rather than by the inputs – what it swallows up.
6 By focusing on the customer, government will ensure that the needs of the customer and not the bureaucracy are being met.
7 Government should become an enterprise, earning rather than spending money.
8 Government should be proactive rather than reactive, looking to prevent problems rather than trying to cure them.
9 Government should be decentralised and participatory management encouraged.
10 Market mechanisms should be preferred to bureaucratic mechanisms.

Osborne and Gaebler provide numerous examples from local and national government in the USA of how government can become more entrepreneurial and more innovative in the ways that it seeks to govern the community and to respond to the wishes of that community.

The need for innovation was recognised by the OECD in 1986:

> The tasks confronting all advanced countries over the next decade call for a culture of flexibility and adjustment, a culture of innovation. (Quoted in Dror, 1988, p. 25.)

Recognised here is the need for all organisations to change in much the same way as Moss Kanter argues for private sector organisations and Osborne and Gaebler for those in the public sector.

Voluntary sector organisations have demonstrated innovation, flexibility and responsiveness for many years and there are lessons for those working in local authorities who increasingly have to form relationships with the voluntary sector for the provision of services such as those required in community care.

However, caution needs to be expressed in defining entrepreneurial. If it is identified with seeking new opportunities, taking new initiatives or looking to be innovative then this is wholly appropriate for a public sector organisation. If it is identified with risk-taking then it is a moot point whether risks should be taken with public money or in sensitive areas such as child care.

To move from bureaucratic government to entrepreneurial government, to steer rather than to row, requires a change in the culture of the organisation and a change in the task of the bureaucrat. Bureaucrats will need to:

- initiate ideas and seek opportunities;
- anticipate changes in the external environment;
- expect success;
- be open-minded;
- convince and not enforce (see Fisch, 1988).

Compare these with Weber's criteria for the appointment of bureaucrats that we listed in Box 3.1!

CONCLUSION

The concept of bureaucracy has been fundamental to thinking about how public sector organisations have been structured. Its advocates argue that bureaucracy is an appropriate form of organisation for the performance of certain tasks where dependability and reliability are of the essence. However, it cannot be universally adopted with unquestioning enthusiasm. The literature on bureaucratic dysfunctions reveals that it produces unintended consequences and may not be the most efficient form of administration. Bureaucracy is not a neutral machine for the transmission of politicians' policies into practice. This is not to deny the influence of bureaucracy. To quote Peter Self: 'The Weberian model of a hierarchical, rule-dominated administration still has some validity for some parts of the system but not for others. Public administration has become a patchwork quilt of complex relationships and numerous decision points, on which new forms of politics are brought to bear.' (1977, p. 4.)

In recent years the bureaucratic form of organisation has come under challenge from all quarters, and by politicians who see it as inefficient and a barrier to the effective implementation of their policies. Added to this, there has been frequent public criticism that it is remote and disabling, and bureaucrats themselves have argued that it stifles their initiative. In later chapters we will examine the challenge to bureaucracy and how the public sector has developed new administrative structures to deliver public policies.

FURTHER READING

Pugh's (1984) helpful collection of readings provides the reader with excerpts from the more significant work on the structure of organisations. Beetham's (1987) book *Bureaucracy* provides a useful introduction as does the more dated book of the same name by Albrow (1970). More specific public sector applications include Brian Smith (1988), Page (1985) and Haynes (1980). Eva Etzioni-Halevy (1985) provides a thorough review of the literature on the conflict between the political process and the bureaucratic process.

CHAPTER 4

The formal organisation

INTRODUCTION

The previous chapter was concerned with bureaucracy as a form of government. In the next two chapters we shall be examining a number of different perspectives on organisations. These perspectives fall under two main headings – the formal and the informal approaches to organisations. In this chapter we link the discussion of bureaucracy to the wider concern with formal organisations in general and examine the formal relations, structures and processes that exist within organisations. In contrast to this, the informal approach to organisations which concentrates upon the informal relations that exists between individuals and groups within an organisation is dealt with in the next chapter.

We need to be aware of formal relations operating at different levels within the public sector and we need to show how public service organisations relate to each other. Unlike in the private or voluntary sectors, public authorities often owe their existence to statutes and often have limited discretion about the range of services they provide. Local authorities are obliged to have certain appointed officials to discharge certain functions, for example to maintain registers of councillors' interests. Executive agencies in the civil service owe their existence to an act of political choice without the requirement of legislative authority. This has the effect of making formal structures particularly important and, in part, explains why there has been an ongoing concern for structural organisation in the public services.

Local government exists at different levels and there are formal and informal relationships between the different tiers. In the case of the shire counties created in 1974, district councils are responsible for collecting refuse and county councils are responsible for its disposal. We also need to be aware that local government exists within a wider network of quangos, agencies and voluntary organisations (see Rhodes, 1988). More importantly, local government exists within the context of central government domination.

Within each level of government we may find competing tensions inherent in the relationships between the different sectors. Thus, for example, within local government there appears to be an increasing tendency to move towards a more decentralised service provision and organisational structure; at the next level of government the centre may be wishing to increase its control over what local government does. A second dimension that we need to be aware of is one of organisational change and the reasons for it. We can ask 'Why are new departments created?' or 'Why are old ones abolished?' We may like to think that such changes enable the organisation to be more efficient and effective in achieving its goals and yet it may well be that such changes arise as a result of trying to satisfy an individual's political ambitions or to undercut the ambitions of a rival. Organisational change may be the result of these kinds of issue rather than in response to some logic of organisational design.

The so-called 'classical approach' to management has, as we shall see in the next chapter, been challenged by its critics who argue that it ignores the human dimension of organisations. While the classical approach has advanced the rational approach to organisations, it is worth adding the caveat that the implementation of classical principles may be frustrated by other considerations as Lord Armstrong, a former head of the home civil service, observed: 'There are some general principles of organisation, but the application of them is constantly interrupted by short-term political considerations. In my experience politicians have a contempt for good organisation.' (Quoted in Ponting, 1986, p. 124.)

A further dimension that we also need to be aware of is the development of organisational structures over time. Local government outside London experienced wholesale reorganisation in 1974 with the implementation of two-tier structures of counties and districts. In 1986 the metropolitan counties and the Greater London Council were abolished and in 1992 the Local Government Commission was set up to consider the structure of local authorities in England. Similarly, reorganisations of the National Health Service in 1974 and 1982 attempted to impose a form of uniform pattern on the structure.

It is more difficult to trace a common pattern or rationale for the present structure of government departments. Each department has its own history, traditions and culture, and to impose a general framework to account for their development is not easy. The title of Chapman and Greenaway's history of government departments is *The Dynamics of Administrative Reform* (1980), and it captures the ebb and flow of central government changes. This is understandable when we consider differences in the following:

- **Size**. There are approximately 2,400 civil servants in the Department for Education and there were 96,000 in the old DHSS before its split into two separate departments in 1988.
- **Functions**. The Department for Education is concerned with advice and monitoring rather than the actual provision of education, which is now delivered by a range of organisations with varying patterns of accountability. In contrast, much of the work of the Department of Social Security is dealing with clients through agencies which are part of the department.
- **Organisation**. Some departments, such as the Welsh, Scottish or Northern Ireland Offices, are organised on a territorial basis while others such as the Treasury are primarily centred in Whitehall.

● **History**. The Treasury can be traced back to the eleventh century whereas the Department of the Environment was created in 1970 by combining a number of functions including housing and local government which were previously located in smaller ministries. It is important that we bear these differences in mind when we attempt to analyse the formal nature of public sector organisations.

THE CLASSICAL APPROACHES

We have discussed the importance of Weber in understanding the workings of bureaucratic organisations. There are other classical studies that attempt to understand how organisations work with a view to improving performance.

Scientific management

As the name suggests, this approach is concerned with the application of the methods and techniques of science to organisations. It is the belief that universal and general principles can be applied to every organisation. The approach suggests that organisations can be viewed as essentially the same and that there are few differences between organisations that cannot be overcome by the application of general principles. Two of the leading exponents of this approach to organisations were F.W. Taylor and H. Fayol. Unlike the academic approach of Weber, however, Taylor and Fayol were not content just to analyse organisations. Both were concerned to offer prescriptions as to how organisations should be run with a view to particular management ends, in particular, how to improve performance.

Taylor was an engineer by training and his approach to understanding organisations reflected both his scientific background and the belief in science as the solution to society's problems that was so characteristic of the late nineteenth century. Taylor (1967) examined the traditional working methods of individual workers in a number of studies covering such simple tasks as bricklaying or shovelling materials. He believed that it was possible to apply scientific principles to each task which would replace the old rule-of-thumb method of working. He believed that the workforce should be selected on the same scientific basis. Such an approach would lead to a more efficient worker and hence to a more profitable organisation. He also believed that the worker was rational and would respond to financial incentives as a way of increasing productivity. Hence the payment by piece-rate for the individual worker. Taylor believed in the division of labour since tasks could be broken down into simple repetitive jobs. This would allow the individual to specialise in a particular job and the division of labour would lead to a clear distinction between management and the workforce. The modern versions of Taylorism are expressed in terms of job design and work study. Similarly, the concepts of the division of labour and organisation through specialisation still hold sway within many organisations. Indeed, Pollitt describes the approaches to public management adopted by Reagan and Thatcher as neo-Taylorist:

The chief feature of both classic Taylorism and its 1980s descendant were that they were, above all, concerned with *control* and that this control was to be achieved through an essentially *administrative* approach – the fixing of effort levels that were to be expressed in quantitative terms. (Pollitt, 1990, p. 177.)

Although Taylor was carrying out his research at the beginning of the century and despite the fact that his conclusions did not meet with the universal approval of either the workers or the management he left an important legacy which later theorists built upon:

- the application of universal scientific principles;
- specialisation;
- division of labour;
- clear hierarchies;
- ethos of management control.

Those familiar with either central or local government within Britain will, no doubt, recognise some of these features as characteristic of their own experiences:

- emphasis upon routine tasks;
- clearly defined tasks;
- clear hierarchical control.

The concern with the scientific approach to organisations was developed by Henri Fayol (1949) whose scientific background was in biology rather than engineering. He was apt to use biological metaphors to explain the workings of organisations. His principles of management were as follows:

- The division of labour and the stress upon the advantages that such specialisation brings.
- The stress upon authority.
- The stress upon discipline and the penalties incurred when discipline broke down.
- The concept of the unity of command – a dual-command system leads to dissension and chaos.
- The unity of direction since, to use one of Fayol's biological metaphors, 'a body with two heads is a monster'.
- The subordination of individual interests to those of the organisation as a whole.
- The fair remuneration for the workforce. Like Taylor before him, Fayol believed in the motivating force of money.
- The principle of centralisation. Centralisation, like the division of labour, is, according to Fayol, a feature of the natural world.
- A scalar chain or line of authority, both vertically and horizontally.
- A concern with order. This is the idea that there is a place for everyone and everything.
- Equity in the form of equitable treatment for the workers.

- Initiative.
- Stability of tenure.
- 'Esprit de corps'. This is the notion that union is strength. The modern-day equivalent of this is the idea of an organisation having a corporate image such that all those within the organisation can respond to and identify with.

Fayol suggested that management is concerned with planning, with organisation, with command, co-ordination and control and with an emphasis on formal authority.

There is a sense in which scientific management is concerned with a way of thinking about organisations irrespective of the individual prescriptions of individual writers and researchers. It links into organisational structure in so far as structure is concerned with:

- specialisation;
- standardisation of rules and procedures;
- standardisation of employment practices;
- formalisation of rules clearly specified;
- centralisation;
- configuration, i.e. whether the chain of command is long or short.

The advantage of this formal approach to organisations is that it shows how organisational objectives can be reached by:

- Formally allocating people and resources. Individuals may feel happier if they have a clearly specified job within the organisation and know exactly where they fit into the workings of the organisation. It helps if we know where to go for formal approval of decisions, or know who is responsible for what. Accountability and responsibility can be clearly located.
- Such an approach also clearly specifies operating procedures and mechanisms laid down in a formal manual for example. In local government the existence of standing orders, codes of conduct and conditions of service clearly stipulate what can and cannot be done in certain circumstances. This is particularly important when we consider that much of the work of government is legal in nature involving the carrying out of statutory responsibilities.
- It also indicates the decision-making procedures which show how and where decisions are made within organisations. Again the formal committee structure of local government indicates where authority is located. We shall see later, though, that in practice this may not always be where power is located.

A more recent organisational theorist illustrates the enduring qualities of these principles. According to Child (1977) the major dimensions of an organisational structure consist of:
- the allocation of tasks and responsibilities to individuals;
- the designation of formal reporting relationships;
- the grouping of individuals into units, units into departments and departments into larger units. It allows the compartmentalisation of tasks and jobs;

- the location of authority:
- channels of communication, interpretation and participation.

We can conclude this section then by picking out a number of criticisms of the scientific management approach to organisations.

- It may prove difficult to co-ordinate the many specialised tasks and divisions that are required by the division of labour.
- It may prove difficult because individuals may not be able to see the whole of the organisation since they are so wrapped up in their own specialised part of it.
- The organisation may prove to be inflexible and unable to respond to changing circumstances.
- It may be too bound by rules and not allow individuals to exercise discretion within their work.
- It may lead to lack of motivation. Individuals may be seen as 'cogs in the machine' and one of the major criticisms of Taylor's approach was that he had a tendency to treat workers as automatons who would respond to financial incentives automatically.
- Individuals lower down the organisation may be given little responsibility with few decisions delegated down the organisation to them.

The mechanistic and the organic organisation

Burns and Stalker (1961) offer a more sophisticated version of this approach by suggesting that we also need to take into account the context within which different types of organisations operate. They compare two different types of organisation, what they term the 'mechanistic' and the 'organic'. The mechanistic organisation is characterised by:

- a hierarchical system of control and communication;
- functionally specialised and precisely defined jobs;
- information flows up the organisation;
- decision and instruction flows down the organisation;
- loyalty and obedience.

We can see the similarities here between the scientific approach to organisations and the bureaucratic model that we looked at in the previous chapter. However, in contrast to those who can see nothing good in this type of organisation, Burns and Stalker argue that this type of organisation may be appropriate to an organisation operating within a particular environment. If the organisation is in a stable environment then such formality may be advantageous. However, if the organisation is in an unstable environment then a different, more flexible, organisational structure is necessary. As we shall see later this is one of the reasons behind the call for changes in the civil service and local government in Britain. It is argued that the traditional bureaucratic mechanistic structure that has been operating for so long can no longer cope with the dynamic environment that we now live in.

Burns and Stalker contrast this type of organisation with the organic organisation, which is characterised by:

- jobs losing much of their formal definition;
- less rigid demarcation of functions;
- lateral as well as vertical interaction;
- the content of communications being information and advice rather than instructions – participation rather than control.

Burns and Stalker argue that this type of organisation is more likely to survive in an uncertain environment. Thus, using the distinction between mechanistic and organic organisations we can argue that in so far as we live in an uncertain world where political consensus is not guaranteed and economic stability is not assured then our public sector organisations ought to be moving more towards an organic and away from a mechanistic structure.

Whatever the structure, an organisation needs people to make it work and hence the need to take into account the roles of individuals, their beliefs, values, motivations and how they interact with each other and with groups. This is examined in the next chapter and it forms the basis of the human relations approach to organisations. To what extent, however, can the principles that we have looked at so far help us in designing an organisational structure?

ORGANISATIONAL DESIGN

The concern of the writers that we have looked at in the preceding pages are with a number of organisational variables:

- specialisation of tasks;
- standardisation of rules, procedures and work practices;
- formalisation in terms of clear duties and responsibilities;
- centralisation and control;
- configuration in terms of the different levels within a hierarchical structure;
- communication and instruction;
- co-ordination of the different activities.

All organisations will have to address these issues and the way in which they do so will depend, to some extent, on what kind of environment they are working in – be it stable or unstable.

A second set of concerns is with the structuring of the organisation and the way in which it groups its activities. Mintzberg (1983, pp. 48–52) suggests that different criteria are available:

1 **Knowledge and skills** – a university may be divided into departments based upon knowledge in a subject area. We thus find Departments of Philosophy, Mathematics, Politics and so on. Hospitals are often composed of groupings based around particular medical skills such as physiotherapy or radiology. In central government we have, for example, the Central Statistical Office offering statistical expertise; local authorities often have centrally organised planning units.

2 **Functions** – many organisations are divided into departments centred around the function that they perform such as personnel, finance, research and marketing. Local authorities are often composed of these kinds of functional departments such as education, social services, environmental health and so on.

3 **Time** – some organisations operate on a shift system so the structure is based around a particular shift. This is often the case with a continuous production plant, but we also find it in hospitals and also in the police force.

4 **Output** – some firms will have departments reflecting a particular product such as furniture, soft furnishings or kitchenware. Social security operations are divided into types of outputs, for example pensions and overseas divisions.

5 **Clients** – an organisation may be constructed around the clients. This would take the form of one department being responsible for all the services affecting a particular client group. A recurring theme in government reorganisation is whether or not to have, for example, a Ministry of Children, or a Department of Senior Citizens. Some local authorities have committees organised upon a particular client group basis such as women, ethnic minorities, the disabled and so on.

6 **Place** – very simply the organisation is divided on a geographical basis. Thus we have the Welsh Office, regional health authorities, and county councils. The problem is, when reorganising in terms of place, to make sure that people's wishes are taken into consideration. The new county of Cleveland created after the local government reorganisation of 1974 has failed to create a sense of identity amongst its inhabitants and many of those living south of the River Tees still feel a sense of belonging to Yorkshire. The Local Government Commission, created in 1992 is attempting to address their problem by identifying appropriate boundaries for local communities.

The Haldane Report (1918) on the machinery of central government, which dominated thinking on the design of central government, examined a number of these criteria and recommended the distribution of government work on the basis of functions performed. Such a basis is fairly common throughout Western Europe. Most governments seem to have departments of defence, transport, education, the environment and so on. As we have indicated earlier, though, the dynamic of administrative reform seems to have been fairly arbitrary in terms of central government. Within the same department we might find more than one of these criteria in evidence. For example, the social services department within a local authority is a functional department. Its internal structuring, however, may be on a geographical basis in terms of area offices and on a client basis in terms of individual officials having a number of cases to deal with.

Thus, not only are there ambiguities in practice in terms of the organisational design of public sector organisations but they do not tell us very much about the power and status that attach to particular departments. The Treasury is only a small department in terms of the number of civil servants that work there but it has tremendous power as a result of its financial role at the heart of government.

ORGANISATIONAL CHARTS

Almost all organisations of any size have organisational charts which show how the organisation is expressed in formal terms. Such charts purport to indicate where control is located, the degree of centralisation, the division of labour, tasks, hierarchies and so on. Thus, in local government we often find charts modelled on the pattern indicated in the Bains Report (1972) on the management and structure of local authorities. Bains encouraged the idea that there is one ideal form of organisational structure which can be applied to all organisations. As we have already indicated the reform of local government in 1972 attempted to impose uniformity on to the pattern of local government in England and Wales. Bains recognised the diversity of local authorities but suggested that certain basic structural features should be common to all authorities. Thus the structure of a district council may look like Fig. 4.1.

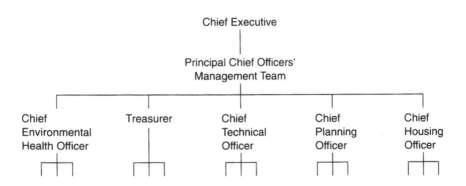

Fig. 4.1 Structure of a district council

Below the chief officers the rest of the department's staff will be arranged on the same hierarchical basis. The tradition within local government is to have a parallel structure for the councillors. The officers are arranged in terms of both functions dealing with housing or environmental health but also support services dealing with finance or personnel. However, such a structure does have a number of weaknesses:

- It tells us nothing about which departments or chief officers might be more important than others.
- Such charts are fairly simple in nature and do not indicate the complexity of the organisation. Thus an organisation may need departmental or unit charts to show all the jobs and tasks that go on within an organisation.
- Such a vertical representation tells us nothing about the relationships that go on between the centre and field offices. Thus an education department may be organised on an area basis so that the centre plays only a co-ordinating role. In the provision of services the field or area offices may be more important than the centre.
- It tells us nothing about where power is located. We have seen charts for the police service that omit the lowly police constable. For the public this may be the most important part of the organisation.
- Such charts also tell us nothing about decisions, real channels of communication (it assumes these to be formal) and relationships (it assumes these to be hierarchical). In reality individuals will often bypass these formal structures in order to get things done by contacting their opposite number in another department directly. Like the formal approach to organisations, such charts give us a picture of how an organisation works but it is only a partial picture and misses out on the crucial aspect of how people behave within organisations. Charts such as these may be unable to capture the complex patterns of organisation that exist in local government today with new forms of relationships such as purchasers and providers of services and local management of schools.

Most organisational charts reflect vertical relations. A more sophisticated approach is to adopt a matrix structure which also examines horizontal relations. Indeed the Bains Report advocated the use of programme teams which cut across the traditional departmental structure of local government. This would ensure communication and co-ordination horizontally as well as vertically. A matrix structure can indicate how relationships may be brought together across functional departments which in practice is how organisations are more likely to operate. Thus, for example, in deciding to build a new school there will be other departments than just the education department involved, as shown in Fig. 4.2. There will be a need for the technical support services, for new roads to be built for access, for liaison with police, social services and so on. To ensure co-ordination a project team may well be set up which draws upon the various departments.

	Education	Architects	Planning	Transport
Project A (New School)				
Project B (Extend Playing Fields)				

Fig. 4.2 Matrix structure

Likewise in central government the creation of task forces to deal with specific problems such as those associated with the inner city will cut across departmental boundaries. Here the structure is determined by the problem to be solved rather than by trying to fit a particular problem or project into a formal structure. It shows how in reality there is a need to communicate horizontally as well as vertically. Such an approach forces managers to communicate with one another and it helps break down rigid departmental boundaries. It does, however, sacrifice one of the classical principles of organisational structures which is the unity of command.

SYSTEMS THEORY

Systems theory is a more modern perspective upon organisations and sees organisations as a system interacting with the environment within which they operate. The work of Burns and Stalker that we briefly introduced earlier is an example of an approach to organisations using the concept of a system. We can define a system as an organised unitary whole composed of interdependent parts or sub-systems and with boundaries separating it from its environment and other systems.

Systems theory borrows ideas from the physical sciences and economics and applies them to organisations. For example, we can characterise the human body as a system which is comprised of a number of sub-systems. The reproductive system, the digestive system, the thinking system all go to make up the overall system. Similarly, a motor car is a system which takes the driver and passengers from point A to point B. It is also made up of a number of sub-systems – the braking sub-system, the heating sub-system, the gearing sub-system and so on. If one of these sub-systems does not work properly it will affect the working of the system as a whole and the motor car will not function to the best of its abilities.

Both the human body and the motor car interact with the environment. The motor car uses inputs such as petrol, oil and human effort and produces outputs such as movement, noise and other forms of pollution. The human body will use inputs such as food, oxygen and ideas and produce outputs such as activity and carbon dioxide. The concept is expressed diagrammatically in Fig. 4.3.

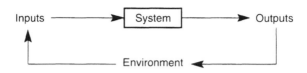

Fig. 4.3 Systems theory

We can apply this thinking to organisations and look at how they interact with their environment and with other organisations. Thus we can talk of a local government system which is different from a central government system but nevertheless interacts with it.

Systems theory proposes that there is a continuum between closed systems and open systems. Using the distinction between a mechanistic and an organic system, a mechanistic system is relatively closed and an organic system is relatively open to the environment. It assumes that local government is a relatively open system operating in an environment where environmental factors include:

- **legal**, e.g. changes in the law;
- **economic**, e.g. decrease in resources;
- **political**, e.g. policies of political parties;
- **demographic**, e.g. the changing birth rate;
- **technological**, e.g. new computer systems.

Local government then operates in this environment, transforming inputs such as labour, policies and finances into outputs in the form of the provision of services such as education or housing. Its ability to do this depends upon what goes on within the system itself, i.e. who has power, who makes decisions, who implements decisions and so on. Systems theory helps us to understand the context in which an organisation exists and how it transforms inputs into outputs. This is a theme that we will follow throughout the rest of this book.

Organisations need to be adaptive to respond to the changing inputs and therefore the process of management and organisational structuring will need an environmental orientation. Sometimes the boundaries between systems are not entirely clear. Do we define a system as one local authority or is it the system of local government as a whole? Is it a Training and Education Council or the whole system of training? Is it a prison or the whole criminal justice system? Perhaps these kinds of questions are best answered by knowing what we want to analyse. If we want to understand the functioning of a payroll system of a local authority we could see it as a system and the near environment will include the other departments of the local authority as well as the banks, building societies and other financial institutions. If we wish to examine the problem of recidivism amongst offenders, to look at the prisons alone would ignore the crucial roles played by the courts and the Home Office in the determination of sentences and the prison system we have.

Where there is a blurring at the boundaries, managers need to be sensitive to boundary disputes and to be able to work across boundaries with other organisations. For example, in delivering community care, local authority managers will need to be aware of the interests of the health authority, general practitioners, private sector providers, the voluntary sector, users and carers and so on.

THE CONTINGENCY APPROACH

The perspective adopted by the 'contingency' theorists rejects the view that there is one best model for an organisational structure. Rather, such theorists suggest that for any particular organisation the most appropriate structure is that which best fits the particular organisation, depending upon the relationship between a number of variables. These variables will include size, technology, people, purposes and environment. Within an organisation, depending upon these variables, it may make sense to have different organisational structures. Thus a local government department offering central support services such as a training department may require a different structure than one which is decentralised and based around service provision. A number of studies based primarily upon private sector organisations have analysed the impact that these variables will have.

- Child (1977) has examined the relationship between size and the economic performance of the organisation.
- Perrow (1967) has examined the relationship between technology and structure.
- Woodward (1958) has looked at the relationship between technology and organisational performance in the manufacturing industry.
- Lawrence and Lorsch (1967) analysed the internal structure of firms in the plastics, container and consumer food industries in terms of differentiation and integration. Differentiation refers to the different relationships, departments and goals that exist within an organisation and integration is the degree of co-ordination and co-operation between different departments with inter-departmental tasks. The matrix structure that we examined earlier would take account of these two variables.

Unlike systems theory, the contingency approach examines particular organisations. The theory argues that we cannot develop one universal scientific approach to create the perfect organisational structure, but rather we have to look at a number of variables and see how they interact with each other within particular organisations. Thus a reorganisation of central government without taking into account the many different functions that the individual departments perform will not work. Any change has to be designed to fit the particular needs of particular departments. The problem is the difficulty of selecting the key variables and then analysing the relationships between them.

Organisational performance tends to be multi-faceted. Changing the technology in an organisation may have no impact unless there is a willingness on the part of staff to adapt to it or unless the operating processes take account of the increased speed of communications that new technology can allow. Which is more important and can we clearly identify the key variable? Similarly, there may be no control over the consequences of changing the different variables and there may be unforeseen consequences. We also need to take into account other variables, particularly when concentrating upon the public sector. Thus, Hinings *et al.* (1975) note the importance of political values and power. The contingency approach does, however, draw our attention to the fact that different structures may be necessary for the different activities that an organisation performs and takes account of the differing environment within which organisations operate.

Summary

The stable mechanistic organisation form is more appropriate when the following conditions hold:

- the environment is relatively stable;
- the goals are well defined and enduring;
- the technology is relatively uniform and stable;
- there are routine activities;
- decision making is programmable and co-ordination and control processes tend to make a tightly structured, hierarchical system possible.

The adaptive organic organisational form is more appropriate when the following are true:

- the environment is relatively uncertain and turbulent;
- the goals are diverse and changing;
- the technology is complex and dynamic;
- there are many non-routine activities in which creativity and responsiveness are important;
- the systems of communication and co-ordination are informal and non-hierarchical. (Kast and Rosenzweig, 1985, pp. 111–17.)

DECENTRALISATION

Finally we need to spend some time considering the role of decentralised administration in the public sector. This is of particular importance as more and more government activities are being provided at a more localised level. Such moves have taken a number of different forms:

- In the National Health Service clinical budgeting and resource management have been introduced so that the doctors are responsible for the financial consequences of clinical decisions.
- In education the introduction of the local management of schools will give many of the decisions affecting individual schools to the school itself and away from the local education authority.
- There is a long history of decentralised management in the field of housing where local offices on council estates have their own budgets for minor repairs and other aspects of service delivery.

Mintzberg (1983, p. 99) identifies three different types of decentralisation. Firstly, *vertical decentralisation* which entails the dispersal of power down the chain of command and is more commonly referred to as delegation, means involving those people lower down the organisational hierarchy in decisions rather than concentrating power at the very top level of the organisation. In the civil service, the Financial Management Initiative involved the delegation of responsibility for budgets and staff down the hierarchy on the assumption that this would result in more effective decisions. Linked to this is the notion of accountability which we discussed in Chapter 2.

Secondly, *horizontal decentralisation* involves transferring decision-making powers to people outside the line structure. For example, it may involve the transfer of responsibility for the maintenance of computer systems to an information technology support group. This may have the advantage of allowing the line managers to concentrate on what they define as core activities, leaving technical work to specialists.

Thirdly, *dispersal* involves the physical location of services in a particular place. This does not involve the relocation of decision making and is akin to what Smith (1985, Chapter 8) describes as field administration. For example, a library service may be concentrated in one large library in the centre of town or dispersed into a number of smaller libraries in the suburbs and mobile libraries to serve smaller villages.

In practice, decentralisation often involves a combination of these three elements. For example, a local authority may decentralise decision-making structures by having area-based policy-making committees as well as decentralised offices in localities where officers are responsible for making operational decisions about service delivery.

We can contrast centralisation with decentralisation. The advantages of *centralisation* will include:

- easier implementation of a common policy for the organisation as a whole;
- prevention of sub-units becoming too independent;
- easier co-ordination;
- improving economies of scale and a reduction in overhead costs;
- greater use of specialisation;
- improved decision making which might otherwise be slower and a result of compromise because of differentiated authority;
- uniform and equitable treatment of clients;
- control in the hands of those at the top of the organisation.

The advantages of *decentralisation* are:

- it enables decisions to be made closer to the operational level of work;
- it encourages motivation and is good for morale;
- it allows responsiveness to the customer or the client;
- it will break down bureaucratic procedures;
- it will allow increased accountability since it will be more difficult to pass the buck up the organisation.

Decentralisation is thus seen as an alternative to the bureaucratic practices that we investigated in the previous chapter.

According to Hambleton and Hoggett (1984) decentralisation allows:

- the improvement of services;
- greater accountability of services;
- easier distribution of services;
- increased political awareness by encouraging participation.

Decentralisation has supporters from all parts of the political spectrum. On the left it is believed that it will encourage political participation, and on the right it is believed that it will get the central state off the backs of individuals and allow greater individual choice. We can ask, though, to what extent does it allow individuals to have control over day-to-day operational matters, control and influence over strategic decisions and control over finance?

In both the private and public sectors there is increasing attention devoted to, and criticism of, the length of hierarchies: The chain of command in the civil service is approximately twelve tiers from the permanent secretary to the administrative assistant. In the police service there are at least eight ranks of police officers, more in the Metropolitan Police. There is pressure to reduce the length of these widely criticised hierarchies (see, for example, Sheehy, 1993). The development of government by contract as opposed to government by command requires new sets of relationships, often with services delivered from outside the traditional public sector by, among others, private contractors. Also, approaches such as total quality management emphasise individual responsibility for quality of work thereby making supervisory levels of management redundant.

However, hierarchy is not universally condemned. Elliott Jaques argues that management hierarchies are necessary if complex tasks are to be achieved in large organisations. For Jaques, hierarchies allow the allocation of tasks to competent people with systems of accountability for performance. He concludes:

> Managerial hierarchy or layering is the only effective organisational form for deploying people and tasks at complementary levels, where people can do the tasks assigned to them . . . Trying to raise the efficiency and morale without first setting their structure to rights is like trying to lay bricks without mortar. (Jaques, 1991, pp. 117–18.)

CONCLUSION

There are a number of tensions inherent in organisational structures and the formal approach to organisations needs to recognise the tendency for different organisational principles to pull in different directions. These tensions are between the following.

Central control and decentralisation

Although we have indicated the growing strength of the movement towards decentralisation we have to embrace this with caution. We used the example of the local management of schools to indicate devolved decision making to the school itself. And yet, at the same time, central government has imposed the national curriculum on the state education system which seems to move in the opposite direction, seeking to impose a nationally determined agenda for education.

Integration and differentiation

Lawrence and Lorsch (1967), as we saw earlier, developed this tension in their contingency approach to organisations. In central government there are a number of mechanisms for co-ordination. There are also a number of inter-departmental committees based in the Cabinet and there is Cabinet itself to co-ordinate government policy. There are also co-ordinating departments such as the Treasury in central government and the Chief Executive's Department in local authorities. Such co-ordinating mechanisms are required to counter the tendency of functional departments to pursue their own goals and interests even when in conflict with the interests of the organisation as a whole.

Continuity and adaptability

We have indicated that organisations exist within a changing environment and they have to respond to this environment. At the same time they also need to ensure continuity. This is particularly important for public sector organisations where a change in the ruling political party may mean a change in policies and priorities. One of the advantages of the bureaucratic structure is that it can ensure continuity through the use of standard work practices and also provide some measure of stability. Other contributions to continuity will be the existence of professional norms and values that persist over time, the need to be responsible and accountable to Parliament and the constraints placed upon radical change by legal requirements.

The picture that is emerging is of dynamic organisations existing within changing environments with the need to balance competing tendencies to survive. This picture is added to in the next chapter where we examine the informal relations that exist within organisations, and in Chapter 6 where we examine power.

FURTHER READING

Most of the introductory texts to organisational theory will have a chapter on the classical, systems and contingency approaches to organisations. Mullins (1989) is particularly thorough. The selected readings in Pugh (1984) include excerpts from the classical texts. Mintzberg (1983) is especially good on organisational design. Haynes (1980) is extremely good on the local government context; likewise Pitt and Smith (1981) on government departments. A wealth of material on the history and organisational structures of central government can be found in Hennessy (1989a). Child (1977) examines the notion of organisational structure in depth. Hambleton and Hoggett (1984) raise many of the issues associated with decentralisation in local government.

CHAPTER 5

The informal organisation

INTRODUCTION

The main emphasis of the classical approach to organisations which we examined in the previous chapter was upon the formal characteristics of organisations, particularly in terms of organisational structure. Little attention was paid to the individuals within organisations in terms of their beliefs, values and their relations with each other. This chapter begins by examining these informal relations and assesses their importance in terms of our understanding of how organisations operate. This informal perspective is not meant to replace the formal approach but rather to supplement it and to develop a fuller understanding of how organisations operate. The classical approach used the methodology of the physical sciences to illustrate a view of organisations. Those that study the informal aspects of organisations tend to do so from perspectives drawn from the social sciences, particularly sociology and psychology.

THE HUMAN RELATIONS APPROACH

This approach is associated with the famous Hawthorne experiments at the Western Electric Company in America between 1924 and 1932 (see Mayo, 1971 and Roethlisberger and Dickson, 1939). The original intention behind the research was to measure the effect of variations in the work conditions on the individual worker. The researchers used control groups from amongst the workers to assess the effect upon productivity of such variations. The first phase of experiments was concerned with the variation in the lighting. The results of this first phase were, much to the researchers' surprise, that productivity increased no matter how much the lighting was varied. The conclusion drawn was that it was the fact that the group was working as a team that was important. Also the workers felt a certain status and a privilege to be singled out for special treatment. Thus, it was argued that the increase in productivity was a direct result of improved relations among the workers. Subsequent experiments tested the effect of rest periods, the duration of work and the use of a payment by piece-work system. The results of these experiments seemed to indicate that:

● informal group dynamics were important;

- informal group norms would develop which could undermine formal working relations. The researchers found that the workforce would work more easily with one supervisor rather than another;
- informal group norms developed over what was to count as an acceptable day's work despite what management thought. Those individuals that worked above or below these group norms risked being ostracised by their fellow workers;
- such informal group norms were important to the workers even to the extent that an individual worker might refuse promotion if it meant leaving the group;
- if management took an interest in the workforce and allowed them some control over their environment then the workforce would feel less alienated from the workplace;
- where norms of co-operation and high output are established because of a feeling of importance, physical conditions may have little impact.

The methodology, the results and the interpretation of those results have all been questioned and criticised (see Parsons, 1978) but the Hawthorne experiments do suggest a number of considerations:

- Individuals will interact in much more unpredictable and complex ways than the classical writers would have us believe. Taylor assumed, for example, that workers were rational and would be motivated by an increase in wages and hence by linking wages to productivity the worker would produce more. The Hawthorne researchers argued that this does not necessarily follow.
- Productivity may be affected by the dynamics of changing social relations at work.
- Working in a group and feeling part of a team is important.

The human relations approach, as its name suggests, thus concentrates upon the people dimension within organisations and how they interrelate with each other. We shall return to this later in the chapter when we examine the impact of groups and of culture within organisations.

THE INDIVIDUAL

A number of writers have concentrated upon the psychological make-up of individuals and indicated that the individual's nature needs to be understood to analyse individuals in organisations.

Maslow's hierarchy of needs

Maslow (1943) argued that individuals have a number of basic psychological and physiological needs which an individual tries to satisfy. These needs are:

- physiological: for food, drink, shelter, etc.;
- safety and security;

- social: to relate to others, have friends and so on;
- esteem: to have the respect of others;
- self-actualisation: to achieve full potential.

Maslow argued that as one need is met then the individual moves on to the next need. Thus as the need for basic sustenance is met we move up the ladder to the next step, which is the satisfaction of the need for safety. As each need is met the individual moves up the hierarchy. We shall examine these ideas in more detail when we come to look at motivation and morale within organisations. For the moment we need to take account of individual needs coming into the picture.

McGregor's Theory X and Theory Y

McGregor (1960) argued that within organisations the style of management is also important in determining how an organisation operates. He suggested that there are two different approaches based upon the basic perceptions that the manager has of the workforce. The first perspective, Theory X, assumes that (a) the average person is lazy and does not care to work; (b) most people must be coerced, directed and controlled if the organisation is to benefit by employing them; (c) the average person lacks ambition and has no interest in taking on responsibility.

In contrast to this, Theory Y assumes that (a) for most people work is natural; (b) people are interested in their work and will exercise self-direction; (c) given the right conditions then people will seek responsibility; (d) people are committed to organisational objectives since rewards are associated with the achievement of these objectives.

The importance of this approach is to suggest that it is perceptions that are important and depending on how the management views the worker then different styles of management will develop and different sets of relationships between the management and the workforce will exist.

Herzberg on motivation and hygiene

Herzberg (1966) argued that we need to take into account not just the needs and motivations of the individual worker but also the context within which they are operating. He thus developed a theory which argues that there are two sets of factors at work. The first set of factors are concerned with the *content* of work and the amount of job satisfaction that an individual receives – the motivation factor. This factor includes:

- the sense of achievement;
- the sense of responsibility;
- the sense of recognition;
- advancement at work;
- the content of the job itself.

The other factor is associated with the *context* of work and the work environment. Herzberg terms this the 'hygiene' or 'maintenance' factor. He argues that by maintaining the job environment at an acceptable level then feelings of dissatisfaction can be avoided. The hygiene factor includes:

- the level of salary;
- the quality of supervision;
- working conditions;
- interpersonal relations with supervisors;
- company policy and administration.

In Chapter 8 – on motivation – we shall examine research on the civil service which draws heavily upon the two-factor analysis developed by Herzberg.

Argyris on self-actualisation

Argyris (1957) suggests that whilst the individual may seek to actualise or achieve his or her full potential the organisation does not always allow this to happen. This is particularly the case for individuals working in the kind of formal organisations that were described in the previous two chapters. The individual is frustrated by the formal constraints imposed by formal organisations and creates informal activities. The individual becomes apathetic and disinterested, reducing the speed of work and the care taken over work. Group norms are developed that condone such behaviour. Eventually the organisation will modify its form in order to take account of the individual.

GROUPS IN ORGANISATIONS

Although psychological explanations tend to concentrate upon the individual worker within the organisation, we can also examine the role of individuals as members of groups and note how the existence of different groups, both formal and informal, have an important role to play in developing our understanding of organisations. According to Mullins (1989) a group consists of a number of people who share (a) a common objective or task; (b) an awareness of group identity and boundary; (c) a minimum set of agreed values and norms.

The classical writers completely ignored the existence of such factors. Organisations consist of both formal groups and informal groups. Thus, formal groups are created to achieve specific organisational objectives and are concerned with the co-ordination of work activities. Formal groups can be split into:

- team groups such as research teams or inter-departmental working parties;
- task groups centred around administrative tasks such as finance or personnel;
- technological groups centred around a piece of technology such as in assembly line production. In local government this might take the form of computer services;

- decision-making groups such as committees (particularly prevalent in local government and an integral part of local government structure);
- problem-solving groups cutting across different divisions such as working parties or task forces;
- representative groups such as the British Medical Association representing the views of doctors, or trade unions representing the views of their members.

We would expect individuals to belong to more than one of these groups. Problems may arise when loyalty to one group may be in conflict with membership of another group. We can imagine the dilemma that an individual might face if, for example, he or she works in the personnel department of an organisation and has to give redundancy notices to members of the same trade union. Such formal groups do, however, perform a number of useful functions:

- Certain tasks can be performed only through the combined efforts of a number of people working together, e.g. a police or a medical operation. Sometimes such tasks require groups working together. A car accident, for example, may involve all the emergency services such as the police, fire service, ambulance service and surgeons.
- Groups may encourage companionship and provide a source of mutual understanding and support from like-minded colleagues.
- Membership of a group may provide an individual with a sense of belonging. Maslow, if we recall, suggested that this is one of our basic needs. Similarly, a trade union might assist people in meeting safety needs.
- The group may provide guidelines for behaviour such as a professional ethic or a code of conduct.

Strong and cohesive work groups can have beneficial effects for the organisation where they share common goals and values. At the same time the existence of strong groups may have a detrimental effect upon the organisation where the group puts forward its own interests at the expense of the organisation as a whole. The Hawthorne experiments that we discussed earlier indicated that peer group pressure was more important in determining an acceptable level of output irrespective of the demands of management.

Homans (1950) suggests three concepts for understanding individual behaviour in social groups: activity, interaction and sentiment. The more the people share activities, the more likely they are to interact with one another. The reciprocal is also true; interaction in one sphere of activity often leads to shared activity in unrelated spheres.

Increasingly, the importance of group working within organisations is recognised and much of the work of public sector organisations has a team element. For example, the National Health Service uses quality circles to ensure quality in its service. A quality circle usually involves relatively permanent small groups of between five and fifteen people from the same work group who meet periodically to consider quality problems. The features of such groups are trust, involvement, the commitment to improvement and recognition for success. (See Chell, 1987, pp. 214–19.)

PROFESSIONAL GROUPS

Within the public sector we find that professional groups usually have a tremendous impact upon the culture of an organisation and their influence is felt widely throughout the decision-making channels. It is, therefore, worth exploring in some detail their role. Dawson (1988) indicates that the characteristics of professional groupings include:

- Membership of a professional body. Accountants, lawyers, doctors all have well-established professional associations which control entry to the profession.
- Rigorous and lengthy training – usually over a period of years so the non-committed will fall by the wayside.
- A restricted entry – usually through the attainment of other educational qualifications, such as a university degree.
- Prescribed codes of ethics and standards of behaviour – there are both formal and informal codes which indicate how the member of the profession is expected to behave. Serious breaches of these codes can result in a member being struck off the professional register.
- A proclaimed concern for client groups – doctors exist to serve their patients, teachers to educate their students.
- Peer group evaluation, control and promotion – the work of the professional is usually assessed by other professionals.
- Possession of a status and a mystique associated with the profession. Doctors are held in high regard by society, teachers used to be and social workers strive to be.

Such professional groupings have a number of implications for organisations. Firstly, we can ask, given the existence of a professional code, to what extent is the professional committed to the profession before the organisation? An architect working in local government may insist upon designing buildings that conform to a professional standard rather than to fit the needs of the authority or the community that the authority serves. Winning design awards may be more important than building affordable, practical housing estates. The architect may wish to design the most aesthetically pleasing school using the best materials, the educationalist may be concerned that the school has appropriate classroom sizes for the different educational activities, and the accountant will concentrate upon costs.

Such different perspectives may lead to organisational conflict between the professional group and the organisation as a whole. The professional may insist upon controlling the work that he or she does rather than allowing the administrator to impose control. Doctors may not, for example, be happy with interference in their work by somebody who lacks their medical expertise. Self and peer evaluation seem to indicate that professionals are unwilling to be held to account for their actions by outside individuals or groups. The medical profession will argue that an individual without medical expertise cannot pass judgement on their performance. Finally, different professional groups have distinct cultures, norms and values and these cultures may come into conflict. The administrative civil servant may operate within a legal culture with a concern for following regulations and statutes. The architect or the engineer working within the civil service may believe this to be unnecessary red tape and their culture may be dominated by a concern to do the best possible job conforming to the highest professional standards.

The role of the professional within the civil service has traditionally been that of the 'specialist on tap'. In other words the generalist administrator calls upon economists, statisticians and engineers for information and advice but it is the generalist who is 'on top'. This tradition of generalist domination of the decision-making process was heavily criticised by the Fulton Report (1968) on the civil service. The report argued that the specialist should be encouraged to develop managerial skills and be allowed to play a bigger role in the strategic decisions of the organisation. Such a view has more recently found favour in the National Health Service where the medical profession is encouraged to develop managerial skills. The local government dimension is slightly different with specialists normally in charge of the different departments. Thus the chief housing officer will have expertise, experience and relevant professional qualifications, normally through the Institute of Housing. It is also the case that the generalist administrator is becoming more 'professionalised' with qualifications available through the Business and Technology Education Council (BTEC), the Institute of Personnel Management (IPM), the Institute of Chartered Secretaries and Administrators (ICSA) and so on.

Ultimately our interest with professional groups within organisations is a concern with power and the extent to which professionals have power as a result of their expertise. Following on from that is the question of accountability. If an important concern in the public sector is with accountability then we can question whether peer accountability is sufficient. In the public sector there has to be accountability to the public or the client. A major theme in local government is to control the power of the professional. The concern with professional power is developed in Chapter 6 and our concluding chapters show how the recent changes in public sector organisations may affect the power of the professionals.

DISCRETION

In Chapter 3 we examined the role that formal rules may play in bureaucratic organisations. It is also the case that discretionary powers are vested in people, groups and organisations. This may be formally vested via legislation or may be informal. For example, professionals such as social workers may be required to make judgements based on the available evidence. Alternatively, a group may have informal discretion over such matters as the pace of work, the attitude to work or the willingness to perform tasks. Smith (1981) defines the issues:

- **How is discretion defined?** Discretion is concerned with the element of choice that an individual has when making a decision. The mechanistic following of rules would leave little scope for discretion to be exercised. Thus:

  > A public officer has discretion wherever the effective limits on his power leave him free to make a choice among possible courses of action or inaction. (Davis, 1969, p. 4.)

- **How is it controlled?** In practice there will not be complete freedom of choice for the individual. Group norms and values will act as constraints and even informal rules can be as rigid as formal rules. Professional codes of conduct will constrain individuals and ultimately the law will deter extreme interpretation of rules.

- **What are the consequences of widespread discretion?** Discretion will allow officials to exercise some autonomy in their work and may allow the official to respond to the individual needs of clients rather than applying a set of standard rules. It may encourage, though, the arbitrary nature of decision making so that, for example, the receipt of benefits comes to depend on the attitude of the official and how he or she interacts with the claimant.

- **What factors will influence the use of discretion?**
  1 *The need for accountability* – no matter how much discretion those working in the public sector exercise they will ultimately be accountable for their decisions either to superior officers or to the public through the tribunal systems or judicial review.
  2 *Resources* – the reason why discretion is used in the first place may be because of limited resources. If all minor traffic offences were prosecuted the courts would be overloaded.
  3 *The clarity of formal rules* – if the rules are clear, specific and cover every eventuality there would be no question of them being open to interpretation. Often, though, legislation is general in nature allowing interpretation by officials to meet individual cases.
  4 *Professional power* – professional groups seek to control areas of work rather than having their activities circumscribed by those outside the professional group. Thus one of the principal characteristics of work carried out by professionals is its highly discretionary nature.

Any organisation will have a mixture of formal and informal rules and will allow discretion. However, we need to be aware that they all influence behaviour.

CULTURE

A more recent approach to the informal organisation is to consider the beliefs and values of individuals and groups as part of an organisational culture. Writers are concerned with such issues as: Does culture belong to the organisation or to the individuals within it? Is it thus greater than the sum of the individual parts? We also need to consider the extent to which organisations have one dominant culture, or the extent to which they consist of sub-cultures. In the light of the previous discussion we would be concerned with the extent to which professionals have their own sub-culture which is distinct from the organisational culture as a whole. However, Schein (1987) suggests that organisational culture is concerned with the

> . . . *basic assumptions* and *beliefs* that are shared by members of an organisation, that operate unconsciously, and that define in a basic 'taken-for-granted' fashion an organization's view of itself and its environment. These assumptions and beliefs are *learned* responses to a group's problems of *survival* in its external environment and its problems of *internal integration*. (Schein, 1987, p. 6.)

Our first concern is with deciding what culture does. Here we can offer a number of different possibilities:

● Culture will specify the goals and objectives of the organisation. In the private sector, an organisation's corporate identity will perform this function by emphasising, for example, 'customer service' or using slogans such as Ford's 'Everything we do is driven by you.' Some universities and colleges compete to convince us that they are 'centres of excellence'. The NHS is 'working for patients' and the local authority is 'serving the public' or 'caring for the client'. Such phrases try to give us an image of what the organisation is about and individuals within the organisation are expected to adopt such a culture and to pursue the goals that it prescribes.

● Culture will specify the relations that exist within the organisation and define what is to count as legitimate or illegitimate behaviour. In the Hawthorne experiments that we discussed earlier it was group pressure that determined the appropriate behaviour of individuals rather than formal guidelines, and informal sanctions were imposed if the individual did not conform to the group norms and expectations. In the civil service, the relationship between the civil servant and the politician is partly governed by the need for confidentiality. Civil servants who leak information are criticised by politicians for a breach of trust. After the Ponting case (1985) the head of the civil service, Sir Robert Armstrong, issued a code of conduct in an attempt to guide the behaviour of officials (Armstrong, 1985).

● Culture also specifies what qualities are valued within organisations such as loyalty, confidentiality, dynamism, hard work, the ability to sell a product, and so on. Each organisation, and different groups within that organisation, may value different qualities. Difficulties arise when individuals are asked to develop qualities which they do not possess or which they have previously dismissed as irrelevant or not worth possessing. Thus to ask the civil servant to cut costs irrespective of the effect on the quality of the service provided may be difficult not only if the civil servant does not possess the appropriate financial skills but also if the civil servant takes pride in the quality of service provided. Similarly, if the official is expected to trim advice so that it is politically acceptable he or she may find this unpalatable if there has been a tradition of impartial advice.

All organisations exist within some wider context and we would expect an organisation's culture to reflect this. We would expect a match between the organisational culture and the wider culture of society at large. Thus it may be unrealistic to expect a democratically run workplace when the prevailing political and social ethos is authoritarian. We can pose the question: to what extent is the traditional hierarchical nature of bureaucracy at odds with a less deferential and more egalitarian society? Can we expect individuals to enjoy equal rights and participation in their social lives and yet work under an authoritarian structure at the workplace that gives them little responsibility and allows them little scope for participation in decision making?

Apart from the societal context within which the organisation operates we would also expect the history of the organisation to influence its present culture. Past values and beliefs are transmitted to new members through formal induction programmes and informal working practices epitomised in such phrases as: 'We do things this way in this office.' The transmission of values ensures continuity and allows the organisation to survive changes in personnel. The former head of the civil service, Lord Bridges, describes departmental life in the civil service and suggests that:

> . . . in every Department a store of knowledge and experience in the subjects handled, something which eventually takes shape as a practical philosophy, or may merit the title of a departmental philosophy . . . in most cases the departmental philosophy is nothing more startling than the slow accretion and accumulation of experience over the years . . . Every civil servant finds himself entrusted with this kind of inheritance. He knows that it is his business to contribute something of his own to this store of experience; and that he should play his part in moulding it and improving it to meet changing conditions. Equally he knows that it is something he will ignore at his peril. (Bridges, 1950, p. 16.)

It may happen that individuals are taken over by the organisation and by groups within it, particularly where the corporate identity and image is a strong one. This transmission of culture is aided by the tendency to recruit in 'one's own image' where members of interview panels tend to look for qualities that they themselves possess when recruiting new members. The Oxford and Cambridge arts and classicist graduates at the top of the civil service may, consciously or subconsciously, favour individuals from similar backgrounds because such candidates will possess similar qualities to themselves. Not to do so is to admit that one's own qualities are not required by the organisation. Politicians may apply the same criteria. Margaret Thatcher is supposed to have applied the acid test of 'Is he one of us?' when making her senior appointments.

Thus we are concerned with organisations as social systems that have shared understandings, norms and values and have a common language. The new recruit into any organisation ·or group has to learn these norms and the codes of speech that groups employ before they can feel part of the group. Young and Sloman discovered this sense of intimacy in the Treasury. They quote an Under Secretary commenting upon informal communications networks: 'Some of these people I've known for twenty-five years and we can of course communicate with each other almost in code.' (Young and Sloman, 1984, p. 25.)

The difficulty arises, as we saw with professional groupings, of sub-groups existing within an organisation that do not all share the same goals or values. To what extent does an organisation exhibit a common, homogeneous culture? We can imagine that a small advertising agency may well share a common culture, but a large government department, such as the Home Office, with multiple functions and goals is unlikely to exhibit the same homogeneity. Similarly, the picture we have of the civil service drawn from such programmes as *Yes Minister* only depicts a small number of mandarins at the top of the civil service. We can legitimately ask what does a senior official based in Whitehall and acting as a policy adviser to a minister have in common with an administrative officer working in a local branch of the Department of Social Security other than the fact that they are both civil servants? Of course, it may well be that there is a dominant culture within an organisation which is formed at the top and is transmitted downwards through formal and informal mechanisms. This point is important if it is the case that the leaders at the top of the organisation are the ones who create the image and identity of the organisation.

Handy (1985) has analysed the different types of organisational culture and offers a four-fold typology:

- **The power culture**. The organisation stresses the role of individuals rather than committees. Individuals are power-oriented and politically aware. Control is exercised at the centre and it is characterised by informal webs of influence rather than formal procedures. It is not characterised by bureaucracy.
- **The role culture**. Here the stress is upon formal rules and roles and authority is vested in these roles. It is characterised by formal procedures and offers the individual security, stability and predictability. It is, therefore, characteristic of a bureaucracy. Wilson (1989, pp. 174–5) argues that procedural organisations such as armies in peace time are dominated by formal procedures and supervision. Soldiers repeat meaningless tasks at the expense of staff morale.
- **The task culture**. This is job-oriented and is concerned with getting the job done. It is concerned with utilising resources to meet the organisation's objectives and is characterised by the requirement of efficiency. The culture adapts itself to change and is driven by the need to provide goods and services for the customer. Increasingly, public services are expected to be output driven, to be seen to achieve clear objectives (see Chapter 9).

- **The person culture**. The individual is at the heart of this organisation and this culture, according to Handy, is not often found. The organisation serves the individual rather than the other way round. Control mechanisms or hierarchies are virtually impossible and influence is shared. A commune would possess this type of culture.

Interestingly, as public service organisations have to work with and through each other, it is essential that managers appreciate the culture of the organisation with which they are dealing. For example, the local authority has to be sensitive to the people-centred culture of many voluntary organisations through which it is delivering community care.

Traditionally bureaucracy has been described as a role culture, but there is no reason to suppose that the different cultures cannot all exist within the same organisation, particularly if the organisation is as large and diverse as a government department or a local authority. Indeed the contingency approach to organisations would argue that, depending upon the dominant activity, an organisation should consist of different sub-cultures reflecting different activities.

In the public sector the concept of a role culture would seem to have some relevance. However, we may wish to use a different set of criteria:

- **A political culture** – given that government takes place within a political context then we may wish to consider the political dimension as the most important. Thus, we might be interested in the relationship between the politician and the official; the relationship between the different parties particularly where there is a hung council; the role of interest groups and their relationship with departments and so on.
- **An administrative culture** – which is concerned with rules, roles, authority and fits in with the concept of a role culture.
- **A legal culture** – particularly important in local government where much of the work may be governed by statute, or may involve the regulation of activities.
- **A market culture** – where public sector organisations are exposed to the market through competitive tendering, contracting out, internal markets and so on.

Each of the different cultures may express the roles that organisations perform. Problems arise where there is a clash of cultures. It would be unrealistic to expect officials to be responsive to the market when their traditional activity has been conditioned by the need to follow statutes. The creation of the Training and Enterprise Councils by central government to run the bulk of the country's training has encountered problems of culture clash. Business people brought in to run the councils have been frustrated by the tight operating and financial practices imposed by the Department of Employment. Such practices sit uneasily alongside the entrepreneurial freedom that business leaders are used to.

Within government there will be strong traditions which have to be overcome if a new culture is to develop. Depending upon the strength of the existing culture then change is not easily brought about. The strength of the civil service culture is commented upon by Hennessy who suggests that, after three decades of travelling up the hierarchy, senior civil servants become indistinguishable from each other:

> Their habits, modes of thought, patterns of speech, style of drafting will have rubbed off on one another to the point where but a few free or tough or independent spirits resist mutation into a sludgy administrative amalgam. (Hennessy, 1989a, pp. 521–2.)

CONCLUSION

In this chapter we have examined the informal side of organisations. This approach adds to our understanding by moving beyond the formal structures to examine a range of factors that influence human behaviour. In order to make this understanding more complete we need to examine two aspects of the human relations side: leadership and motivation and morale. Following that we need to add one further ingredient – that of power. Although we have introduced the concept of a power culture, from the work of Handy, it can be argued that all organisations are really concerned with power. From this perspective, all organisations are political in that they are characterised by bargaining, compromises and conflicts between individuals and groups.

In the later chapters of the book we examine the changing nature of the public services. Those who have sought to introduce change and make the public services more dynamic and responsive have repeatedly emphasised the importance of ensuring not just changes in structures and rules but a change in the cultural orientation of the organisation.

FURTHER READING

Most introductory textbooks on organisational theory will have chapters on the human relations approach to organisations. Litterer (1969) is generally good on the informal organisation. Schein (1987) is very detailed on the relationship between culture and leadership. Adler and Asquith (1981) edited a very good collection of essays by different authors on welfare and discretion. Ham and Hill (1984) link discretion to the policy process. Kakabadse (1982) examines culture in a social services department. Handy (1985) explores the concept of organisation culture in detail and is also good on the workings of groups.

CHAPTER 6

Power and conflict within organisations

INTRODUCTION

All organisations, whether in the public or the private sector, are political. This may be more explicit within the public sector because government organisations are led by politicians and their work involves the implementation of a political party's policies. And yet private sector organisations are also political in the sense of competition between ideas and individuals within the organisation. There is conflict between departments, within hierarchies and over decisions that are made. All organisations are concerned with who makes decisions, who controls resources, who determines which issues are discussed, who sets the agenda and how conflict between individuals and groups is resolved. We are also concerned with the political environment within which all organisations operate. Decisions taken by politicians concerning the economy, for example, will affect those organisations engaged in business.

Politics occurs at different levels. One level might be 'insider' politics characterised by bargaining and conflict within organisations. A second level might be described as 'public' politics centred on party manifestos, elections and determining economic and social policies. A third level exists as 'system' politics which is concerned with shaping the political system itself (see Dunsire, 1984). Level one politics impacts upon all of us who work in organisations; level two politics, for most of us, is evident once every general election, whilst level three politics rarely involves other than a small minority.

We need, therefore, to examine who has power within society and locate that within the context of the power of the state. Through such an examination we can see who has power over decisions and which groups and individuals can achieve their aims. There are a number of general theories that are concerned with such issues and we shall briefly investigate these before moving on to an examination of power within organisations. Such theories are focused on system politics. All the theories that we examine have variations and we shall be concerned to pick out the main themes that the different interpretations of these theories have in common.

PLURALISM

Pluralism suggests that, within society, power is fragmented between different groups all of whom are in competition with each other. Depending upon the issue, different groups will get their own way and no one group dominates power within society. Political power can result from a variety of factors including wealth, control over information, status, popularity and legality. Pressure group politics is a manifestation of this where individuals organise into groups to achieve their aims. Examples of such groups range from trade unions and professional associations through to environmental groups trying to save the whale or local groups that are concerned with juggernaut lorries travelling through a small village. The issues are numerous and diverse but groups form to try to influence decisions concerning these issues.

Pluralism is a development of democratic theory and recognises that often individuals can best get their views heard by combining in groups to give them a stronger voice. Pluralism presupposes that groups have access to the decision-making process and that power is widely spread. Although power is widely spread it does not necessarily mean that it is evenly spread between all groups. However, in society the groups that we might think of as having an influence upon the decision-making processes will be the trade unions, representatives of the business world such as the Confederation of British Industry (CBI), the bureaucracy and political parties.

In organisational terms, a pluralist approach would suggest that organisations are made up of different groups each with access to the decision-making processes and with the ability to influence those processes. Thus, for example, in the National Health Service groups such as the consultants, junior doctors, administrators, nursing staff, GPs and so on, will all be striving to influence policy and to get their views accepted by the organisation. In local government we might find groups composed of councillors, officers, local businessmen and businesswomen, client groups, voluntary agencies, all attempting to get their views accepted. Stoker and Wilson (1986) argue that a range of resources are available to the competing groups involved in local decision making such as access to contacts, position in the hierarchy, control of information and so on. They identify a number of actors involved in the decision-making processes in local government and suggest that the picture of who has power is sometimes not clear.

Similarly, the conventional picture of decision making within health authorities is that of consensus between different coalitions of interests represented by practitioners, politicians and administrators, each with different resources and power bases. Pluralism, then, is concerned with competition between different groups involved in making decisions. Critics argue that this does not seem to be very realistic. Some groups seem to have more power than others. Big business or some trade unions, for example, seem to have exercised power consistently over long periods of time. Similarly, within organisations is it not the case that certain groups consistently seem to be able to get their own way? For example, in the

National Health Service it may well be the consultants that always seem to get their own way and the nurses rarely so. In the civil service it may well be the small number of Permanent Secretaries heading government departments that make decisions. In local government it may well be a small group of chief officers and committee chairpersons that control decisions. More widely, it may well be that central government usually gets its own way over local government. If this is the case then society and organisations, far from being pluralist in nature, are, in fact, élitist so that on any given issue there may be a small group that exercises a great deal of power. Indeed many of the pluralist writers were acutely aware of inequalities in the distribution of power.

ÉLITISM

Élitist theories argue that power is always in the hands of a minority. Within society power is in the hands of a small number of individuals and groups who may be prominent in industry, in financial or in political circles. It is these élites that dominate society. Those who support the arguments of the élitist theories will point to the tendency for senior politicians from all parties to come from similar social and educational backgrounds. Similarly, it is often the case that senior officials within the civil service all seem to come from the same sort of background. The virtual absence of women and members of ethnic minorities and the continuing dominance of Oxford and Cambridge arts and classicist graduates amongst the senior civil service and the 'high fliers' are said to support these criticisms. C. Wright Mills (1956) advances the notion of a power élite composed of men from similar social and educational backgrounds sharing similar values.

We can legitimately ask, however: What is wrong with this state of affairs? Indeed, Schumpeter (1976) argued that democracy is really about competition between competing élites for the votes of the people and that democracy did not require mass participation. From a different perspective it can also be argued that it is right and proper that, for example, the mandarins of the civil service should have power, because, after all, they have the expertise and knowledge in government matters. The politician may have been democratically elected but the politician does not have the same experience as the career official. We can characterise this as rule by the non-elected with power in the hands of a bureaucratic élite. Those familiar with the television programme *Yes Prime Minister* will recognise this characterisation. Similarly, it can be argued that consultants and their professional body, the British Medical Association (BMA), should dominate decision making within the National Health Service since they have the medical knowledge and expertise which the politician, the manager and the patient do not possess. Such arguments are powerful ones and, as we shall see later, possession of specialised knowledge is an important source of power.

There are also strong arguments, however, to suggest that a more pluralistic decision-making process is the best way for society and organisations to operate.

Expert knowledge may be too narrow in its focus. A decision made in the light of wider considerations may be a better decision. To what extent can it be the case that a decision-making process that is dominated by white, male, middle-aged and middle class civil servants is likely to be appropriate for all areas of social and economic policy? Such decision makers may have little experience of the issues that affect women or ethnic minorities, for example. In the long run a more efficient and effective – not to say democratic – decision may be one that draws upon different points of view and has considered several possibilities.

MARXISM

To do justice to the many writings of Marx and the vast body of work that has accumulated around his writings is impossible within the confines of this book and we shall, therefore, merely attempt to discuss one or two ideas and indicate their impact upon organisations.

Marx was very much concerned with conflict; indeed for him the driving force of history is based upon conflict between different groups or classes within society. This conflict comes about because of economic differences between different classes based around who has control over economic production. For example, one of the most important features of capitalism is the pursuit of profit and owners can increase profits by exploiting the workforce. This inevitably leads to conflict between these groups. Within organisations such conflict may take the form of strikes or go-slows because of the attempt by owners and managers to control wages and conditions of employment.

Inevitably, as capitalism developed it made sense to introduce more machinery, to move to a division of labour and to a conveyor-belt system of production. We saw in our discussion of bureaucracy that such developments can lead to a more efficient and effective organisation. And yet the individual worker is forgotten in all of this. In a drive for improving productivity and hence greater profit the values, needs and concerns of the worker are ignored. The worker becomes, in Marx's terms, 'an appendage of the machine' and is alienated from the workplace, from the job and from fellow workers. The provision of welfare benefits merely preserves an exploitative and inegalitarian system and Marx argues that the bureaucracy becomes merely the tool of the ruling classes.

Braverman (1974) argues that scientific management and the work of individuals such as F.W. Taylor, that we looked at in Chapter 3, encouraged the development of the control of the worker by management and that the transformation of work advocated by scientific management led to the de-skilling and to the degradation of the worker. Such effects also apply to the office worker who similarly experiences an increased division of labour, the mechanisation, simplification and routinisation of tasks, and strict management control.

CORPORATISM

Corporatist theories argue that major interest groups are incorporated into the decision-making apparatus of the state. Conflict is kept to a minimum by allowing such groups to share power. An example of corporatism at work may be that of Britain in the 1960s when the unions, represented by the Trades Union Congress, and big business, represented by the Confederation of British Industry, seemed to have easy access to government. Corporatism is a development of pluralism that allows for the domination of a small number of powerful groups. Schmitter defines corporatism as:

> . . . a system of interest representation in which the constituent units organised into a limited number of singular. compulsory, non-competitive, hierarchically ordered and functionally differentiated categories, recognised or licensed (if not created) by the state and granted a deliberate representational monopoly within their respective categories in exchange for observing certain controls on their selection of leaders and articulation of demands and supports. (1979, p. 13.)

In Britain in the 1960s, for example, government recognised the legitimate right of the Trades Union Congress to be consulted over issues which affected its members. In return, government expected the Trades Union Congress to respect that right and to control its members. Rhodes (1981) utilises this definition of corporatism in an examination of the policy networks within which public sector organisations operate. Rhodes (1988) argues that policy networks exist across a range of different areas including territory, issues, professions, inter-governmental associations and producer groups. Depending upon the policy, different members of the network will wish to have an influence. Policy networks illustrate the complex, dynamic and diversity of policy making. One example is the way in which policy decisions are formulated and implemented in Wales as a result of complex relationships involving politicians and officials in the Welsh Office, local authorities, quangos and Whitehall.

We have thus examined some of the general theories of power within society and within organisations. We now need to narrow our focus and concentrate upon the concept of power itself. We shall accordingly define the concept, examine its usage, and investigate the sources and limits of power.

THE DEFINITION OF POWER

Immediately we have difficulties since there seems to be no generally accepted definition of power. In the language of political philosophy, power is deemed to be a concept that is 'essentially contested' which means that although the concept has featured prominently in political philosophy over the centuries and is now a major concern of organisation theorists, we are still left with disputes over its meaning. We can, however, offer a very general working definition, which seems to feature in most discussions. Thus we take power to be the ability of one person or group A to get another person or group B to do as A wants. From this very general definition we can see that power is relational in character. Power is not something that is possessed such as blue eyes or red hair but manifests itself in terms of relations with others. Indeed it is often the case that a powerful person is not necessarily somebody who is physically strong but will depend upon the extent to which that person can get others to do as he or she wishes. It may well be that the most powerful person is someone who does not have to resort to physical force at all. We can see this idea expressed in international relations between states: the USA could not defeat Vietnam despite the fact that in terms of military equipment the USA had the most powerful weapons. Military hardware alone is not sufficient to ensure military victory. We have to take into account the skill of the leaders, the morale of the troops, the influence of world opinion and so on. In organisational theory Pfeffer (1981) argues that power is a relational concept that can only be understood in terms of interactions between individuals and groups.

We can see that power is related to other concepts such as force, influence, authority or manipulation. Power is one of a cluster of concepts that are all concerned with the ability of one person or group to affect another person or group as expressed in our general definition of power. However, we do not need to embark upon a lengthy discussion of differences between these concepts as such differences will be explained as they bear upon our concern with power in public sector organisations (see Connolly, 1974, for treatment of these conceptual issues). What we can do is examine the concept of power from a number of different perspectives.

THE BASIS OF POWER

Power in any form will be based upon something. In general terms we can suggest that power is based upon a number of different factors.

Economic power

This will be based upon the possession of scarce resources such as coal or oil or skilled labour and the extent to which those resources are in demand. Also the existence of alternative resources will limit the power of the individual or the group. Thus the power of a group like the miners will depend upon the demand for coal compared to other forms of energy. Hence their power to influence the government will depend upon the extent to which alternative forms of energy are readily available. The economic power of the individual may also depend upon the possession of a particular skill or knowledge that others want and are prepared to pay for. For example, the government may offer extra financial rewards to try to recruit scarce science teachers.

The basis of power may change. What is to count as a scarce resource, for example, may change over time. In times of low unemployment labour will be in a strong position because it is in demand by employers and is not easily substituted. At other times labour will be in a weak bargaining position if, as in times of high unemployment, the employer can easily acquire alternative sources of labour off the dole queues. Individuals who possess certain skills may also find their power diminished if those skills are made redundant by developments in new technology.

Political power

This will be based upon legitimacy, i.e. that which is accepted within a particular society as conferring the right to rule. Sometimes 'might is right' has been accepted as a legitimate form of political power, whereas at other times and in different societies hereditary succession has been accepted as the legitimate source of political power. In democratic societies the will of the people, as expressed in elections, is deemed to be the appropriate legitimation for political power. Thus our elected representatives are entitled to make decisions on our behalf. We may not like what our representatives do; we may even have not voted for the party or individual that wins the election. We do, however, agree to play by the 'rules of the game' and accept their decisions as binding upon us. If we wished to change the rules of the game we would involve ourselves in level three politics that we discussed earlier (see page 73).

The basis of power will depend upon the context within which it is exercised. Thus the will of the people as a basis of power may not be accepted easily in a society with a tradition of monarchical rule.

Organisational power

What then is organisational power dependent upon? We can identify a number of factors.

Information

Organisations rely upon information in order to function and it is likely that the individual or group that has control over information will have power. Part of the explanation for the power of the official over the politician may well be the extent to which the politician relies upon the official for information in order to make decisions. Critics argue that because of the control of information officials are in a position to slant their recommendations to the course of action that they prefer. If, on the other hand, there are alternative sources of information and advice then the monopoly position of the official will be undermined. Politicians may thus seek to use special advisers or use research units or policy units outside of government for their advice. The Conservative governments since 1979 have taken advice from the Centre for Policy Studies and the Adam Smith Institute in drawing up their policy proposals. Similarly rival political parties also have their own policy teams which draw up policy documents.

Knowledge

Linked to the power acquired through the control of information is that acquired through the possession of some specialised knowledge or skill, particularly where that knowledge cannot be easily substituted. The power of the officials stems from their understanding the processes and procedures that characterise the bureaucratic organisation. The politician may not possess this knowledge. A minister stays in a government department for only a limited period of time, on average two years, and this is considered insufficient time to master the workings of a complex government department. Other examples include the power of the medical profession within the National Health Service as a result of their medical expertise and the power of the professionals in local government, be they accountants, architects or social workers. The power of such groups will be enhanced if the organisation requires their expertise in order to function. The type of knowledge required within organisations may, however, change over time. In times of financial stringency and the adoption of 'value for money' strategies in government those with financial expertise may acquire power. Similarly, in those organisations that are becoming increasingly reliant upon information technology then those with computing skills may become more powerful.

Personal power and charisma

Power may depend upon the personal skills or charisma of certain individuals who, because of their particular characteristics, induce others to follow them. Successful politicians may have it; captains of industry may have it; captains in sport may have it. We can legitimately ask to what extent such personal qualities are important as a source of power within the public sector. According to Weber, bureaucracy is characterised by rational-legal authority rather than by charismatic authority. Given the constraints placed upon officials by formal rules and regulations we may wonder to what extent there is the opportunity for officials to express personal qualities. The attributes of the official are traditionally considered to be formal, anonymous and impersonal in character – hardly the stuff of charisma. And yet even with formal organisations there will be some discretion and there will be opportunities to impose oneself on the organisation. The police constable on the beat will occasionally be in situations where leadership skills have to be shown; team leaders will need to elicit the support of other team members, and some supervisors are more readily followed than others.

Resources

According to Leftwich:

> Wherever one finds human groups, one finds such collective activities: all of them, productive or social, in some way involve activities concerned with organising the use, production or distribution of resources. That's politics. (Leftwich, 1984, p. 64.)

Those who control resources – such as money or people – will have power within organisations. We have seen how the control of resources, particularly scarce ones, within society will determine who has power. The same arguments can be applied to organisations. The resources of organisations will include people and money and those who control these in terms of salaries, promotion or budgets will have power. Middle management will have power over those lower down the organisation if middle management determines pay, promotion and bonuses. This argument presupposes that others seek and value these resources. If, for example, an individual does not seek promotion then it will be difficult for those who control promotion to have power over that individual. Where such resources are controlled at the top or are determined by national agreements, as with much of public sector salaries, then the power of middle management will diminish. A further dimension is where one organisation is dependent upon another for resources. Local government depends upon central government for much of its finance and such dependency will limit the scope of local government work. At the same time local government is responsible for implementing central government policy and hence we may find mutual dependency between organisations. Rhodes argues that any organisation will be dependent upon other organisations for resources. He uses the term 'power-dependence' to describe this mutual dependency and suggests five resources that are used in the relationship between central and local government. These are:

- constitutional-legal resources that are allocated between local authorities and central government by statute;
- hierarchical resources which may take the form of, for example, central government circulars that guide the work of local authorities;
- financial resources;
- political resources, such as the access to decision making bestowed on politicians by their election into office;
- informational resources, so that the group or individual who has these resources is in a powerful position.

Rhodes also suggests that central government and local government will be dependent upon each other 'to different degrees in different circumstances' (Rhodes, 1981, p. 101).

Professionalism

We have seen how public sector organisations are made up of professional groups and have briefly discussed their importance for organisations. We can locate that earlier discussion within the context of power by arguing that membership of such groups can confer power upon individuals, particularly if that group has status and prestige. Doctors have a high status based upon their profession and the perception of that profession by the public at large. In contrast, social workers may not have the same status and their power will be less. The concept of a profession is, as we have seen, based upon claims to specialised knowledge and skills developed over time through training. Where certain skills and knowledge are not valued then the profession will have little status. We can expand the argument concerning the power of occupational professions to cover any group. Thus a trade union will have power within an organisation if the union represents all workers and those workers have skills and knowledge that are in short supply. Organisations may also be made up of different groups and professions and when these groups seek to assert themselves then the organisation may well be characterised by competition between groups. This argument fits in with the pluralist notion of power which we will discuss in the next section.

Authority

A final source of power is that of authority. There are individuals within organisations who have power by virtue of the fact that they occupy a certain position within the organisational structure. This power is not necessarily dependent upon their personal qualities nor will it depend upon their control of information or their expertise. We may not like or respect our superiors, for example, but they will have power over us just because they occupy a position above us in the organisational hierarchy. Of course, the higher up the organisation an individual progresses it is likely that they will possess skills and expertise, but it does not necessarily follow. In theory, Parliament is the supreme legislative authority in the United Kingdom, but it could be argued that real power, as opposed to authority, is located elsewhere in the hands of the Cabinet or Prime Minister or leaders of industry. The power of Parliament will be limited where a government has a working majority in the House of Commons. Similarly, in the case of a local authority, formal authority to make decisions will rest with the full council; but in reality it may well be that power is in the hands of a few councillors and chief officers such that the locus of decision making may be far removed from the full council meeting.

Power, then, is not the same as authority, even though the two will be closely related. Indeed it may well be that power is not linked to the position of an individual within the formal structure of an organisation at all. An example here may be the power of the receptionist within an organisation to project an image of that organisation since the receptionist is often the first point of contact that the public has with organisations. Not only that but the receptionist may control access to individuals within the organisation and hence play an important role as 'gatekeeper' to the organisation. The civil service recognises this: 'Reception staff will convey the image of the office to the public, and they should therefore be carefully selected for the task.' (Cabinet Office, 1988, para. 2.23, p. 12.)

Despite this, receptionists are usually low down in the formal organisational structure and poorly rewarded in terms of pay and status.

POWER AND DECISION MAKING

We have examined the concept of power within organisations and we now need to see how it is exercised. Power is only seen when it is put to use. This often manifests itself within decision making in terms of who gets their own way within organisations. We can approach decision making from several dimensions. We will follow the approach adopted by Lukes (1974) who suggests three different dimensions.

First dimensional view

This view is associated with the pluralist view that we discussed earlier. An early version of pluralism and decision making was developed by Dahl in *Who Governs?* (1961). This book was a study of decision making in the town of New Haven, America, in the 1950s over issues such as urban development and public education. Dahl focused upon the making of decisions over which there was an observable conflict of opinion and he studied how that conflict was resolved between the different individuals and groups involved. Dahl argued that power was fragmented between the different groups involved in the decision-making process since different groups got their way on different issues. Thus when there is an observable conflict between different groups then whosoever gets their way has power. It may well be a different group on different issues. We might, therefore, examine different groups involved in the policy process concerned with, say, education. Such groups would represent parents, teachers, political parties, the local education authority, local business, school governors and the Department for Education. According to Dahl, we can see which group gets its own way on a particular issue and conclude that this group has power. Following Dahl, we would expect different groups involved in the policy process to have power on different issues.

Second dimensional view

This first view was criticised, in particular, by Bachrach and Baratz (1962) for being too narrow. They argued that some groups can consciously or unconsciously put up barriers to the public discussion of issues. Dahl concentrates upon issues over which there is an observable disagreement and yet it may well be that certain issues are kept off the agenda altogether. Some issues may be filtered out because they are too controversial and hence public discussion may be confined to relatively safe or non-controversial issues. We need, therefore, to be aware of the power of the group or individual who decides what is discussed in the first place. Stringer and Richardson (1980) show how information can be managed and how the presentation of statistics by government departments can keep problems off the agenda. One example they give is that of Home Office statistics on drug addicts that show only those addicts that are registered. Low numbers might indicate that there is no drug problem. Yet what about all those addicts that acquire drugs illegally and hence are not registered?

Another example of the differences between the two views is the location of power within central government in Britain and the role of the Cabinet. The first view would suggest that in Cabinet issues are 'up for grabs' and whichever minister gets his or her own way on an issue has power. The second view would point to the fact that in reality it is the Prime Minister who, in setting the agenda for Cabinet discussion, decides what is to be discussed in the first place and consequently has power.

The relationship between central government and local government further illustrates this point where local government will have the power to make policy and spend public money but only within the limits set by Parliament and central government.

Third dimensional view

This is the most radical view and is the view endorsed by Lukes himself. Lukes argued that both the previous views are unsatisfactory in that power is only seen to operate where there is conflict. Yet a person or group may have power by shaping beliefs, values and desires. Thus the power of advertising is such that we believe that our lives will be unbearable unless we possess the latest dishwasher, video recorder or television set. This, Lukes argued, is the most insidious form of power in that we can be manipulated into a course of action or believing in a set of values without realising it. From this perspective, political power in Britain is in the hands of the government not just because it controls the agenda but also because we would never question its right to do so. Ultimately the attempt to undermine the power of the government can be portrayed as an attempt to undermine the whole system of parliamentary democracy as we know it and this will not even be considered. We are 'indoctrinated' into believing in the value of parliamentary democracy just as we are indoctrinated into believing in the merits of this or that soap powder. The extent to which the majority believe in parliamentary democracy or advertising will be an indication of how much power those who propagate such views have.

Similarly, those within organisations who can persuade others to put the good of the organisation before that of the individual or group will have power. Thus, nurses are persuaded that they must put organisational goals such as the welfare of the patients before individual and group goals. Any attempt to win better pay or conditions through industrial action is criticised by the government as selfish and, in so far as many nurses agree with this, then such prevailing beliefs are a very powerful tool in the hands of government.

The major problem with Lukes' view is that if there is no observable conflict then how do we know that power is being exercised at all? It is all very well to use the language of manipulation or indoctrination but how do we know that this in fact is what happens? Individuals may freely endorse an organisational culture or set of values and who is to say that they have been indoctrinated?

A more fruitful line of inquiry is to examine the concept of conflict within organisations and to show how power is exercised in practice.

POWER AND CONFLICT

If organisations are pluralist in nature such that different groups and individuals can influence the decision-making process then we would expect groups representing different interests to compete with each other. Competition may be no bad thing if it encourages the development of new perspectives, sets standards and encourages groups to improve their performance. Conflict, on the other hand, may lead to tension, to inter-personal friction, and to the pursuit of individual or group goals rather than the pursuit of organisational goals. Competition characterises a healthy organisation and conflict an unhealthy organisation. However, there is another view that is gaining in prominence. As organisations, both in the public and private sectors, increasingly rely on good relationships with other organisations to either supply goods or deliver services then co-operation rather than competition will be required. Kanter (1990) has argued that becoming PALS (Pooling, Allying and Linking) across companies is the key to corporate success. As more of the public sector is contracted out then good relations between the contractor and the contractee are important. We examine the challenge of managing such relations in Chapter 13.

Competition will be channelled into avenues that benefit the organisation, and one of the major tasks of management is to manage and resolve conflict. From the perspective of power we can suggest, similarly, that power can be used to aid or hinder the organisation.

What then are the possible causes of conflict within organisations? Hall argues that there will be four components in a situation of conflict:

- the parties involved;
- the field of conflict;
- the dynamics of the situation, or how the parties react to each other;
- the management, control or resolution of that conflict. (Hall, 1972, p. 153.)

In the first instance we can suggest that individuals will enter into organisations from a diverse range of social, economic and educational backgrounds which will give them different perspectives and different values. At the same time individuals will enter into organisations for different reasons and will have different expectations of that organisation. Some will see the organisation as offering a career; others as a stop-gap before moving on; still others as a means to earn as much money as possible in order to pursue life outside the organisation. These differences will inevitably lead to disagreements within the organisation. There will be conflicts and disagreements arising from the organisation itself which will result from a number of factors.

Incompatible goals

Individual goals may well be in conflict with organisational goals even where there is a strong commitment to one goal by the organisation. It is worth repeating that there may be competing goals within the organisation itself. Thus, for example, the prison service may wish to pursue the twin goals of the punishment of offenders while at the same time seeking to rehabilitate them. These two goals may prove to be incompatible and yet each will have its supporters. Within the National Health Service there may well be a commitment to provide the best possible medical care that the state of medical knowledge will allow and yet this may be tempered by the requirement to act within tight financial constraints. The two goals may be in conflict. Many organisations will face the problem of which goals to prioritise in the light of competing goals.

In the public sector there is also the added dimension of the politician–official relationship. The goals of the politician may well be in conflict with those of the official. When the politician pursues the goal, for example, of reducing the size of the public sector, is it likely that there will be a whole-hearted commitment to this goal when this may directly threaten the job security and promotion prospects of the official?

Centre versus periphery

There may well be conflict between the different parts of an organisation as a result of its geographical and physical dispersal. There will be conflict between central and local government and also within the same authority or department. The region or local office may feel that it is being dictated to by a central office that has no understanding of local needs and conditions. A decision made in Whitehall may look very different in the North East of England. At the same time, the central office may argue that local offices are too parochial and the imposition of a uniform provision of service has to be of paramount importance.

Interdepartmental conflict

Different departments may wish to pursue their own interests at the expense of other departments or of the organisation as a whole. Within central government there will be conflict between the spending departments and the non-spending departments. Between the spending departments there will be competition for resources. Indeed, as we have seen elsewhere, public choice theory is based upon the premise that bureaucrats are in competition with each other to expand their budgets. Each year there will be competition between the departments of Health, Social Security, Defence and so on, to ensure a slice of the public expenditure cake. Within local authorities there will be similar competition between personnel and finance, between education and social services.

The professional versus the official

If different groups within the organisation resent or do not understand the work and contributions of other groups then there will be conflict. The National Health Service administrator may be critical of the doctor who is profligate in the use of equipment and resources and at the same time the doctor may resent having to account for expenditure to the administrator who may lack the medical expertise to understand why such equipment and resources were used. Similarly, within the civil service the engineer or architect may resent being bound by the rules and regulations of administrative practices and accountability rather than those of the profession.

Structural differences

Disagreement may occur between different levels within the organisation where one level controls the resources that the other wants in terms of information, salary increases, promotion and so on. These differences may be exacerbated in a more formal hierarchical structure where clear divisions exist between the different levels. As organisations, particularly in local government, are restructured into business units, cost centres or purchasers and providers, formal agreements come to replace informal ones. Service Level Agreements (SLAs) are entered into as quasi-contracts which determine the relationships between the different parts of the organisation. In the past a manager may have contacted a colleague in another department informally for information or for a favour. Under SLAs a common response is to treat such informal requests as outside the terms of the agreement and, perhaps, to charge for them.

Personal differences

It is likely in any organisation that individuals will have different opinions and values, there will be personality clashes and there may well be conflicts of interest where an individual is required to pursue a particular course of action that they cannot, in all conscience, perform. The public sector is likely to throw up issues that may require the individual to go against the organisation's instructions. The former civil servant, Clive Ponting, was taken to court for disclosing information about the sinking of the Argentine ship, the *Belgrano*, during the Falklands conflict. Ponting's defence was that he was acting in the public interest since he felt that the government was trying to mislead Parliament. As an individual who had access to this information he felt that he could not, in all conscience, keep quiet about it.

Finally, we can suggest that there will be:

- competition for resources in terms of budgets, status, prestige and staff;
- competition for goals, particularly where those goals remain unclear or there is no agreement on objectives or priorities. The goal of a local authority may be expressed as 'Serving the public' but this is rather vague and can be interpreted in any number of different ways;
- competition for territory. Handy (1985) makes the point that organisations can be seen in territorial terms, characterised by empire building. There will be violation of territorial boundaries and jealousy of the resources or territory that another group or department has at its disposal. For example, the Civil Service Department was created in 1968 to oversee manpower and training issues within the civil service. These functions had previously come under the Treasury. The Civil Service Department eventually lost a running battle with the Treasury and was disbanded in 1981, with some of its functions returning to the Treasury. There may also be overcrowding in some areas. Certain issues quickly become topical and every group wishes to be involved. At the end of the 1980s environmental issues rose to the top of the agenda and suddenly we were all 'greens' as attention was directed towards environmental issues.

One of the most comprehensive accounts of power concerning organisations is that given by Mintzberg (1983). One of the themes he develops is the relationship between power, organisational structures and styles and the relationships between internal and external stakeholders. Mintzberg identifies six power configurations which he sets out in declining order of the concentration and clarity of power:

- **The instrument** is dominated by outsiders, with little freedom of action for internal stakeholders. Its internal organisation is bureaucratic and it tends to exist in a stable environment, performing simple, standardised tasks.
- **The closed system** tends to be dominated by senior managers within the

organisation. Again it is bureaucratic, performing tasks similar to the instrument configuration and is unable to respond to a changing environment.

- **Autocracy** is dominated by the charismatic internal leader. It exists in young organisations and may prosper where a small organisation exists in a dynamic environment.
- **Missionary** organisations are dominated by a strong internal coalition with shared goals and culture centred around a distinctive mission.
- **Meritocracy** tends to be dominated by professionals within the organisation with a clear mission and a culture based upon expertise.
- **The political arena** involves multiple internal and external stakeholders. It may be dominated by short-term goals, perhaps involving organisational paralysis, and temporary political alliances.

CONCLUSION

To what extent, though, is the exercise of power, the endless competition, healthy or unhealthy? As was suggested earlier, competition may generate new ideas, stimulate and channel energies, set standards for others to follow. It may also waste time and energy; it may be unproductive; it may lead to hostility and to low morale. Whatever the form power takes or the extent to which conflict exists, it is important for us to recognise their existence within organisations. It is in this sense that we can say that every organisation is political and every organisation is concerned with the use, and abuse, of power. Bacharach and Lawler (1980) argue that organisations comprise bargaining systems and we need to understand how they work to understand organisations fully. The research by Thompson (1986) on decision making within district health authorities found much evidence of bargaining, not just between the different coalitions of politicians, administrators and the medical profession but also within these coalitions. Perhaps this is not surprising if we agree with the English philosopher, Thomas Hobbes, who argued that the pursuit of power is part of human nature.

FURTHER READING

For general theories of power and the state the book by Cox, Furlong and Page (1985) is very useful. Pfeffer (1981) and Bacharach and Lawler (1980) both examine power within organisations. Rhodes (1981) examines power in the context of relations between central and local government and is well worth reading. For those interested in a case study approach then Thompson (1986) is most illuminating. Finally, for those interested in the radical approach to power, Lukes (1974) is required reading.

CHAPTER 7

Leadership

INTRODUCTION

Increasingly the qualities of leadership are deemed to be desirable for those working in the public sector. In the private sector the quality of leadership has long been recognised as a key factor affecting organisational performance. The Local Government Training Board publication *The Leadership Audit* (1987b) recognises the importance of leadership for local government officials. Management development within British Rail has been built around a leadership programme for their top managers. A recent scrutiny of public sector job advertisements reveals such phrases as: 'You will be expected to take a lead on all aspects of work in the Division.' 'The General Manager will be required to play a leading role.' 'You must be able to demonstrate leadership.'

We shall examine the different theoretical approaches to leadership and apply these approaches to public sector organisations while asking a number of questions:

- How do we define leadership?
- Who are the leaders?
- What does leadership consist of?
- What do leaders do?

Each of these questions will be addressed in turn.

HOW DO WE DEFINE LEADERSHIP?

Writers often distinguish between management and leadership. Ackerman (1985) argues that there are a number of important differences. He suggests that management is synonymous with organisations but that leadership can exist outside of the organisation. According to this author, management may be related to formal authority within an organisation and managers get others to do their bidding because of their organisational position. Individuals follow leaders because of the additional attribute of charisma and the personal attraction of the leader. As Stewart puts it:

> Managers have subordinates. Leaders have followers: people who recognise and find attractive the leaders' sense of purpose. Leaders are those who can get the people with whom they work, whether subordinates or not, to be convinced co-operators. Leaders

make others feel that what they are doing matters and hence makes them feel good about their work. (1989, p. 4.)

There are many different definitions of leadership, but they do seem to have certain features in common and a useful general definition is that given by Kossen: 'Leadership is the ability to influence the behaviour of others to go in a certain direction.' (1983, p. 201.)

Kossen's definition of leadership is a wide one and may encompass leadership in a range of situations, including:

- the military leader who is concerned to win support of the troops to pursue the goal of military victory;
- the political leader who is concerned to persuade the citizens that his or her way is the right way;
- the team leader at work who is concerned to ensure that members of the group are all pulling in the same direction towards greater productivity or an improved service.

Another feature of this definition is that it does not specify at what level within the organisation the leader is. Thus, if an official lower down the organisation can influence those at the top to move in a certain direction then we could designate that person a leader. This may occur where a lower level official may have specialised knowledge or is considered an expert in some area.

Leadership, traditionally, has been seen as a form of activity that is expressed in terms of a relationship – that between the leader and the led. More recent theories, which we shall examine later, suggest that the idea of individuals being led is too passive and that the capacity for leadership may be in all of us. We shall need to study, not just the individual characteristics of leadership, but also the reaction to leadership by others. Leadership is apparent in many different spheres of activity – the military, the political, the organisational and so on – and it may exist at different levels.

If we return to the definition of leadership as the ability to influence others to go in a certain direction then this ability may be required at many different levels within the organisation. At one level it may be expressed by a commander-in-chief who is determining the strategic objectives of the military and has to convince the generals. At a different level it may be the squad leader who has to define these overall goals in operational terms and who has to lead the squad in battle. In the same way the chief constable in the police service may be concerned to define strategic goals for the police force as a whole while the individual police constable may need to exercise leadership in an operational situation and direct others in that situation. Here we might use the term 'street-level' leadership. Similarly, the manager in charge of a local authority department may need to give a lead to others in defining the role and objectives of that department.

The ability to give direction to people is necessary not just at the top of an organisation. Its necessity will depend upon the context and the situation. Stewart

(1989) argues that, despite the traditional subordinacy of the nurse to the doctor, nurse managers, for example, will need to demonstrate leadership not least in terms of acting as a role model for younger nurses and for maintaining morale. There are situations, like the operational one that the police find themselves in, where an individual has to take the lead. We can expand, therefore, Kossen's original definition so that our definition of leadership is the ability to influence the behaviour of others to go in a certain direction within a given context.

WHO ARE THE LEADERS?

Traditionally, we have understood leadership as belonging to those at the top of organisations and have described others within the organisation as followers, subordinates or the led. This is likely to be the case in formal hierarchical organisations where it is felt that the proper locus of decision making is at the top. With decentralised structures and accountable management we would expect individuals lower down the hierarchy to take on more responsibility. The traditional view of the leader may, then, be questioned and our model of leadership may have to be widened to encompass the different locations of leadership. Indeed, Bradford and Cohen (1984) argue that the image of the leader as hero is inappropriate for today's organisations. There is a mythology of the 'good leader' where such a person:

- knows what is going on at all times within the department;
- has more technical expertise than those lower down:
- should be able to solve any problem that crops up;
- should be the primary person responsible for how the department is working.

This image, according to Bradford and Cohen, is outdated. It is the image of the tough, resourceful 'lone ranger' figure who rides in to rescue the town from the wicked cattle baron. What happens when our hero is not there? Surely it is better for the townsfolk themselves to develop the necessary skills to fight their own battles? Our 'post-heroic leader' will allow others to take responsibility, develop their own skills, solve their own problems and develop their own goals. Our leader, according to this approach, will allow others to develop, to act as an enabler rather than as a director of subordinates.

This view, though, has implications for the public sector where convention has it that it is the role of the politicians and not the officials to provide a vision and determine goals. Indeed the idea of civil service leadership is a contradiction in terms within a democracy. The problem with decentralising responsibility and accountability within public sector organisations is that traditionally it is the politician who is held to account rather than the official. Thus if leadership is to be practised throughout the organisation then it has to be consistent with political objectives and compatible with the role of the politician.

At the same time Painter (1989) argues that senior officials within the civil service need to be aware of their responsibilities in offering professional leadership and articulating the values of the civil service as an organisation. Senior officials have a duty to protect junior officials and to set standards for those lower down.

WHAT DOES LEADERSHIP CONSIST OF?

We are all familiar with the cliché 'Leaders are born and not made', and whether this is true or not it does suggest to us that leadership is dependent upon an individual possessing certain characteristics. This idea has received much support and it is known as the 'trait theory' of leadership. The theory states that individuals possess certain characteristics so that they are predisposed to act in a certain way within a given situation.

Trait theory

Kossen (1983) has suggested that possession of certain characteristics is required for leadership:

- the ability to solve problems creatively;
- the ability to communicate and listen;
- a strong desire to achieve;
- many interests and sociability;
- a positive and sincere attitude towards subordinates;
- self-confidence;
- enthusiasm;
- self-discipline;
- manners;
- emotional stability.

Kossen also says that these characteristics can be learned and developed, thereby suggesting that leaders can be developed as well as born. One problem, though, is that there is no general agreement on what these characteristics should be. A workshop on leadership skills in local government produced a list of ten key skills:

1 **Vision** – creating a sense of what the organisation is about and where it is going.
2 **Prioritising** – the ability to distinguish between, for example, the urgent and the merely important.
3 **Motivation** – through recognising achievements and rewarding staff.
4 **Inter-personal skills** – such as listening, suggesting, being positive.
5 **Political sensitivity** – to the needs of councillors and to organisational power.
6 **Resilience** – to remain steadfast in the face of adversity.

7 **Charisma** – difficult to define but it attracts others.

8 **Risk-taking** – in areas such as delegating work to other staff.

9 **Flexibility** – to respond to new ideas and practices.

10 **Decisiveness** – when the situation demands it. (Local Government Training Board, 1987b.)

In her work on the National Health Service, Stewart (1989b) produces a similar list:

- pointing the way or creating a vision;
- symbolising what matters in terms of the values of the organisation;
- getting others to share these values;
- creating pride in the organisation;
- making people feel important;
- realising people's potential;
- self-sufficiency and relying on oneself.

The problem with such lists is that they do not specify any order. Is flexibility any more important than decisiveness? May the two, in fact, be in conflict with each other? We can imagine a situation where a decision needs to be made quickly and the official does not have the scope to take into account individual or local circumstances. Likewise, we may not wish a budget-holder to take risks with taxpayer's money and, to ensure equity, the official may need to follow formal rules rather than respond flexibly to each new case.

It may also be that we look for different attributes in different parts of the public service. In the civil service, for example, recruitment is dependent upon the selector's perceptions of:

- penetration of thought;
- fertility of ideas;
- judgement;
- written ability;
- oral expression;
- personal contacts;
- influence;
- drive;
- determination;
- emotional stability;
- maturity. (See Chapman, 1984.)

Once again, though, such a list may be too general and does not indicate any order of preference. It may be that for any individual to succeed in any organisation then he or she will need some or all of the qualities listed above. Likewise the ability to listen or to communicate or show enthusiasm and self-confidence know no organisational boundaries.

There is one feature that is included in the local government list of characteristics that may be unique to the public sector and that is the requirement that our public sector officials have political sensitivity. Thus our official, in dealing with the politician, needs to be aware of the political impact of his or her advice and be sensitive to the needs of the politician. In drafting reports, for example, the official will need to be aware of the ruling party's political values. This issue has been of particular importance within central government in recent years as the traditional task of the civil service – that of offering objective, impartial advice – has come under scrutiny. Recent Conservative governments have stressed a greater concern with commitment to putting policies into practice and getting the job done. However, any organisation has to be aware of the environment within which it operates. The business man or woman has to be sensitive to the needs of the customer or to the demands of the shareholders.

The approach to leadership purely in terms of individual characteristics is also deficient in that it does not take into account the relationship between the leader and the followers. However, the approach remains influential. Recent initiatives in the education and training of managers in both the public and private sectors have emphasised the need for employees to display specified attributes or qualities. Two initiatives, the Management Charter Initiative (MCI) and National Vocational Qualifiications (NVQs), require candidates to provide evidence of specified competences before qualifications can be awarded. We discuss this approach further in Chapter 13.

Style theories

If we recall our definition of leadership we stressed that leadership involves a relationship. This relationship may take a number of different forms. There are a number of theories that discuss this relationship and they are generally known as 'style theories of leadership' where the focus is upon the style that a leader adopts in dealing with others.

A common approach is to suggest that there are different styles of leadership such as:

- **autocratic** – identified with a strong domineering leader where power and control are centralised;
- **participative** – the leader gives up some power and authority to subordinates;
- *laissez-faire* – the absence of direct leadership. The leader may believe that the most important role for them to play is that of a co-ordinator.

An example of the first might be Mrs Thatcher, in so far as it is said that she dominated her Cabinets. However, she could not control every aspect of government and she reluctantly had to give up some of her authority to, for example, the Chancellor of the Exchequer where financial matters were concerned. Thus it may be that style theories are too simplistic. Different situations may require different styles of leadership and a good leader may be one who uses a combination of different styles. Where there is a task to be completed and deadlines to be met an autocratic approach may be appropriate. Where the issue is one that requires a consensus decision it may be that a more participative style is required.

Not only is the particular situation important but also important are the attitudes towards the leader by the followers. A leader may believe that individuals need coercing into following a particular direction, or alternatively may believe that encouragement is the key. The model of the post-heroic leader that we discussed earlier is certainly based upon the premise that individuals will respond to encouragement.

One of the better known theories concerned with leadership styles is that put forward by McGregor (1960). As we saw in Chapter 5, he suggested that the style adopted depends upon the perception that leaders have of their subordinates. Leaders who believe that their subordinates are lazy, lacking in ambition, self-centred and resistant to change will adopt an autocratic style of leadership. The emphasis here is on securing the compliance of the subordinate through direction and control. McGregor calls this Theory X. In contrast to this is Theory Y, where he argues that if the leaders see subordinates as willing and able then the leader will be less inclined to pursue an autocratic style but instead prefer a participative style of leadership and encourage subordinates to accept responsibility and authority. Blake and Mouton (1964) argue that leadership behaviour is based upon a conflict between two opposing forces within the individual – a concern for the *task* to be done and a concern for *people*. Blake and Mouton construct a matrix with concern for task on one axis and concern for people on the other axis. They identify five main leadership styles to be plotted on the matrix, depending upon the various commitments to either people or the task.

So far, then, leadership can be seen as a number of different factors, comprising:

- an individual's characteristics;
- the organisational context – different organisations may value different characteristics;
- different styles that leaders prefer;
- different styles appropriate to different situations, depending upon whether the situation is task-oriented or people-oriented;
- the perceptions by leaders of the qualities and values of those they are seeking to influence.

Contingency theory

This group of theories suggests that leadership will be a combination of different factors, depending upon the situation. Different leaders will choose different approaches, depending upon the context. It depends upon what 'best fits' the situation. This is an expression used by Handy (1985) who suggests that there are a number of leadership variables and the best combination is one appropriate to a particular situation. The variables that Handy uses are:

- the leader's style, which may change;
- expectations of the leader's behaviour;
- the objectives of the group;
- the environment of the organisation.

Fiedler (1967) suggested that the elements of a leadership situation are threefold:

- leader–member relations and the extent to which there is support for the leader;
- the task itself – is it simple or complex?
- position power – to what extent does the leader have the power to reward or punish other members of the organisation?

A leader must assess whether favourable factors exist, e.g. good relations, high task structure and strong position power, before selecting an appropriate style. Fiedler found that extremely favourable or unfavourable conditions required a task-oriented or autocratic style of leadership. Those situations deemed to be moderately favourable required a people-oriented style. Leaders can then be matched to the situation which suit their style or the situation could be changed to suit a particular style.

A more recent approach emphasises not just the relationship between the leader and others but also stresses the changing nature of this relationship.

Developmental approach

This approach stresses the fact that as individuals 'mature' in an organisation then the leader should take account of this and allow the relationship to develop as a consequence. Thus we might expect to move gradually to a more participative or *laissez-faire* approach. Banner and Blasingame (1988) suggest that there are nine stages in this developmental process:

1 **Attention** – leaders initially pay attention and give time to subordinates.
2 **Support** – help the employees in their work.
3 **Feedback/information sharing** – show how the employee's work fits into the wider scheme of things.
4 **Nurturing** – move towards the sharing of ideas.
5 **Emerging autonomy** – the employees begin to define their own role but still need guidance.
6 **Setting limits** – autonomy plus limits determined by the leader.
7 **Personal competence** – employees are highly 'mature', i.e. they are high achievers who take responsibility for results.
8 **Independent personal and professional growth** – employees begin to lead themselves.
9 **Loyalty and commitment** – the leader and the organisation are now seen as 'family' by the individual.

This approach takes into account the changing nature of the relationship between the leader and others and indicates how it may develop. It is a more sophisticated account than the simple trait and style theories that we began our account with.

WHAT DO LEADERS DO?

Leadership is concerned with performing a number of different tasks and below we explore some of these tasks in detail.

Providing a vision

We have discussed the notion that leaders will influence others to go in a certain direction. In order to do that our leaders must, themselves, have a clear idea of where that direction lies. Increasingly, management theory stresses the most important role is that of the visionary where the leader:

- creates a vision;
- communicates it to others within the organisation;
- shows its relevance to their work;
- ensures commitment to that vision.

Peters and Austin (1986) use the image of the leader as 'chief salesperson' where leadership is involved in creating an image of the organisation and symbolising what it stands for. Within the public sector we tend to think of politicians as providing the vision for the organisation, expressed in terms, depending upon the ideology of the party in power, which include:

- reducing poverty;
- promoting equality and freedom;
- pursuing justice;
- caring for the welfare of the population;
- promoting enterprise;
- educating the population.

Perhaps we should also expect the officials to provide a vision for the organisation even though less grandiose in scope. We can imagine a departmental head in a local authority urging his or her staff to be the most efficient and effective, the most caring or the friendliest department. Such visions can be utilised at all levels within an organisation and are not the sole prerogative of those at the top. Indeed, they may be considered to be much more practical than the visions given to us by politicians and hence may be more likely to have support. It is difficult to operationalise the politician's intangible objective of promoting freedom and equality.

Providing an overall perspective

Linked to the notion of creating a vision is connecting that vision to the overall perspective of the organisation. Both require standing back from the day-to-day running of the organisation and examining the wider picture. One of the major criticisms that is made of senior management is its unwillingness to let go of the reins of an organisation, to delegate routine tasks and to concentrate upon the longer term. Leaders have to see the work of the organisation within a wider context and to be aware of the environment within which the organisation is working. Garratt (1987) suggests that leaders need to be aware of the wider economic, social and political contexts, the uncertain world within which organisations operate, and to take account of this external environment. Stewart (1989) argues that the call for leaders in the National Health Service is precisely because the National Health Service increasingly operates within an uncertain and changing environment. Departmental heads will need to be aware of other departments within the organisation, will have outside relationships involving clients or customers, and will need to work with other agencies. People in departments dominated by the professions will need to be aware of developments within the professional field and keep up-to-date with the latest techniques or equipment. At whatever level it manifests itself, leadership is concerned with standing back from the day-to-day routine of affairs.

The Fulton Report (1968) on the civil service was critical of the generalist class within the civil service and suggested that a greater role in management should be found for the specialist classes. However, recent writings on leadership would seem to support the retention of the skills of the generalist administrator. A feature of leadership is the ability to stand back and take the wider perspective; this means not being bound by the commitment to a narrow specialist view. The generalist administrator is concerned to take this wider view and not be bound by a narrow perspective. This role would fit easily into the modern view of leadership.

Similarly, in local government the tradition that senior officers are specialists with professional expertise has been questioned. The suggestion is that there needs to be a move away from the narrow professionalism of the past towards a more generalised and politically aware professionalism. The concern is with taking a wider perspective, looking outwards rather than inwards.

Transmitting the vision

We suggested earlier that leadership is concerned with influencing the behaviour of others. This may take a number of different forms:

- coercion;
- manipulation;
- threats;
- promises;
- explanation;

- persuasion;
- setting an example.

The more extreme forms of influence, such as coercion or threat, are unlikely to be sustained over any length of time. If a leader constantly has to threaten individuals, it is unlikely that those individuals will come to share the vision of the leader. Of course, it may be that under certain circumstances a more autocratic relationship is appropriate. For example, where a decision has to be made quickly then it may be more appropriate to tell an individual what to do rather than use persuasion. This may be appropriate in an organisation like the army where discipline and the carrying out of orders is essential to the success of that organisation. Here there also may be more compliant subordinates who prefer this more authoritarian style – there may be individuals in any organisation who do not want responsibility and who prefer to be told what to do. We suggested earlier that leadership will need to take account of different situations and the different relations that leaders will have with others. The perceptions that individuals have of the leaders is also important here.

The developmental model that we discussed earlier argued that the relationship between the leader and others will develop through various stages and it is up to the leader to know what is appropriate at any given time and with any given individual.

Relations with others

We have stressed the notion that leadership is concerned with a relationship and we have indicated what forms this relationship might take. Many difficulties faced in the public sector will stem from the formal, hierarchical structure within which such relationships take place. As we have seen, such organisations tend to be dominated by formal rules and by hierarchical modes of accountability which may lend themselves to a more autocratic style of leadership. Hence it will be necessary to take account of the structure in determining what leadership role is most appropriate. It will be pointless advocating a more participative style of leadership if the structure does not allow participation and informal rules to develop.

A further problem is that the promotion, pay and career development of officials may be outside the control of immediate superiors and hence it may be difficult for the departmental head to have much impact upon the work, the responsibilities, the morale and the development of individuals within the organisation. As we saw earlier with Fiedler's model of leadership, position power is an important factor. In the civil service it may not exist lower down the organisation. The developmental model of leadership advocated by Banner and Blasingame will require greater responsibility and the identification of leadership lower down the organisational structure than has traditionally been the case within either central or local government.

CASE STUDY: THE LOCAL AUTHORITY CHIEF EXECUTIVE

Prior to the 1972 reorganisation of local government, the paid administration of each authority was headed by a town clerk with a number of relatively independent service departments. Writing in 1972, at a time of relative stability, the Bains Committee on management in local authorities (1972) advanced the case for a more corporate approach to management. They recommended that all authorities appointed a chief executive as 'leader of the officers of the authority and principal adviser to the Council on general matters of policy' (cited in Alexander, 1982, p. 69). When it came to the detail of the role, Bains was less clear. It was proposed that

> His first task is to gain the respect and esteem of his colleagues, because his true powers will come more from his own qualities and character than from anything written into his, or the Chief Officers' terms of appointment. (Cited in Widdicombe, 1986, p. 143.)

Fifteen years later approximately 95 per cent of authorities had a post approximating to that of chief executive (Audit Commission, 1989c, p. 3). In practice, chief executives of larger authorities often played the role of administrative co-ordinator with a clear view of management but in smaller authorities they were often nothing more than *primus inter pares*, following the role of the old town clerk. It was only in the larger metropolitan authorities that the chief executive (usually) played the role of corporate manager and policy planner (see Widdicombe, 1986, p. 143; Dearlove, 1979, pp. 171–2).

Significantly, the Widdicombe Inquiry into the Conduct of Local Authority Business moved away from the emphasis on personal attributes placed by Bains to a stress on managerial responsibility. Widdicombe considered that the role of the chief executive should be enhanced, becoming a statutory position with 'overall managerial responsibility for the discharge of functions by officers' (1986, p. 145).

In contrast, Greenwood (1987) offers two styles of local authority, assertive 'prospectors' and conservative 'defenders'. In assertive authorities, he expects chief executives to be outward looking, assessing the external environment and seeking to make the best interface between the organisation and its environment. In contrast, defenders do not see the importance of scanning what they perceive to be a stable external environment. Instead they tend to have chief executives who are inward looking, focusing on internal operations and efficiency.

The Audit Commission, considering the role of chief executives in the context of an era of change, emphasises the need for them to demonstrate leadership qualities to guide authorities into an uncertain future, addressing an increasingly competitive environment.

> Yet there is a clear need for leadership for corporate thinking and corporate decision-making. In the Commission's view the chief executive must be both the authority's centre of continuity and its agent of change. So whatever other responsibilities attach to the post, he or she must

1 Manage the interfaces between politics and management and also, increasingly, between clients and contractors.
2 Convert policy into strategy and then into action.
3 Develop processes, people and management skills to ensure that the authority is, and will continue to be, capable of delivering its strategy.
4 Review performance against stated objectives.
5 Think and plan ahead. (1989c, p. 8.)

They conclude by asserting that 'local government will need leadership to restore a sense of direction. A strong chief executive can provide much of that leadership and direction, if he or she is allowed to do so.' (1989c. p. 12.)

CONCLUSION

We have examined the various models and explanations of leadership, from the traditional concern with leaders and their subordinates to a more recent approach which suggests that leadership needs to be more enlightened and to allow individuals to develop their own leadership skills. We illustrate these points diagrammatically in Figs 7.1 and 7.2.

Fig. 7.1 The traditional model of leadership

If we were to compile a checklist of leadership it would comprise the following:

- take an integrated view;
- learn to delegate tasks and responsibility;
- know the staff;
- help and allow individuals to develop;
- provide direction;
- be constructive and positive rather than destructive and negative;
- trust and have faith in the staff;
- treat staff with respect and value their abilities.

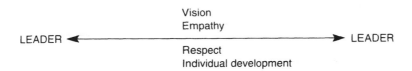

Fig. 7.2 The 'enlightened' model where individuals are seen as equals within the organisation

Stewart's prescriptions for the leader in the National Health Service urge:

- do not be afraid to think of yourself as a leader;
- have a strong belief in what needs doing;
- be willing to convey the vision to others;
- show enthusiasm and commitment in pursuing the vision;
- show a passion for excellence;
- show a positive attitude to setbacks;
- encourage others and do not let disappointments show. (1989, p. 17.)

Finally, then, we also need to locate our concept of leadership within: (a) the political environment within which the organisation operates and hence be aware of political objectives; (b) the organisational structure that exists; (c) the 'fit' between the structure of public sector organisations, and the preferred leadership style. It is no good advocating a more participative style of leadership if the organisation is dominated by a bureaucratic structure.

FURTHER READING

There are many general textbooks on the subject of leadership. The ones that we have found useful are Kossen (1983), Selznick (1957) and Chell (1987). There are also a number of texts that are prescriptive in giving guidelines to improving leadership performance. Bradford and Cohen (1984) and Wright and Taylor (1984) both fall into this category. A similar approach based upon research in the National Health Service is offered by Stewart (1989). We found Local Government Training Board (1987b) instructive for the local government context. The short article by Painter (1989) is also useful for the dimensions of leadership in the civil service.

CHAPTER 8

Motivation and morale

INTRODUCTION

Lack of motivation and the existence of low morale is of concern to all organisations. From an organisational perspective. motivation is linked to performance. A highly motivated individual will perform better than one with a low level of motivation. Organisations, therefore, have an interest in ensuring that people are motivated and morale is good throughout the organisation. Within the public sector one of the implications of attempts by government to reduce the size and change the structure of public sector organisations has been declining morale – or so commentators would have us believe.

> There is ample evidence that pay levels in the NHS are too low and that there are insufficient rewards. These pay levels have resulted in low morale within the Service and have made it increasingly difficult to recruit and retain staff. (Institute of Health Services Management, 1988, para 2.8.)

We find similar accounts in the press. The Sheehy Report (1993) on police pay and conditions which recommended performance-related pay and short-term contracts produced an outcry from those it was intended to affect. One police officer commented:

> Officers' work would be concentrated on only those activities which could be readily quantified. The ever present threat of redundancy on 'structural grounds', irrespective of performance, would be a further demotivating factor. (D. Hale, letter to *The Guardian*, 26 July 1993.)

Problems arise when we attempt to *measure* motivation and morale. An approach to understanding organisations that concentrates its focus on people within organisations needs to take account of what it is that motivates people within those organisations. We have already examined the Human Relations approach to organisations, and this is a precursor to examining what it is that motivates people to perform within organisations. We shall be concerned with a number of general questions about motivation and morale:

- What is motivation?
- Why is it important within organisations?
- Is it linked to performance?
- Can we measure it?

- Does motivation vary between individuals and between different types of occupations?
- Is there anything distinctive about motivation and morale within the public sector?

In order to answer these questions we need, in the first instance, to examine theories of motivation and then discuss their practical relevance.

THEORIES OF MOTIVATION

A number of theories are built upon some conception of human nature. The theories make certain assumptions about individual needs and desires and how individuals are motivated to satisfy these needs and achieve our desires. Depending upon what view of human nature we take then we will arrive at different explanations of what motivates us.

Maslow's hierarchy of needs

We discussed Maslow's theory in Chapter 5 and so we do not need to reproduce his basic arguments. But it will help our present purposes if we show his theory of basic needs in the form of a diagram (see Fig. 8.1).

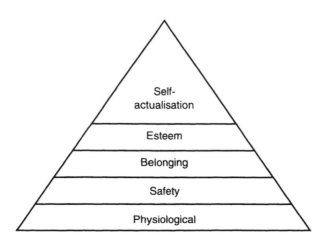

Fig. 8.1 Theory of basic needs

Although Maslow was not concerned specifically with individuals within organisations, we can suggest a number of implications of his theory:

1 Our needs change so that our motivation will change. It may well be that throughout our careers we are motivated by the desire to satisfy different needs.
2 As careers progress what motivates us may also change.
3 Motivation is a reflection of our role within the organisation. If we are at the bottom of the organisation we may be motivated by the desire to satisfy physiological needs. In the first instance we go to work in order to eat and drink and provide ourselves with shelter. As we take on more responsible and satisfying work we may be motivated by the desire to satisfy self-actualisation needs.
4 Managers need to be aware of these different needs and recognise the stage at which individuals have reached in the satisfaction of their needs. Giving an employee more money may not motivate him or her if that individual needs to satisfy the desire for respect and the esteem of colleagues. That may be satisfied by giving the individual more responsibility or more challenging work.
5 Satisfaction in terms of needs says nothing whatsoever about improving performance. Individuals may be more content and morale may be high, but does this necessarily lead on to an improved performance?

Although Maslow offers us useful insights into individual psychology, his theory is open to a number of criticisms:

● The basic components of Maslow's theory are often presented as a pyramid, but this seems to imply that those needs situated at the top of the pyramid are more important than those at the bottom. This is open to debate. It also seems to imply that relatively few of us ever reach the stage of self-actualisation.
● What exactly is self-actualisation? Although it can be linked to the idea of attaining personal meaning through work, much of our potential may be attained outside of work in terms of sport or hobbies.
● Are there only five basic needs? Do we know what they are? Can we prove it? There is no evidence to suggest that Maslow's assumptions are correct or incorrect.
● Are there clear dividing lines between the different levels? It may be that people wish to satisfy a number of needs at the same time.
● It may be that individuals can satisfy their needs outside the organisation altogether. Thus, an individual's need to belong may be satisfied by close family and friendship ties.

McGregor's Theory X and Theory Y

As we saw in Chapter 5, McGregor argued that the style of management adopted is a function of the manager's attitudes and assumptions about human nature. We can wonder to what extent McGregor's Theory X is appropriate for the modern organisation since it implies direction and control through a centralised system of organisational structure. In other words, this theory will apply to the traditional, formal organisation. Under Theory X motivation occurs only at the physiological and security levels of Maslow's hierarchy. In contrast, Theory Y focuses upon the top three tiers of Maslow's hierarchy and implies the integration of individual goals with those of the organisation.

An important feature of McGregor's approach is that it shows how management assumptions are important in determining motivation and morale. It is in this sense that the scientific management approach and that of the human relations school that we discussed in earlier chapters are both managerialist in that increased efficiency of the organisation is the context for both approaches. McGregor's approach suggests that motivation also depends upon relations with others as well as the individual's own nature. However, we need to be aware that:

- individuals respond differently to different types of management style. Thus, some individuals may welcome the opportunity to exercise responsibility whereas others may not be interested and prefer the security of being directed by others;
- situations may also respond to different styles of management. For example, in a police operational matter it may well be that one individual must make a decision and make that decision quickly. Clear direction has to be given and control over colleagues exercised.

Recently we have seen the introduction of performance-related pay for managers across the public services including university lecturers and many civil servants. This, of course, rests on the assumption that money is a motivating force. An alternative, a Theory Y based approach, would be to focus on job enrichment.

Downs and bureaucratic motivation

Although rarely included in standard textbook discussions of motivation, the work of Downs (1967), as representative of public choice theorists, is important. Public choice theorists explicitly examine the motivation of bureaucrats and suggest that, in crude terms, the most important motivator is the desire to increase one's share of the budget which leads to increased status. The assumption is that it is much more difficult to assess the work of a public manager than it is of a private sector counterpart. There are no sales or profit figures to judge the bureaucrats' work. Public choice theory argues that bureaucrats are judged by the size of the budget that they control and by how much they can increase it. It is a fairly cynical thesis and its advocates offer plentiful prima-facie evidence to support it.

Downs argues that bureaucrats do exhibit personality traits but these may differ. Not only that but they do have different ways of achieving their maximum personal utility. He goes on to argue that:

- Bureaucrats are made up of different types of officials.
- These officials can be characterised in two ways: those who are purely self-interested and those who have mixed motives.
- The purely self-interested officials are of two types. The first type are the climbers, motivated by power and prestige and the pursuit of both. This type of individual may 'stab you in the back' to achieve their ends. The second type are the conservers, motivated by the desire to retain the status quo. They resist change because they feel threatened by it and are the ones who constantly refer to the rules and regulations before they will do anything. They tend to be characterised by the phrase 'its more than my job's worth . . .' and often may be seen as petty officials.
- Mixed-motive officials are of three types. The first are the zealots, who are especially obsessive about particular pet policies even though no one else may share their enthusiasm and although it may be detrimental to the organisation as a whole. The second type are the advocates, who are concerned with getting things done and are loyal to a broader set of policies. The third type are statesmen, who are concerned with the good of the state or society as a whole. They comprise the classical concept of the public official who is anxious to promote the 'public interest'.

The assumption is that organisations are made up of different types of individuals who have different motives. Not only that, but motivation can be expressed in terms of self-interest, however that may be perceived, and this may be different from organisational interests.

We can offer a number of criticisms of this approach:

1 Only the most senior officials may be in a position to have some impact upon determining their own work interests. The vast majority of officials will not be in a position to push their own interests to the top of the agenda.
2 If public choice theory as a whole is based upon the concept of maximising budgets it may be the case that most officials have no control over budget allocation. As Dunleavy (1985) argues, different kinds of government bodies will vary in their control over their budgets.
3 There is little empirical evidence based on thorough research to support this thesis.

Herzberg's two-factor theory

From Herzberg's theory we can suggest that motivation is concerned with both the content and the context of work. According to Herzberg (1966), job enrichment, where responsibility is increased and more challenging work undertaken, can lead to job satisfaction. If we received job satisfaction, we would be motivated to work harder. At the same time if the hygiene factors were a poor working environment, poor salary and poor supervision then we might ask: 'Why work here?' We might be able to do the same job elsewhere under better working conditions.

However, like many of the theories we have been looking at, it leads to over-simplification. What satisfies one individual may not satisfy the next. Some workers do not seem to be particularly interested in the job content of their work. As long as the context of work allows good working relations and a pleasant environment then morale may be high but individuals may not be particularly motivated to seek responsibility.

Expectancy/valence theories

These theories attempt to link the value of rewards, the probability of receiving these rewards and the effort put in. This simple proposition is linked most closely with the work of Vroom (1964) and Porter and Lawler (1968). Expectancy theories are concerned with the relationships among the inputs that make up motivation.

The motivation to perform is seen as a function of the beliefs that individuals have concerning future rewards multiplied by the value they place on those rewards. Individuals desire certain goals and they put a value on these goals. To determine motivation we need to break the model down into two components: expectancy and valence (or the value which an individual places on an outcome). Thus:

- Individuals believe that acting in a certain way will lead to certain outcomes (the performance – outcome expectancy).
- Individuals believe that these outcomes have positive value for them (valence).
- Individuals believe that they are able to perform at the desired level (effort – performance outcome). Here 'Can I do it?' is the question.
- Expectancy is the perceived probability that effort will lead to perceived outcomes.

The individual will want to know the answer to two questions:

1 What am I most likely to get out of this if I do it? (*Expectancy*)
2 How much do I value what I am likely to get out of it? (*Valence*)

The theories are based upon individuals' perception of what they expect out of work and recognise that individuals place different values on rewards and the effort that they have to expend in order to achieve those rewards. There is believed to be a direct correlation between expected rewards and performance.

However, such theories have limited predictive capability in that we cannot measure the individual's perception of values. Unless we assume that all individuals are the same then presumably we may all have different values and different perceptions of how to satisfy these values. We can also legitimately ask to what extent people are rational in the sense of making some kind of calculation concerning the best way to satisfy their needs.

Although we have offered a fairly simplistic version of these theories we can still see that even a simplified version is very complex.

Adams and equity theory

This theory brings in the element of comparison such that an individual will compare his or her ratio of input (effort) to output (pay) with a similar ratio for some other relevant person. Other theories are based upon the individual. This group of theories is based upon how we perceive others in comparison to ourselves. We desire to be treated equitably (Adams, 1965). Thus:

- It is perceived equity that motivates behaviour and provides satisfaction.
- Perceived inequity will lead to dissatisfaction and conflict between individuals.
- The individual is motivated to change the situation back to an equitable one.

The theory is based upon exchanges and the equity of those exchanges. If we work extra hard for our employers we expect some kind of reward in return. Not only that, but we expect that reward to be a fair and just one. The organisation must ensure that employees *believe* that they are being treated fairly in comparison with others. This comparison may be based upon pay since this can be easily measured. It may also involve comparison with other professions and other occupations and not just with rewards to other people within the organisation.

The administrative officer working within the civil service may compare pay and conditions with similar jobs in the private sector such as a building society. Indeed this may more likely be the case if there is a uniform salary within the civil service which is not based upon performance.

However, most of the research in this area is based upon employee reactions to pay inequalities. This may be too narrow a base if pay is only one factor in determining levels of motivation. It may be used by the employer to induce individuals to be over-competitive with each other.

A major problem is that there is no reason why we choose the referents that we do other than the fact that they may be someone we know or whose occupation we have information about. Thus, there is no particular reason why we should choose one referent rather than another. We may choose a professional sports person as our referent and bemoan the fact that our salaries do not compare despite the fact that we may have as much talent in our chosen fields. It is difficult trying to build a theory on such subjective criteria.

Summary

Each set of theories offers us insights but none is conclusive. However, we are left with a number of general points:

- views on human nature are important;
- the role of management is crucial;
- the content of work is important;
- the context of work is important;
- individual perceptions of reward and the relation between performance and reward are important;
- the notion of a fair or equitable reward compared to others is also important.

IMPLICATIONS FOR MANAGERS

Increasingly it is recognised that the role of management is of crucial importance in securing motivation and morale. The Griffiths Report (1983) on management in the National Health Service suggested that the presence of a general management process is important in: 'securing proper motivation of staff. Those charged with the general management responsibility would regard it as vital to review incentives, rewards and sanctions' (para. 9c, p. 13).

Given the theories that we have explored above we can suggest that the manager needs to:

1 Be aware of the individual needs of employees (Maslow).
2 Be aware of the assumptions that they are making concerning human nature (McGregor).
3 Be aware of the organisational context of work and not just concentrate on the job itself (Herzberg).
4 Calculate that outcome which each employee values (*expectancy*).
5 Make sure that the desired levels of performance are attainable (*expectancy*).
6 Link desired outcomes to required performances (*expectancy*).
7 Make sure that employees are treated equitably (*equity*).

Such a role for management assumes that:

● it is possible to measure motivation;
● rewards are linked to performance;
● management has the time and the expertise to assess individual performance;
● organisations can be individualised and take account of the many different needs of employees.

THE PUBLIC SECTOR

As we indicated at the beginning of the chapter, there is a growing interest in issues of motivation and morale within the public sector. The extent to which it is being seriously addressed throughout the sector is less clear. However, efforts in this direction are increasingly being reported on:

● Lawrence and Santry (1989) reported on the work being done in a division of the Department of Trade and Industry and indicated the techniques used. These included the introduction of specific work targets, a more open and informal management style and the establishment of a quality circle.
● The Local Government Training Board (1988b) reported that morale and motivation can be improved by defining the core values of the organisation and communicating these to employees.

One piece of research by Livingstone and Wilkie (1981) looked specifically at the civil service. The exercise was concerned with the motivation of junior and middle managers within the civil service and in broad terms used Herzberg's two-factor analysis described briefly above. Livingstone and Wilkie presented a number of factors leading to dissatisfaction:

- failure to achieve;
- lack of a challenge;
- the feeling of being an unimportant cog in a large machine;
- ungrateful or demanding clients particularly in the – what was then – Department of Health and Social Security;
- the lack of autonomy and responsibility;
- the lack of promotion prospects;
- salary – a low proportion identified this as a source of dissatisfaction; dissatisfaction was mostly aimed at individual anomalies or inappropriate differentials within the organisation rather than those outside;
- the manager's inability to delegate responsibilities or to communicate to those lower down;
- the lack of training to carry out the job;
- departmental practices were often unworkable.

Livingstone and Wilkie also identified a number of factors leading to satisfaction, the most important of which were:

- a sense of achievement – successfully completing a task or overcoming a challenge;
- recognition;
- decent colleagues;
- the physical environment;
- a degree of autonomy in one's work.

Livingstone and Wilkie make a number of comments concerning their findings. They suggest that relatively junior and often youthful staff do not shirk opportunities for taking responsibility when the opportunity is there and they, in fact, associate responsibility and autonomy with a high degree of job satisfaction. Thus an improvement in performance is often related to the content of the job rather than to pay. An interesting, worthwhile and challenging job was deemed to be a motivator. Unfortunately the tradition in the civil service is to bring about changes in structure rather than changing job content or levels of responsibility. Just to redesign the structure misses the point.

Many respondents felt that the most effective barriers to change were the attitudes, beliefs and behaviour of senior management itself. In the civil service the prevailing ethos is one of control of subordinates rather than allowing discretion. Paradoxically, attending courses at the Civil Service College often led to more dissatisfaction when contrasted with the reality of civil service life. Livingstone and Wilkie conclude by arguing for the decentralisation of control and the democratisation of work processes.

The sample may be biased in so far as Livingstone and Wilkie used middle management as their study and it may well be that at this level individuals are reasonably well paid and hence money is not as important as other factors. If they had interviewed the – what were then termed – clerical officers and assistants, they may well have come up with different results. In the Department of Trade and Industry case, reported above, junior staff were short of money and welcomed the opportunity to earn more through overtime.

However, their work does cast doubt on two recent developments within the civil service. Firstly, merit pay: if it is the case that money is not the most important motivator then linking pay to performance, as with merit pay, is not likely to improve performance. Secondly, recent changes in the structure of the civil service with the development of the agency model through the Next Steps programme will not improve matters unless it is linked to changing roles and relationships. Changing the structure alone is insufficient to improve performance. Indeed the Next Steps Report found that: 'People who had recently resigned from the Civil Service told us that frustration at the lack of genuine responsibility for achieving results was a significant factor in encouraging them to move to jobs outside.' (Efficiency Unit, 1988, para. 2.3, p. 3.)

A surprising feature of the Livingstone and Wilkie research is the lack of a commitment to the public service ethos. Certainly in certain professions such as teaching, nursing or social work it is generally considered that a desire to serve the public is of paramount importance.

A more recent report from the Department of Social Security indicated low morale and a lack of confidence in the organisation. It suggested that lack of job satisfaction is related to:

- **pressure**, with too much work and too little time;
- **recognition and regard**, with efforts going unnoticed by both employer and the public at large;
- **career development and training** – where it exists it leads to a happier employee;
- **communications**, where people prefer formal communication from the department rather than relying on the 'grapevine';
- **pay**, which was perceived to be poor both in terms of the duties involved and pay for similar jobs elsewhere;
- **the quality of service**, where the feeling of providing a quality service improves morale. (1988, pp. 16–17.)

HUMAN RESOURCES

Since the early Hawthorne studies, which we examined in Chapter 5, the recognition of the importance of the human element of organisations has never really been off the agenda. The most recent version of the concern with people as an important organisational resource is human resource development.

Unfortunately, there appears to be no clear definition of what this is. In one, limited, sense it is old-style personnel management with a new name. In a more radical sense it involves incorporating individuals into the strategic management of the organisation and recognising that long-term labour planning and development makes sense. According to Storey there are four dimensions to this approach:

- it is linked and integrated into corporate strategy;
- it is intended to ensure commitment of employees and not merely their compliance;
- in order to ensure this commitment, greater attention should be paid to the recruitment, training, appraisal and rewarding of staff;
- the management of human resources should be carried out by line managers and not by personnel specialists. (Storey, 1989, p. 20.)

Of course, it is one thing to state that people are an organisation's most important resource and should be included in the strategy of the organisation and another to operationalise this. One approach is through organisational development which focuses upon the individual. It is argued that if employees can be encouraged to be more flexible then change is more easily brought about. The objectives of organisational development are:

- the personal growth of individuals through the enhancement of skills and personal attributes;
- the creation of an organisation where problems can be discussed freely and openly;
- to locate decision making lower down the organisational ladder;
- to build an atmosphere of trust throughout the organisation;
- to increase the sense of individual ownership of organisational goals;
- to increase self-control and self-direction;
- to change authority relations so that those with expertise, as well as those who occupy certain hierarchical positions, have authority. (Golembiewski, 1977.)

Such an approach relies upon the commitment of senior managers to develop the potential of those lower down the organisation and it requires an appropriate organisational setting. We return to organisational development later in Chapter 13.

These issues appear to be increasingly important in the public services. The Department of Employment Group has produced a human resource development strategy which defines three key undertakings:

- To make the development of people one of the Group's corporate objectives.
- To include human resource development in operational planning at all levels.
- To give everyone the opportunity to agree personal development objectives.

The Group will:

- be clear about its aims and objectives and communicate these to staff;

- have a strategy for developing its staff in the light of these objectives;
- recognise the importance of developing its staff to be adaptable and able to manage change;
- be fully committed to giving human resource development proper priority and making available the necessary time and resources;
- have a range of easily accessible opportunities for individuals to develop, both in their own interests and in those of the organisation;
- promote equality of opportunity for all, irrespective of race or sex; identify and remove barriers to the development of individuals and give particular regard to the needs of the disabled;
- create a climate in which individuals are encouraged to seek out development opportunities;
- seek to provide staff with incentives and rewards for performance and development;
- manage the succession to key identified posts. (Department of Employment Group, p. 3.)

However, commentators on other parts of the public sector are sceptical as to how far, in practice, the development of people has gone. Fitzgerald suggested that in the National Health service, management development was 'embryonic' (1990, p. 34).

With government backing many public services organisations are introducing staff appraisal systems which link individual performance with organisational objectives. The National Audit Office (NAO) makes the case for appraisal which is now widely adopted throughout the civil service:

> It can be a powerful management tool capable of motivating staff, improving organisational performance, and providing the main link between an organisation's strategic objectives and the role of individual members of staff. (National Audit Office, 1991, p. 1.)

The NAO recommends that individual performance is rated on the scale set out in Box 8.1 and that staff are assessed for their suitability for promotion and set job plans for the coming year.

Box 8.1 National Audit Office scale for rating individual performance

---

1 Outstanding.
2 Performance significantly above requirements.
3 Performance fully meets normal requirements of the grade.
4 Performance not fully up to requirements, some improvements necessary.
5 Unacceptable.

(National Audit Office, 1991.)

Of course, any appraisal system that is based upon qualitative judgements is only as good as those that are doing the assessing and there is always the possibility of subjective judgements based upon personal dislike coming into play. Indeed, the union response to such schemes has been to point out possible problems with such appraisal systems.

Often with governmental backing, appraisal has also been linked to rewards through the introduction of a performance-related element in people's pay. Opsahl and Dunnette (1966, p. 302) argue that the success of performance pay depends on the worker's ability to see the link between effort and reward. Herriot argues that such strategies may be dysfunctional if they fail to assess performance at the appropriate level: '. . . if the performance culture values and rewards individual performance, then it is likely to militate against supportive teamwork' (1992, pp. 91–2).

Osborne and Gaebler cite several examples of how performance-related reward systems can fail. They can:

- involve subjective judgements and favouritism;
- involve setting low, easily achieved targets;
- result in people chasing numerical targets rather than achieving the objectives behind the targets;
- result in goal displacement, for example by focusing on departmental objectives rather than organisational goals such as customer satisfaction. (Osborne and Gaebler, 1992, pp. 156–9.)

Argyris (1990, pp. 96–8) describes research by Putnam and Thomas showing that managers tended to give high ratings to poor performers in order to avoid upsetting staff. Also, it was found that performance systems did not encourage risk-taking and innovation and, as a result, staff tended to focus on job preservation and the accumulation of overtime. Other consequences that Putnam and Thomas cite are:

- increases in the wage bill;
- progression to the top of the performance scale;
- protection of the acceptance of mediocre performance;
- use of grievance procedures;
- mistrust.

Osborne and Gaebler suggest that groups should be rewarded in addition to or instead of individuals. The difficulty of assessing the performance of individuals is that it is sometimes impossible to determine an individual's contribution to what may be a group activity. Looking after the health of a patient is never the responsibility of one person but will involve a range of individuals which may include consultants, nurses, cleaning and catering staff, ambulance staff, physiotherapists and so on.

In the USA, just as in the UK, there is a controversial debate about performance pay for teachers. Osborne and Gaebler suggest that those teaching staff in schools who perform well and are popular with parents should be rewarded. They add the caveat that the socio-economic status of the school needs to be taken into account – a factor that did not appear in the calculation of the controversial school 'league tables' in England and Wales in 1993.

CONCLUSION

There are a number of problems in discussing motivation and morale. Firstly, how do we measure motivation and morale? We can measure productivity but with motivation we can only make certain assumptions that improved motivation may lead to improved performance. It is probably easier to measure lack of motivation. Thus, for example, a high level of absenteeism may be a sign of low morale; high staff turnover and the inability to retain staff may be a sign of low morale (witness the number of teachers that leave the profession every year); industrial action or strikes may be an indication that morale and motivation are low. Thus if we want signs of low morale in the civil service, for example, we could point to the 1981 civil service strike.

A second general problem is associated with the esteem with which a profession is held by society as a whole and, as far as the public sector is concerned, the attitude towards it of the government of the day. Thus, commentators have suggested that the Conservative Party came into power in 1979 and was committed to reducing the size of the public sector. Not only that but a change in methods of working, in its ethos and what were seen as its privileges, such as index-linked pensions, was to follow. There is evidence to suggest that this did in fact happen.

Within the civil service the Priestley pay bargaining system which linked civil service pay to rates in the private sector was abolished in 1981. Equity theory that we examined earlier suggested that a feature of motivation was the individual's perception of equity compared to others. At one stroke the Conservative government undermined that principle.

The banning of trade unions at the Government Communications Headquarters (GCHQ), the naming and blaming of civil servants in the Westland Affair, and the Rayner Scrutinies were all seen as undermining the morale of civil servants. The former Labour Party leader, Michael Foot, suggests that there may be another reason:

> Does not the Prime Minister appreciate that one of the reasons for the very low morale in the Civil Service is that she has appointed so many confirmed Thatcherites to some of the best jobs? (*Hansard*, 18.2.1988, p. 1152.)

In local government developments such as compulsory competitive tendering and the introduction of the national curriculum in schools have been said to undermine morale.

Thirdly, there are a number of factors that are to be considered when looking at motivation and morale within public sector organisations and these operate at many different levels. These factors are both external and internal to the organisation and are a reflection of individual needs and the organisational context. We can represent this as in Fig. 8.2:

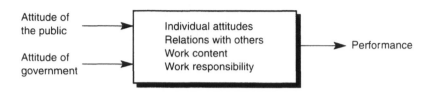

Fig. 8.2 Motivation and morale factors

FURTHER READING

Steers and Porter (1979) offer a good general introduction to the concept of motivation. The collection of essays in Vroom and Deci (1970) also provide a useful introduction. The article by Fowler (1988b) describes the history of performance-related pay and offers a guide to the future use of such systems. The Livingstone and Wilkie article (1981) on motivation in the civil service and on the application of one of the main theories of motivation is well worth reading.

CHAPTER 9

Planning and decision making

INTRODUCTION

The concept of planning can be applied in its various ways to a whole range of activities. The common theme is that planning is used to solve problems. Because of the wide range of problems that the public sector faces there will be different approaches to planning in different situations.

One view of the administrative task is to see it as planning and decision making (Simon, 1976). If we accept this view, we need to consider what decision making is about and then examine the various prescriptions on how best to make decisions.

This chapter discusses the notion of planning, examines different approaches to planning and looks at the changes in attitudes to planning that have taken place. In so doing, we will look at two approaches to decision making – the rational and the incremental models – and assess their suitability to modern public sector organisations.

PLANNING

According to Wedgewood-Oppenheim, planning 'can be seen as a process whereby aims, factual evidence and assumptions are translated by a process of logical argument into appropriate policies which are intended to achieve aims' (Wedgewood-Oppenheim, 1982, p. 107). This definition assumes that organisations have aims which are clearly stated and they have the capability to gather information and use it in a positive way to develop policies. At this point we must note that policies need to be put into practice – a theme that will be developed later in the chapter.

As we have already stated, decision makers in organisations will formulate aims or objectives which they wish to achieve or, in other situations, a commanding authority will impose objectives on organisations. In order to achieve those objectives, an organisation will need to plan its activities: it will need to take account of factors internal to the organisation such as its assets, the qualities of the staff, the task to be achieved, etc. as well as environmental factors such as demand for services, government policies and so on.

In Chapter 4 we considered the idea of systems theory which enabled decision makers to take a holistic view of organisations and how those organisations relate to their environments. The activity of planning illustrates the usefulness of this approach for organisational analysis. It is often difficult for people in organisations to see the wood for the trees, and it is very easy to concentrate on large amounts of internal detail while ignoring important trends in the outside world. For example, organisations may tend to concentrate on improving minor internal processes while failing to take account of changing patterns of demand for their services.

Organisations need to be adaptive to respond to the changing environment and therefore the process of management and organisational structuring 'should have an environmental orientation' (Haynes, 1980). To be fully effective, managers must concentrate on the total organisation and environmental changes instead of on artificial internal segments.

WHAT DO PUBLIC SECTOR ORGANISATIONS PLAN?

The concept of planning can be applied to a wide range of activities. We identify a number of areas where planning has, or is having, influence. The list of these areas is by no means exhaustive.

National planning

Nations in what was formerly the Soviet Bloc were characterised by national planning. Instead of leaving economic decisions to the free hand of the marketplace, economic decisions were made by highly centralised states which were responsible for resource allocation and the planning of economic activities. This method of planning was widely criticised for its inefficiency and its inability to adapt to changing demands.

Western economies are based on a mix of the free market and state planning and have tended to move towards greater use of market forces. However, the state still intervenes in many areas of social and economic activity including the provision of welfare services – hence the existence of the public sector.

Town and country planning

As Elcock (1986, Chapter 9) points out, town and country planning can be traced back to the Victorian era when enlightened industrialists sought to improve areas such as Bournville in Birmingham and Saltaire in West Yorkshire. The Town and Country Planning Act 1946 formed the basis of the modern planning system, requiring local authorities to make plans for their local areas, and to control land use in those areas.

Though the system has now been modified for some years, local authorities still play a crucial role in the shaping of the local environment by, for example, forecasting the need for roads for travel to work or leisure, and thus plan on the basis of that need. Planners seek to influence behaviour, for example, by deciding that particular zones will be devoted to industrial estates, others to shopping centres and residential use in order to harmonise traffic movement and so on. The Skeffington Report of 1969 emphasised the importance of public participation in the planning process, and local authorities were urged to publicise plans and encourage the public to contribute to the process. Critics of the planning system argued that the resulting system was bureaucratic and slow moving because of the problems of dealing with competing interests and the long cycles of committee meetings that local authorities use. Recent initiatives, such as the creation of urban development corporations, have sought to speed up decision making and involve people with business experience. These initiatives, however, have not been without criticism. In particular, it has been argued that urban development corporations are non-elected bodies and are not subject to public scrutiny in the same way that local authorities are.

Corporate planning

Traditionally, local government exhibited one of the dysfunctions of bureaucracy mentioned in Chapter 3 – that it was run on departmental lines with departments such as housing, education and public works providing services in isolation from each other. As Haynes points out, the planning process reflected this in that it 'usually took the form of a series of isolated, departmental exercises which lacked any common framework of reference apart from the central control of financial input' (Haynes, 1980, p. 82). As the scale of local government grew and the environment began to change more rapidly, it became apparent that services needed to be more closely integrated in order that they would meet the needs of the environment. The late 1960s and early 1970s saw a plethora of government-sponsored reports which sought to influence the way in which local authorities were organised and the services that they provided. For example, the Seebohm Report on Personal and Allied Social Services (1967) pointed to the need to anticipate events and to conduct research on future needs.

The Bains Committee on The New Local Authorities: Management and Structure (1972) recommended that local authorities should adopt a corporate approach which would enable the authority to provide a range of integrated services to meet the changing needs of the local community. Like many other ideas that we consider in this book, it is not an idea which originated in the British public sector. Corporate approaches had their origins in business thinking in the United States of America, were implemented in large multinational corporations in the 1950s, and eventually found their way into public sector thinking in Britain in the late 1960s.

Corporate management and planning required that the local authority adapt its internal organisation in order to provide a set of integrated services to the local community. Particular emphasis was placed on the links with other service providers in the area. For example, the then new local authority social service departments needed, according to the Seebohm Report, to develop close working links with health authorities and local authority housing departments. Following on from Bains the internal organisation of the local authority was to be integrated by appointing a chief executive officer as the senior official of the organisation. A chief officers' management team, as well as parallel political structures including a policy and resources committee (consisting of senior elected members), was recommended to co-ordinate the decision-making process. These proposals were adopted with (often unquestioning) enthusiasm by many local authorities. This, together with the development of central research capabilities, underpinned the transition that local authorities had made from town and country planning to corporate planning.

Strategic planning

Strategic planning involves formulating the organisation's objectives and developing strategies to achieve those objectives. In Chapter 3 we examined the concept of bureaucracy and the features of the bureaucrat. In order for strategic planning and decision making to be effective, a different set of values needs to be held by senior officials. Vision, leadership, the ability to be proactive, flexible and forward-thinking are the essential qualities that need to be present. Senior managers should be able to look to the external environment in order to obtain messages about likely future trends, for example in the demand for services, resources that may be available, changes in the legislative framework, etc. They need to develop strategies to enable the organisation to make the appropriate policy choices and implement them in order to enable the organisation to meet the needs of the environment.

Strategic planners use techniques such as SWOT analysis. This involves an analysis of the internal Strengths and Weaknesses of the organisation and the Opportunities and Threats to the organisation (hence SWOT). The idea is to improve the overall organisational performance by eliminating weaknesses and developing strengths. Opportunities are to be maximised and threats either avoided or turned into opportunities (see Sharplin, 1985, pp. 54–6, 190–4 where it is referred to as WOTS-UP analysis).

As with corporate planning, strategic planning has its origins in the private sector. Argenti's (1980) model of strategic planning identifies a number of stages in the process:

- **Stage 1** involves target setting where objectives are clarified and targets set.
- **Stage 2** involves a gap analysis where future performance on current strategies is compared with targets identified in Stage 1.
- **Stage 3** is the strategic appraisal of the internal and external environment and where competitive advantage is identified and targets redefined in the light of this information.
- **Stage 4** is concerned with strategy formulation where options are generated and evaluated against targets and the internal and external environment, and a decision is taken on which strategy to pursue.

- **Stage 5** is strategy implementation where action plans and budgets are drawn up and monitoring and control mechanisms put in place.

In the light of recent developments in the public sector such techniques may be particularly useful in enabling managers to plan the future direction of the organisation. As National Health Service hospitals enter a market for health care they may begin to see other hospitals as competitors. With the advent of compulsory competitive tendering in local authorities, direct service organisations are forced to compete with private sector organisations for contracts to provide certain services and as a result they are beginning to use strategic planning techniques (see the section below on business planning).

Writing about local government, Clarke and Stewart argue that a strategic perspective 'places a premium on the role of the chief executive and its support; it also demands that senior management of service and support departments set their separate sectional interests within a wider strategic perspective. The latter must give their departmental organisations purpose and direction but this must be rooted in what the authority as a whole is trying to do' (1988, pp. 14–15). An example of a strategic planning cycle is shown in Fig. 9.1. You may note that this cycle develops Argenti's model by adding policy review.

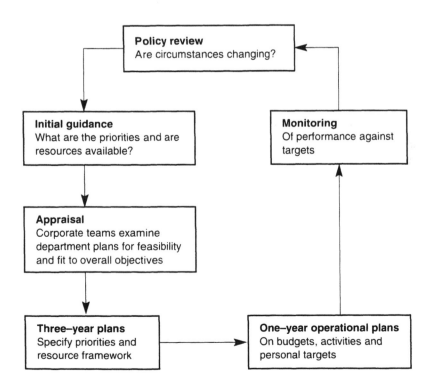

Fig. 9.1 The strategic planning cycle at Kent County Council
(Adapted from Lavery and Hume, 1991)

Policy planning

Governments and other public sector organisations plan and manage policy areas such as housing, education and law and order. The complex nature of policy provision for many policy arenas involves a large number of actors in local authorities, central government, voluntary bodies, pressure groups, inter-governmental bodies, local authority associations, professional bodies and so on (see Hambleton, 1986). For example, Malpass and Murie document the complex machinery which administers housing policy (1987, pp. 136–77).

Increasingly, policy planning has to cross over agency boundaries as organisations have to work with each other in the delivery of public services as in the provision of community care. In formulating policies the needs of different agencies and individuals should be recognised and taken into account. It means agreeing on common objectives, on priorities and recognising the different priorities of different groups. It means creating mechanisms for co-ordination such as joint planning teams and it involves clarifying responsibilities for the implementation of policy. Joint planning is not easy and leads to specific challenges for managers. We address these challenges in Chapter 13.

Business planning

The introduction of compulsory competitive tendering through the Local Government Planning and Land Act 1980 and the Local Government Act 1988 means that direct service organisations may see themselves as agencies with a degree of independence from the actual client, for example, the social service department requiring the cleaning of office buildings. As such they are in a position to see themselves as running a business and may adopt the whole gambit of business techniques when addressing their organisational problems.

It is impossible to make a technical distinction between strategic planning and business planning: both use techniques such as SWOT analysis. Private sector consultants such as Peat Marwick McLintock have offered their services to local government to enable them to apply business planning ideas to strategic and operational levels of the organisation.

Increasingly, public sector organisations are using business plans to aid the setting of objectives and targets for the year ahead. The Contributions Agency, an executive agency of the Department of Social Security, included the following in its business plan for 1992–93:

- Priorities for Action;
- Main Aims;
- Objectives;
- Targets and Assumptions, including financial and performance related to compliance in contribution arrears, maintenance of record of employers' returns and information provision and customer service.

These targets are quantified. The business plan examines the activities of the agency in detail, examines the human and financial resources available, and discusses the management and control systems required.

Expenditure planning

As we have observed in earlier chapters, one of the major concerns of government – one which can be traced back to the last century – is the control of the level of expenditure by the state. Various strategies have been adopted to reduce the level of expenditure. These will be examined in detail in the next chapter.

THE PLANNING PROCESS

The examples above illustrate the fact that different things can be planned. However, planning is only a part of an administrator's work. Ideas need to be put into action. Therefore we need to consider a model of decision making which can be applied to the planning process. The model – known as the rational model – involves a cycle of decisions which need to be made so that an organisation can achieve its objectives.

The rational model

The cyclical process shown in Fig. 9.2 is an adaptation of decision-making models that economists have used to maximise the utility obtained from the use of scarce resources (see, for example, Haynes, 1980, Chapter 4). The model has been used widely by political scientists and, interestingly, underpins the Business and Technology Education Council's guidelines on problem solving on public administration and business studies courses.

It begins with the identification of a problem or issue which requires consideration. At this stage there will be a decision to do nothing or pursue the issue. If the issue is pursued then it needs to be defined and a fuller understanding of the nature of the issue needs to be gained. Analysis based on a partial understanding of the issue is likely to be flawed. In matters relating to the social sciences, the number of variables is large and hence it is often difficult to establish valid theories of cause and effect. This, together with the political dimension, means that it is hardly surprising that problems associated with the inner cities tend to be defined and redefined over the years.

If the rational model is followed, the decision maker is then required to identify possible courses of action to solve the problem. For example the Review of Railway Finances chaired by Sir David Serpell was given the following terms of reference 'to examine the finances of the railway and associated operations, in the light of all relevant considerations, and to report on options for alternative policies, and their related objectives, designed to secure improved financial results in an

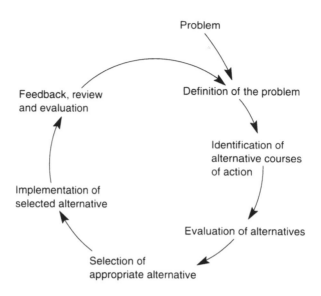

Fig. 9.2 The rational model (1)

efficiently run railway in Great Britain over the next 20 years'. (Department of Transport, 1983, p. 1.)

The terms of reference are reproduced here in full because they provide an interesting example where the overall objective behind the policy development is clear – improved financial results or, in other words, reducing the size of the state subsidy or Public Service Obligation as it is correctly known.

The Committee considered the long-term options for the railway network. They did this by 'producing a set of mathematical models which linked variables (demand, service levels, unit costs and infrastructure) in such a way that, as changes were made in one or more of these variables, the estimated consequences for the others, and for financial results could be evaluated' (Department of Transport, 1983, p. 63). This resulted in the production of a set of options. These varied from what was essentially the retention of the existing system with a few modifications, to an option referred to as a Commerce Railway consisting of about 16 per cent of the existing network (meaning that to travel from Manchester to Leeds one would need to go via London).

Given that decision makers often deal with complex problems, there is a requirement to think beyond the obvious and usual solutions to such problems and to consider innovative solutions. Techniques such as 'brainstorming' and 'lateral thinking' can be used to generate such alternatives (see Mullins, 1989, Chapter 14).

Once the alternative courses of action have been identified they need to be evaluated, and particular attention is devoted to the implications of each option. In the case of transport planning – for example the location of a third London airport – planners used a technique known as cost-benefit analysis in order to establish the costs and benefits of each option. This involved costing up the advantages and disadvantages of each of the proposed courses of action and selecting the preferred option on the basis of the balance of each calculation. Problems arise firstly in trying to forecast events and make realistic costings of programmes, and secondly in making costings of intangibles such as the cost of noise pollution in the case of a new airport (for a thorough critique of this technique see Self, 1975, on the Roskill Commission on the third London airport).

The selection of the preferred option is often a political process and so subject to the values that politicians bring to the process as discussed in Chapter 2. However, once the preferred solution has been selected, we have a policy in the form of a statement, perhaps an Act of Parliament or a government circular. The next stage is to implement it or put it into action. Academic research tells us that this rarely happens perfectly and so we need to examine the effects of the policy in practice. This takes the form of obtaining feedback and evaluation. As we shall see in later chapters the public sector is making increasing use of performance indicators in order to assess the effect of policies. Suffice it to say at this point that because of the complex and changing world in which the public sector operates, implementation of policies may solve certain problems but is likely to throw up further problems which in turn need to be solved: hence the cyclical nature of the policy-making process.

Criticism of the rational model

One of the implicit assumptions of the model is that those who are making decisions are rational actors. We have noted in Chapter 2 that politicians bring values, policies and priorities to the process and these will, of course, influence the process. Peter Self cites a former head of the civil service, Lord Bridges:

> However complicated the facts may be, however much your junior may try to persuade you that there are seventeen arguments in favour of one course and fifteen in favour of the exact opposite, believe me, in four cases out of five there is one point and one only which is cardinal to the whole situation. (Quoted in Self, 1977, p. 3.)

Similarly, administrators may not have the open-mindedness, breadth of imagination, intellectual or organisational resources, or the time to generate the full range of alternative courses of action and assess their implications. A career official may be reluctant to present an option to a political master in the knowledge that it would be politically unacceptable.

Personal experience shows that the best ideas never work perfectly in practice. Lewis Gunn provided civil servants with a number of conditions which would have to be satisfied if perfect implementation of policies were to be achieved (Hogwood and Gunn, 1984, pp. 198–206; see also Hood, 1976). It is helpful to look at these to realise the complexity of planning for the world of public sector organisations.

The circumstances external to the implementing agency do not impose crippling constraints

As we have seen, public sector organisations work in a world where they are heavily dependent on the co-operation of other organisations to get things done. For example, local government depends on Parliament and government to determine the financial framework.

That adequate time and sufficient resources are made available to the programme

For example, the local authorities implementing the NHS and Community Care Act 1990 are dependent on central government making the resources available to complete the changes from long-stay institutions for the elderly to community care.

That the required combination of resources is actually available

The predicted demographic downturn will mean that in the future there will be labour and skills shortages for many organisations. For example, the comparatively low levels of public sector pay mean that schools and benefit offices in the south-east of England have had difficulty in recruiting and keeping staff.

The policy to be implemented is based on a valid theory of cause and effect

In other words, if we do X now then Y will happen. The theory behind the community charge or poll tax was that individual flat rate charges for most members of the community would focus attention on the level of spending by the authority and increase local accountability. Critics say that this is not the case and cite 'poll tax capping' as evidence. If accountability had been enhanced, profligate councillors would have been dismissed from office and replaced by more prudent ones.

That the relationship between cause and effect is direct and there are few, if any, intervening links

Often the theory of cause and effect is extended to cover a whole series of events. For example, we may assume that if we do P then Q will happen; if Q happens then R will then occur. The longer the 'chain of causality', as Gunn calls it, the more likely it that there is going to be a weak link in the chain. For example, if a verbal message is to reach its audience then the reduction in the number of people passing the message will reduce the possibility of the message being distorted.

That dependency relationships are minimal

One of the problems that the Conservative government faced in the 1980s was that it depended on over 400 local authorities in England alone to implement large parts of its policies, for example housing, education and social services. These are political organisations, many of whom were opposed to the policies, some of whom were obstructive to their implementation. One solution that government has used is to replace or override them with more compliant organisations such as the urban development corporations referred to above.

That tasks are fully specified in correct sequence

If an office development is being built, the foundations are built first, the cosmetics such as paint and carpets last. Public services are making increased use of project planning techniques to assist them.

That there is perfect communication and co-ordination

We have already referred to the problems of co-ordination in organisations – individuals and groups within the organisation need to identify with the objectives of the project. The success of the organisation will depend, in part, on the effectiveness of the communications systems in the organisation.

That those in authority can demand and obtain perfect compliance

As Gunn states, this situation is difficult to achieve and is probably undesirable. Leaders of large organisations will inevitably find problems in getting those at lower levels in the hierarchy to comply with their objectives – a problem illustrated by the frequent leaks of confidential memoranda and reports in Whitehall.

As we indicated above. the rational model may generate untried solutions. Organisations may take giant leaps and consequently deal with the unfamiliar. One of the strengths of organisations is the expertise that officials have accumulated over time. This expertise, based on past practice, may not be appropriate to new solutions. Organisations may be less ready to deal with radical solutions because of the dangers of dealing with the unfamiliar.

Alternatives to the rational model

In this section we discuss two points. Firstly, we will introduce an alternative model of decision making – incrementalism – and secondly, we will consider whether it is an approach that can be commended to policy makers.

An increment is a small step from the existing position. Most public sector officials have traditionally been paid on a salary scale which has a number of incremental points on it and each year the official will advance a small step towards the top of the scale. Policy making can be conducted in a similar fashion; indeed, research testifies to its popularity.

Herbert Simon (1976) argues that decision makers seek to be rational and behave like economic actors in maximising the utility of any decision. However, the circumstances in which they operate mean that, in practice, they settle for being satisficers. In other words they aim to satisfy and to perform to satisfactory standards. The barriers to rationality outlined above, in terms of the lack of organisational, intellectual resources and time mean that the well-intentioned official will settle for satisficing or getting by.

In particular, Hogwood and Gunn (1984) cite five types of limitation to explain why the opportunities for rational decision making are limited.

Psychological limitations

Decision makers lack the complete knowledge of the issues, and do not have the skills or understanding of the values that underpin decision making which are necessary to behave rationally.

Limitations arising from multiple values

In situations where there is a collective rationality there is likely to be a conflict of interest and because different people weigh values in different ways, there is no rational way of resolving the conflict.

Organisational limitations

In earlier chapters we have discussed the limitation of organisations as tools for solving problems. The high degree of specialisation in terms of function, the implications of departmentalism and the inadequacy of management information all mitigate against rational decision making.

Cost limitations

Rational behaviour is expensive. As Hogwood and Gunn point out, it is likely that the costs of rational behaviour will outweigh the benefits.

Situational limitations

All decisions are taken in the light of past events, the demands of pressure groups, the expectations of the future – all of which are based on assumptions. We can add to this the uncertain environment in which decision makers operate. For example, local authority treasurers were faced with a high level of uncertainty in planning budgets because of the lack of information on resources available from central government and the uncertainty about the number of community charge defaulters.

So far we have presented a pessimistic view about decision making – that incrementalism is adopted as a decision-making technique because of the impossibility of the rational model. However, writers such as Lindblom (1959) have argued that an incremental strategy of 'muddling through' may be a positive one. Hogwood and Gunn summarise the case in favour of incrementalism:

- Making objectives explicit is a hostage to fortune and the failure to do so may reflect a shrewd awareness.
- Giant leaps into the unknown are dangerous and therefore wiser counsel may preach limited change from the existing position.
- In practice, it is unlikely that problems are solved in one go. A better approach is to adopt a serial approach and solve them over a number of stages.
- Because of the number of agencies and interests in any policy issue, the conflict of competing interests means that rational approaches are unlikely to succeed.
- The nature of policy making means that those involved in the process are open to negotiation and compromise as a method of solving problems.
- Although a rational approach may produce the best policy, there may not be widespread agreement on it. Compromise may be a better alternative. (Hogwood and Gunn, 1984.)

The two models summarised

Figures 9.3 and 9.4 demonstrate how the two approaches to decision making can be used to move from the current state of affairs to a desired situation. Supporters

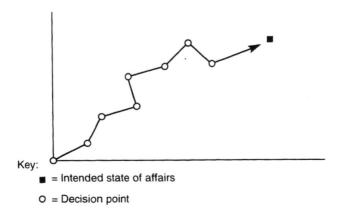

Key:
■ = Intended state of affairs

O = Decision point

Fig. 9.3 The incremental model

of the rational model may seek to move to the desired situation in one strategic move. However, the problems that we have considered mean that it is likely that we may miss the target and actually arrive at an unintended situation. The incremental model demonstrates how a successive number of small steps may enable decision makers to move slowly towards the intended state of affairs with the facility to re-address the situation at each stage in the process.

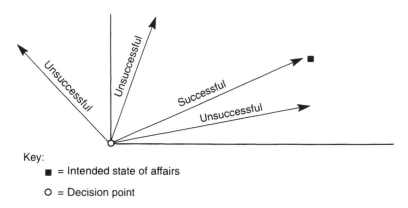

Key:

■ = Intended state of affairs

O = Decision point

Fig. 9.4 The rational model (2)

THE RISE AND FALL AND RISE OF PLANNING

As we have already discussed, planning and the use of rational techniques were highly popular in the late 1960s and early 1970s. This was a period of growth in the size of government in terms of budgets and the areas of service provision. Added to this there was a belief in the economies of scale of large organisations – hence the 1970 White Paper on the Reorganisation of Central Government and the 1972 Local Government Act which reduced substantially the number of local authorities creating much larger organisations. Rational techniques were introduced to try to solve what were perceived to be problems at the time.

Planning and the rational model fell into disrepute in the mid to late 1970s for a number of reasons. Firstly, changing external factors meant that many plans became rapidly out of date and so they could never be implemented properly. These included:

● the economic environment changed with the Labour government obtaining a loan from the International Monetary Fund in 1975 which had conditions attached to it requiring cuts in public expenditure;
● the imposition of cash limits on areas of public spending;
● the election of the Thatcher government in 1979;
● the growing uncertainty of the environment in terms of reductions in the amount of capital and revenue money available;

- the effects of high levels of inflation particularly on the costs of long-term capital projects;
- the changing requirements of central government in terms of what was required through legislation and circulars;
- the changing demands of the clients of public services (or 'customers' as we are now urged to call them).

Secondly, there was growing disillusionment with planning as a technique to solve problems. As we saw above, there are limitations with the rational model as a method of solving problems.

Despite these criticisms, recent approaches to decision making have sought to pursue the rational approach. The new agenda for the public sector emphasises organisational planning – the setting of objectives, measuring performance against those objectives, etc. Business plans are used to achieve economy, efficiency and effectiveness.

CONCLUSION

Public sector organisations take decisions and make plans in turbulent environments and decision makers need to take into account the uncertainty that the external environment offers. Not only that but the internal dynamics of organisations means that the internal environment is often uncertain. As we discussed earlier, organisations are political in nature and are characterised by bargaining and negotiation between individuals and groups. Planning has to be flexible enough to accommodate this dynamism and to be able to respond to the needs and perspectives of these individuals and groups both in the formulation and the implementation of policy. Barrett and McMahon (1990) examine how managing in uncertainty characterises the National Health Service in the United Kingdom.

In this chapter we have examined approaches to planning and decision making. Many factors contribute to the effectiveness or otherwise of the various techniques. These include the formal organisation, the informal organisation and the nature of the environment. We need to examine these issues further. Perhaps the key issue of the 1980s was resources. In the next chapter we examine how resourcing issues have affected organisational performance.

FURTHER READING

The literature on the policy process is examined in Barrett and Fudge (1981), Hogwood and Gunn (1984) and Burch and Wood (1990). A more applied approach is offered by Hogwood (1987). On local government and its relationship with central government, see Hambleton (1986), Chandler (1986) and Rhodes (1988). For a critique of corporate management see Dearlove (1979). Much of the older work remains salient – see Lindblom (1959) on 'muddling through' and Simon (1976) on the administrative man.

CHAPTER 10

Resourcing the public sector

INTRODUCTION

At the heart of the debate about the role of the public sector is invariably the issue of finance. Some critics of the public sector maintain that it is inherently inefficient and unable to control its expenditure. Though this point of view is not a new one, it took on increased importance in 1976 when the Labour government obtained a loan from the International Monetary Fund which was conditional upon a reduction of the level of public expenditure. The Conservative governments elected in 1979, 1983, 1987 and 1992 instigated a range of policies which sought to reduce further the overall level of expenditure. Although this strategy has met with limited success in terms of reducing the overall level (Dunleavy, 1990), it has had severe implications for the management of public sector organisations.

This chapter examines the processes of revenue raising, allocation, spending and control. These activities are considered in the context of the two models of policy making – the rational model and the incremental model – which were examined in the previous chapter. Examination of the budgetary process in the public sector provides interesting evidence on how organisations actually behave and the applicability of these models as descriptions and prescriptions for their behaviour. To this end, three case studies of budgetary behaviour are discussed: resourcing in central government, local government and the National Health Service. As we shall see, the role of finance is inextricably linked to the programmes they are financing.

GETTING: THE REVENUE-RAISING PROCESS

Revenue can be raised from a number of sources. These vary from service to service and will reflect political choice. Some services are financed out of general taxation and are made available for all of us to consume. Alternatively there may be a direct cash relationship between the service provider and the customer. In some cases, such as defence or law and order, we all stand to benefit from the service and it would be difficult to envisage how it could be financed other than out of direct taxation. In other cases, the decision about how to finance a service will reflect the political and ethical values that underpin the policy. For example, the National Health Service was founded on the principle that there would not be a financial exchange between the doctor and the patient. It was thought that if people had to pay at the point of delivery then this might deter some people from using the service. Critics of the Conservatives' policy on health point to the decline in the number of people having eye tests since the introduction of a fixed charge for the service. The so-called ring fencing of local authority housing revenue accounts in 1990 has meant that current spending on housing has to be financed out of the revenue raised from rents alone. This means that the council house tenant will normally pay the full cost of the service while the owner-occupier will enjoy a subsidised mortgage. This reflects the Conservative government's concern that people should not be drawn into what is called the 'dependency culture'. Instead they prefer to promote the values of a 'property-owning democracy'.

The unsuccessful policies aimed at reducing the level of direct taxation (Gamble, 1988) intended to create an 'enterprise culture'. On the assumption that people are motivated by monetary reward, it was argued that this would provide incentives for them to work harder and for entrepreneurs to create wealth and jobs. It was also assumed that if people had more of their gross income to spend as they chose then they would purchase goods and services that they wanted rather than the state spending money on goods and services for which there may be little or no demand.

Other criteria will influence decisions about the sources of finance. The Layfield Committee on Local Government Finance (1976) argued that in order to achieve a vital local democracy, a larger share of the revenue of local authorities must be raised locally, thus enhancing local accountability. Other criteria for a suitable tax are that it is easy to collect, the yield is predictable, it is cheap to collect, and that it is fair. An interesting exercise is to analyse current and possible forms of local taxation against this checklist.

SPENDING

Spending by public sector organisations has to comply with complex and changing legal regulations, and is exposed to scrutiny at a number of levels. It is quite possible for one organisation to be audited at five levels, as well as being accountable to internal decision-making bodies, political masters and the law.

All organisations will make the distinction between capital and revenue or current expenditure. While there are exceptions, capital expenditure is defined as:

'Expenditure on new construction, land, and extensions of and alterations to existing buildings and the purchase of any other fixed asset (e.g. machinery and plant) – including vehicles – having an expected working life of more than one year'; . . . while current expenditure on goods and services 'includes direct expenditure by central and local government on providing services (e.g. health or education) . . .' (Likierman, 1988, pp. 219–20).

In general terms, capital expenditure will commit future current expenditure. For example, it is capital expenditure that will finance the development of a new leisure centre while current expenditure will be used to pay for the running costs, for example staff, heating and lighting, etc. Decision makers therefore need to plan budgets and commit resources for the future if capital programmes are to be undertaken. Equally, when cuts in expenditure are considered, capital programmes are usually the first victims.

In our discussion on accountability in public sector organisations in Chapter 2 we pointed out that a principal focus of processes of accountability was finance. Repeated attempts to cut back the global total of public spending have placed an increased emphasis on control of public spending. We will see that various strategies can be adopted, many of which will be discussed in more detail in the next two chapters.

The creation of the Audit Commission in 1982 has increased accountability. It appoints auditors for local authorities to ensure probity and promotes improvements in economy, efficiency and effectiveness. As well as investigating the activities of individual authorities, it publishes papers which compare practice and offer suggestions for improvement. The National Audit Office scrutinises the accounts of government departments on behalf of Parliament and conducts periodic audits of the National Health Service (Perrin, 1988). In October 1990 the Audit Commission's remit was extended to cover the National Health Service.

THE ROLE OF THE BUDGET

Budgets take place at the macro level: the Chancellor of the Exchequer sets overall revenue-raising and spending priorities. Within that context, public sector organisations will make their own budgetary decisions. The budgetary process will vary from organisation to organisation but all will share the common theme of allocating resources through a political process. It is political, not necessarily because politicians are involved, but because it involves the representation of organisational interests and has scope for bargaining and conflict.

One of the traditionally cited differences between public and private organisations is the role of the budget. In the private sector, a budget will be a set of projections about likely future activity. A motor manufacturer will only be in a position to estimate revenue because it does not know how many cars it will sell. In the public sector, estimates of revenue may often be more precise and known for the forthcoming year. However, it is debatable how well this distinction holds up today. Large commercial organisations need to allocate budgets to programmes such as research and development and design. These will be needed to finance long-term programmes. In the public sector there is a great deal of uncertainty about the assumptions implicit in budgets. Local authorities will be unaware of the yield of the revenue raised through taxation, the level of pay settlements and the level of inflation. Hence budgets are made amidst uncertainty.

ORGANISATIONAL CULTURE AND PUBLIC SPENDING

As we considered in earlier chapters, public sector organisations are divided into large departments and they will develop cultures of their own. At the heart of these organisations is a central finance department, whether it is the Treasury in central government or the treasurer's department in a local authority. Heclo and Wildavsky's study of the Treasury, *The Private Government of Public Money*, portrays the organisation as a nuclear family with a distinct culture and a set of norms and values all of its own. They act as guardians of the public purse when dealing with members of spending departments who seek additional resources. The authors summarise Treasury norms as:

1   Decide by reacting.
2   Let others do the technical work.
3   You know as much as anybody and more than most.
4   Above all, be sceptical – especially of enthusiasts.
5   Probe, delay and question again.
6   As a rule, cut by bargaining rather than absolute no's.
7   A reputation for toughness inhibits would-be spenders.
8   Be on guard against hidden and built-in expenditure escalators. (Heclo and Wildavsky, 1981, pp. 49–50.)

John Stewart demonstrated how the budgetary environment can impact on the culture of public sector organisations. He analysed local government spending and labour-force figures in the post-war period leading up to the late 1970s. He identified two periods – firstly a period of budgetary growth (until 1976), and secondly a period of reduction in growth leading to a standstill and in some cases cutbacks (1976 onwards). He argued that a period of continued budgetary growth is likely to build expectations that the pattern of growth will continue. If growth is perceived as being the norm by those in the organisation then it 'would begin to influence their behaviour and through their behaviour the procedure and structure of the organisation' (Stewart, 1980, p. 11). This is characterised by:

1   The environment will generate demands which could be met by the increment in the budget without challenging the existing budget thus leaving existing programmes of expenditure untouched. The allocation of the increment becomes the key decision.
2   Procedures established to control the level of spending evolve over time to become bidding procedures for the increment. Hence the emphasis on growth at the margins.
3   Organisations tend to emphasise the benefits of policies rather than their costs, looking at the objectives to be achieved rather than the resources available.
4   Uniform provision of services as opposed to discrimination or targeting services towards groups with high needs become the norm.

5 Capital development was a dominant feature in budgets because of the assumption that, for example, in the case of a swimming pool, the revenue expenditure would be available in future years to heat and staff the pool.
6 Choices tend to be about when to implement a given policy rather than whether to implement it. (Stewart, 1980.)

The overall characteristic of a period of growth is that of a consensus among decision makers. The possibility of conflict is reduced because of the expectation of the continued availability of the increment to avoid the questioning of the existing budget (or baseline as it is often referred to). However, if the assumption of growth is removed, then there is a change in the experience of those involved in the process which leads to a change in expectations. The main characteristics of a period of standstill are:

1 The environment continues to present new and changing demands but these cannot be satisfied by the allocation of the increment.
2 Consensus becomes difficult to achieve and decision makers become reluctant to create future commitments. Capital programmes are cut.
3 The budgetary process focuses more clearly on the resource allocation process with more thorough scrutiny of existing commitments. Control procedures are strengthened.
4 Greater control over the staffing levels results in the freezing of posts.
5 Cash limiting of expenditure is used to control the expansion of budgets through inflation.
6 Attention becomes focused on costs of programmes rather than benefits, and resources available instead of objectives to be achieved.
7 Political consensus disappears and relationships become increasingly adversarial.
8 Uniform provision is replaced by targeting of services at the most needy. (Stewart, 1980.)

Thus we can see a very different style of behaviour resulting from a change in the budgetary environment. If we were to move from standstill to cutbacks, we would expect to see further changes in behaviour. For example:

● voluntary redundancies or compulsory redundancies;
● increasingly departments look to protect their share of the budget;
● the use of voluntary and private organisations to save costs;
● increasingly close scrutiny of discretionary expenditure and consideration given to alternative methods of achieving existing goals;
● the use of creative accounting techniques such as lease-back arrangements if legal;
● increasingly power exercised by central budgetary control staff and auditors;
● further adversarial relationships;
● 'sore thumbs' and 'shroud waving' to demonstrate the effect of cuts or potential cuts. (See Elcock et al., 1989, p. 178.)

Thus the environment in which budgetary choices take place will be an important determinant on budgetary behaviour.

In order to understand fully the effect of resource issues on the public sector we need to examine what happens in practice. To this end we present three case studies. It is not our intention to supply the reader with the full details of the various initiatives; instead we seek to examine the effect of these initiatives on organisations.

CASE STUDY: CENTRAL GOVERNMENT

Control of public expenditure until the 1960s was highly fragmented and largely revolved around the consideration of annual estimates: there was little or no attempt to plan expenditure programmes for the medium or long term. Concern about this led to the appointment of the Plowden Committee on the Planning and Control of Public Expenditure which reported in 1961. The committee recommended a system of annual surveys of planned public expenditure for the years ahead. This led to the introduction of the so-called PES system. The PES (Public Expenditure Survey) involved 'the cost projection of existing policies' (Heclo and Wildavsky, 1981, pp. 216–17). The committee (known as the Public Expenditure Survey Committee, PESC) consisted of an inter-departmental group of departmental finance officers and Treasury officials who prepared information for decision makers. They then compared total spending implications of policies against available resources and different expenditures against each other. This was done by costing programmes up to five years ahead. According to one senior civil servant, Otto Clarke, PES was designed to achieve the effective collective responsibility of ministers for public expenditure, regular ministerial appraisal of public expenditure for five years ahead, and increased stability of public expenditure (see Hennessy, 1989a, p. 179).

The idea was then to introduce greater rationality to the public expenditure process. However, the eventual effect was, as Heclo and Wildavsky observe, to enshrine incrementalism. They state: 'If PES makes it less likely that new monetary programmes with large spending implications will be introduced inadvertently, it also helps to assure departments that their ongoing programmes will not suddenly be disrupted' (Heclo and Wildavsky, 1981, p. 238). In other words, it did not lead to the questioning of the validity of existing programmes, but instead re-costed them, thus providing updated costings (see Pliatzky, 1982, p. 98).

In an attempt to remedy this weakness, a further system was introduced – Programme Analysis and Review (PAR) in 1970. Spending departments were to carry out reviews of programmes by questioning existing commitments and to ask whether they should exist at all and not only how they should be carried out (see Pliatzky, 1982, p. 99). It was a system that was widely criticised for making heavy demands on officials, raising sensitive issues and increasing the level of conflict. It required staff with specialist skills – economists and statisticians – who were not available. Both officials and politicians saw the system as an unwanted intrusion and not for them (see Heclo and Wildavsky, 1981; Gray and Jenkins, 1985). Hennessy wrote the following obituary: 'To be brutal and brief, PAR became slow, top heavy, and a victim of the relentless, interdepartmental grind' (Hennessy, 1989a, p. 236).

The election of the Thatcher government in 1979 was to see a new approach to the management of the civil service. The intention was to seek lasting cultural changes in the service to transform it from a reactive bureaucracy to a more proactive business-like organisation. Four initiatives merit examination: the Rayner scrutinies, the Management Information System for Ministers (MINIS), the Financial Management Initiative (FMI) and agency status.

Following her election to power, Mrs Thatcher abolished PAR and introduced a new system of scrutiny of departmental expenditure – the Rayner scrutinies. Sir Derek Rayner (now Lord Rayner) from Marks & Spencer stated that the reviews aimed to:

(i)   examine a specific policy or activity, questioning all aspects of work normally taken for granted;
(ii)   propose solutions to problems and to make recommendations to achieve savings and increase efficiency and effectiveness; and
(iii)   implement agreed solutions, or to begin their implementation within 12 months of the start of the scrutiny. (Cited in Gray and Jenkins, 1985, p. 118.)

The subjects of the scrutinies varied from payment of social security benefits to the organisation of the coastguard (Gray and Jenkins, 1985). The emphasis was on action and results rather than the collection of pages of analysis – the report produced by the scrutiny team was to include recommendations for the minister to act on.

Several other initiatives have been undertaken, often influenced by the work of the Efficiency Unit. Michael Heseltine was unusual among ministers in having an interest in the detail of the management and internal working of his department. This interest led to the creation of MINIS. This was introduced by Heseltine in the Department of the Environment in 1980 and later in the Ministry of Defence. The basis of the system was to establish what was happening, who was responsible, what the targets were and whether they were being monitored (see Greenwood and Wilson, 1989, p. 125). Interestingly, Heseltine recalled that nobody could remember these questions being asked before. The system involved a cyclical process of establishing what is done, how many people do it and what is achieved, linked to a number of performance indicators. These statements were then considered by ministers and senior civil servants who then made decisions which were implemented. The system was received with scepticism both by fellow ministers (despite enthusiasm from the Prime Minister) and civil servants (see Hennessy, 1989a, pp. 608–9).

However, this led to a more widely implemented Financial Management Initiative (FMI). FMI aims to produce:

> a system in which managers at all levels have (a) a clear view of their objectives; and means to assess and wherever possible measure outputs and performance in relation to those objectives; (b) well-defined responsibility for making the best use of their resources, including a critical scrutiny of the output and value for money; and (c) the information (particularly about costs), the training and the access to expert advice which they need to exercise their responsibilities effectively. (Cited in Metcalfe and Richards, 1987, p. 183.)

Greenwood and Wilson identify four features:

- **Top management systems**: the creation of an information system for senior managers particularly concerning resources, activities, and the review of policy programmes.
- **Statement of objectives**: clear statements of what departments were setting out to do were required. This has proved difficult because of the intangible nature of the activities of many departments.
- **Decentralisation and delegation**: particularly the delegation of decision making and budgets to cost centres so that decisions are made by those responsible for carrying them out.
- **Performance measurement**: measuring the relationship between inputs and outputs, and the effectiveness of policy programmes. (See Greenwood and Wilson, 1989, pp. 129–34.)

Our principal concern here is the delegation of decision making down the hierarchy. A key element of the FMI has been the use of delegated budgeting and the creation of cost centres to hold managers to account for their expenditure. This involves a move away from the traditional form of centralised bureaucratic administration and will inevitably meet with resistance from those at the centre who seek control.

However, the thinking behind the FMI was that if the budgetary process works and if officials have the information and the skills to use the process then good management will result. This has implications for the organisation as a whole: 'in the rhetoric of the FMI, departments are expected to move from structures based on centralised but separate responsibilities for finance, personnel, policy, executive operations and performance improvement towards structures that decentralise and cluster these responsibilities in "businesses".' (Metcalfe and Richards, 1987, p. 194.)

The National Audit Office Report on the FMI (1986) found, in practice, that departments differed in the extent to which they had adopted the FMI. It was also found that middle and lower management had reservations about the new arrangements. In the Ministry of Defence, for example, there was very little participation by those at the lower levels of management. Similarly, in the Department of the Environment, managers felt a lack of decision-making capability to accompany the new processes.

The theme of decentralisation is one that is pursued further in the Next Steps Initiative. Described by the Treasury and Civil Service Committee as 'the most ambitious attempt at Civil Service reform this century' (1990, para. 1), it involves the creation of executive agencies to perform the administrative work of large parts of the civil service (see Chapter 12). The project, which aims to cover three-quarters of the service work by the end of the century, is intended to give chief executives of agencies a higher degree of autonomy from central control. Implicit in the idea is a distinction between the policy-making work of advisers to ministers and the day-to-day administration of the departments. The new relationship, which will be set out in framework documents agreed between the minister and the chief executive of the agency, will cover areas such as recruitment and staff management, planning and financial arrangements. It is intended that managers will have greater freedom to make the service meet the needs of the environment. For example, the role of the Employment Service will be very different in an area with high levels of unemployment compared with one with low levels of unemployment. It is envisaged that staff will be consulted on the work that they do. Already 'wish lists' have been made where staff indicate what they want to see from agency status and these suggestions have been acted on.

The project is still at its early stages and it is difficult to predict what the eventual impact will be. Hood and Jones offer four possible fates for the project:

- major changes resulting in total success;
- superficial adoption with mix of success and failure;
- a step to a further radical initiative;
- termination after enthusiasm wears off. (Hood and Jones, 1990, pp. 82–3.)

The key to the success of the project is the relationship between the agencies and the host department, and the degree of freedom that the agencies will be allowed. Given the history of Treasury control over financial matters, it will require a substantial cultural shift if agencies are to have the financial freedom which is crucial to the success of the project.

By July 1993 a total of ninety agencies had been created, including agencies in Northern Ireland, ranging across the whole spectrum of government activities. Some 350,000 civil servants are employed in these agencies, approximately 65 per cent of the total number of civil servants. Twelve of the agencies have trading fund status, which allows the development of a financial regime more suited to a commercial environment. Agencies with this status include Her Majesty's Stationery Office (HMSO) and the Central Office of Information. However, it is difficult to see how other agencies could be run along similar lines. The Benefits Agency still has cash and manpower controls imposed by the Treasury and this constrains the 'freedom to manage' for civil servants in this agency. This dilemma is at the heart of the financial dimension of the Next Steps Initiative. The civil service has traditionally been part of an input-dominated and – increasingly –

cash-limited public expenditure system. It is difficult to transform this to accommodate an entrepreneurial, output and customer-led culture. There is a continuing tension between the need for central control and accountability and devolved responsibility. In theory the centre, i.e. the Treasury and the parent departments, should give up operational control and concentrate on setting the strategic direction and monitoring performance but this appears to be difficult to achieve. Earlier in this chapter we referred to Heclo and Wildavsky's study of the Treasury, and the norms of the Treasury that the authors describe hardly seem appropriate for a more entrepreneurial financial regime in the agencies.

CASE STUDY: LOCAL GOVERNMENT

In the previous chapter we discussed the ways in which local government has changed its approach to planning. Changing approaches to resourcing issues arise out of the same organisational thinking, particularly the experimentation with rational techniques. The traditional local authority budget was characterised by:

- a narrow focus by senior officers and politicians with limited control over the process. Departmental estimates were prepared in isolation from the other departments;
- the core budget of established expenditure went unchallenged – the focus of the debate was the increment;
- because of the isolation of the various departments whilst preparing the budgets, there was little co-ordination, and little prioritisation of bids for new expenditure, and no attempt to assess the overall impact of the individual estimates of the departments. (See Elcock *et al.*, 1989, pp. 69–71.)

Although we do not need to reconsider *all* the issues relating to the corporatisation of local government during the 1970s, it is important to remind ourselves of the widespread adoption of policy and resources committees, consisting of the senior elected members (with sub-committees specialising in land, finance, personnel and performance review). There were parallel structures on the officers' side with chief officers' management teams consisting of the senior departmental heads. The intention behind these structures was to focus thinking on the overall co-ordination and control of the activities and resources of the authority.

This period saw experimentation with rational techniques such as planning, programming and budgeting systems (PPBS). This is an attempt to bring together the annual budgetary process with the policy planning process by linking the analysis of objectives and activities with the outputs of the authority. As Table 10.1 indicates, this is an example of an attempt to implement the rational model of decision making discussed in the previous chapter.

Table 10.1 The PPBS cycle

Stage
1   Identification of needs and strategic problems in the environment.
2   Formulation of objectives related to those needs.
3   Assessment of alternative ways of achieving those objectives.
4   Assessment of the resource and environmental impact of the alternatives.
5   Decision taken and implemented.
6   Results are monitored and, if necessary, adjustments and revisions are undertaken
    in relation to the strategy and overall objectives.
7   The cycle returns to stage 1.

Variants on PPBS such as zero-based budgeting (ZBB) have been experimented with. This technique according to Henley *et al.* (1983, p. 69), is more suited to situations where restraint or cutbacks are called for. It involves the selection of a zero-base which, confusingly, is rarely zero but may equate to a minimum level of service consistent with the law. Hence there is a gap between the zero-base and the existing budget. This is the area which is subjected to scrutiny and would enable the consideration of, say, a reduction in the level of environmental services together with an increase in spending on education. Inevitably this process will address difficult questions and may generate difficult solutions which may in turn have severe effects on existing interests both inside and outside the organisation. For example, it may require the termination of a service, thus affecting the clients of the service.

A number of problems are associated with these techniques. Experience has shown that they call for more work from officials, and that they meet with resistance from officials (see Jenkins, 1978). Haynes states that PPBS makes an 'inherent demand for self-criticism and the need for a creative dissatisfaction with the status quo' (1980, p. 79). Elcock *et al.* (1989, pp. 85–6) point to the sheer volume of paper that ZBB exercises consume, the possibility of losing sight of overall objectives, and thus the possibility of incrementalism by default.

Paul Griffiths' study of the 1986–87 budgetary process in Mid-Glamorgan County Council illustrates the influence of a number of factors in the budgetary process: culture, the environment and the relationship between members and officers. Firstly, the council had a large Labour majority with political decision making often restricted to the Labour group and with little debate in committees. There was a political culture of stability 'thriving on the creation of symbolic dragons – the English, the Tories, the Church of England, Twickenham' (Griffiths, 1987, p. 215), a lack of a corporate revolution and an inherent conservatism reflected by one councillor who believed that borrowing money to finance capital expenditure was tantamount to creative accounting. The changing policies of the Welsh Office meant that a standstill budget would result in a 14 per cent increase in the rate and a 2 per cent cut in the budget would mean a 5 per cent increase.

Following criticisms that budgetary behaviour had been too incremental in the past, one group of officers conducted a zero-based budgeting exercise which assumed a core budget of 85 per cent. The exercise involved the generation of a number of options including a growth in the budget, standstill and a reordering of priorities. The results of the officer-led exercise were presented to the Labour group. They committed themselves to simple pro-rata savings rather than a reordering of priorities, reflecting the changing demand for the education and social services. This was, according to Griffiths, due to some members not understanding the budgetary data and the closed nature of the decision-making process and also the lack of debate in committees. He concludes: 'In the end the rationalist aspiration of the officers was overridden by the conservative political values of the members' (Griffiths, 1987, p. 223).

During the 1980s central government sought to increase its control over spending by local authorities. This strategy has been pursued through a number of means – there were over 40 Acts of Parliament which changed the finance system culminating in the introduction of the community charge. It is not our purpose to review these initiatives, merely to point out that this has been the single most important factor responsible for the change in budgetary climate in local government in recent years.

In addition, the Audit Commission has, as mentioned above, promoted better financial management. One of the major themes of the 1980s was the decentralisation of services to make them closer to the public. This involves the creation of small teams who need to be able to turn their hands to a wide variety of tasks. This move away from the traditional specialisation which was a feature of local government has meant that generic workers need to develop financial skills and take responsibility for budgets. For example, a housing neighbourhood office manager may be responsible for budgets covering empty properties, rent arrears, maintenance, staff such as wardens, office expenses and income from garages (Audit Commission. 1989a).

As indicated earlier, one of the prime stimuli for the push to better financial management has come from central government. In education, for example, this has taken the form of devolving budgets from local education authorities (LEAs) to schools. Following on from the Education Reform Act 1988 greater control of, and responsibility for, budgets was to be given to schools as part of the local management of schools (LMS). Funds were to be allocated to all LEA schools according to a formula set by the LEA but within regulations specified by the, then, Department of Education and Science. Of that formula 75 per cent had to be determined by the number of pupils attending the school, with weighting for different age groups. The remaining 25 per cent could take account of other factors such as the state of the premises or the special needs of pupils. Until the introduction of LMS few senior staff in schools had any experience of managing finances or indeed had been recruited for their financial skills. They – and their school governors – quickly had to develop financial skills. The 1988 Act made governing bodies responsible for managing the school and its budget and holding the head teacher to account.

The role of the LEA has changed and its powers to implement education policies and to intervene in school activities substantially reduced. The funding formula is prescribed by the Department for Education and this limits LEA control. The LEA is expected to retain responsibility for financial probity, to offer support services, to help schools with their business plans, and for LEA managers to develop strategic direction rather than be concerned with the direct provision of education.

The delegation of financial resources in education mirrors the wider tendency throughout the public sector to push responsibility and accountability closer to the point of service delivery. However, as with Next Steps agencies, relations between the centre and the operating arm still have to be worked through and the centre, in the case of education the LEA, has not found it easy to adjust to the loss of control, financial or otherwise.

CASE STUDY: THE NATIONAL HEALTH SERVICE

The National Health Service provides an excellent example of an organisation facing the problem of making a best fit with its environment. Among the problems it faces are:

- the continuing popularity of the service amongst the general public. This has meant that it has become a politically sensitive issue;
- demographic trends show that the proportion of elderly people is set to rise dramatically over the next ten years. This section of the population makes a high demand on health care resources;
- developing medical technology means that more and more types of illnesses can be treated, thus increasing demands for treatment;
- the consensus on which the National Health Service was founded in 1948 was based on a service financed out of taxation. Though charges for certain services have been introduced and increased, the majority of funding comes from central government sources;
- the academic literature on professionalism cites the medical profession as a prime example of a highly professionalised body. Doctors exercise considerable power and often come into conflict with politicians;
- the rate of inflation for the health service tends to be higher than the overall rate of inflation. This means that to stand still in terms of health service provision, funding has to increase over and above that for other services.

The National Health Service is accountable to central government and decision making has to be seen in the context of the central government initiatives on financial control discussed above. Indeed proposals for the service to be administered by local government have fallen by the wayside because of the determination of central government to control the cost of the service. The service has been the victim of organisational reforms in 1974 and 1982, which reflected the conventional wisdom in the administrative thinking of those times. These reforms created a service which was controlled at the top but left some regional autonomy in relation to the allocation of funding and service organisation (see Klein, 1989).

New directions in National Health Service budgeting have emerged during the 1980s. According to Perrin (1988) it is possible to budget by subjective costs (such as staff, supplies and equipment), functions (such as nursing, catering and estates), specialties (such as neurology, geriatrics and general surgery), or by the units that comprise the district. The problem is to devise a system that enhances financial accountability.

The Griffiths Report (1983) saw the introduction of general managers at regional, district and unit levels. This reform was intended to give the service a clearer management direction. In order to enhance management accountability, budgets were allocated to units. As Perrin (1988) points out, improved accountability was dependent on managers having financial skills, and the creation of effective decentralised structures with staff (especially clinicians) able to understand budgetary information.

Following Griffiths, the Körner Report (1984) recommended that district budgets should be linked to specialties such as X-rays or operating theatres. If a patient was sent for an X-ray, the cost would be attached to the department, giving clinicians information on the cost of their work. Again the aim was improved financial accountability. Problems that arise include the unwillingness of clinicians to see themselves as resource managers. They may believe that this conflicts with the clinical autonomy that they traditionally enjoy. Also, the quality of the information may not be sufficiently high to enable effective decision making.

Budgeting techniques are only one solution to the problems of the health service. According to the King's Fund Institute (1988), decision makers are faced with a number of options. Amongst these are:

- **more public expenditure**: the King's Fund researchers provided a tentative estimate that spending would have had to be just under £400 million higher in 1987/88 if it was to match 1981/82 levels, taking into account changing demand and technology;
- **supplementary and alternative sources of funding**: a number of alternatives exist. These range from private insurance schemes, to shops in hospitals and charging for services;
- **the creation of internal markets**: this would allow general practitioners to make decisions about which hospital or clinician to use. It is argued that the doctor would have the information to decide from where the best value for money could be obtained.
- **expansion of private health care**: the private sector in health care has grown considerably. Like all decisions about the future provision of health care, it is

dependent on the value systems of the decision makers. If private provision is considered acceptable, it is highly attractive in deflecting demand away from the public sector. However, the King's Fund researchers argue that limited private sector expansion may lead to 'distortion in NHS planning priorities, cost inflation and possible adverse effects on NHS labour supply' (King's Fund Institute, 1988, p. 24).

Increasingly, within hospitals, doctors are being encouraged to take responsibility for budgets. As such they are encouraged to 'buy in' the services provided by the X-ray department, operating theatres, physiotherapy and so on. Through the devolution of budgets it is intended that doctors should become more aware of the financial costs of their activities. Historically, costing medical activities has been fraught with difficulties but there are now various techniques available to aid the estimation of costs. One such technique is diagnosis related groups (DRGs) which aims to provide a classification system that groups together cases on the basis of expected costs. Along with the rest of the public services, the intention is to collect information about, and thus be able to control, costs. This has meant that doctors have to familiarise themselves with budgets and with costing. This has caused problems since some doctors argue that the acquisition of financial skills was not the reason why they entered the medical profession.

A more significant innovation, following on from the NHS and Community Care Act 1990, has been the introduction of the purchaser–provider split and the creation of an internal market within the NHS. Structural changes have meant that the district health authority and fundholding GPs can purchase services from a trust hospital, from a directly managed hospital of the district health authority, from the directly managed hospital of another health authority or from private institutions. An element of competition is thereby introduced into the NHS. For example, fundholding GPs now have a budget to buy services for their patients, and will thus have to think about costs. Indeed GPs will shop around for the best deal and may even carry out minor surgery themselves to save money. These developments mean that the GP is in a relatively powerful position *vis-à-vis* hospital managers and doctors. GPs now have an incentive to under-refer patients to hospitals as financial as well as clinical considerations come into play. There is also the danger that, as more and more money is allocated to fundholding GPs who will naturally look after the interests of their own patients, the health authority is in a weaker position to develop a health strategy for the area as a whole.

Internal markets form the basis of government thinking about the reform of the National Health Service. This reflects the view that if the logic of the private sector is introduced into public sector organisations then greater efficiency will be achieved. This theme is pursued in more detail in the next chapter.

CONCLUSION

The above three case studies bring out a number of points about resourcing the public sector which demonstrate that resourcing issues are not the sole province of the technical experts in the area: accountants and economists. Instead resourcing issues impinge on all of us. We can make a few more concluding points:

- The environment affects budgetary behaviour. In a period of growth, the increment is the focus of debate; with cutbacks the baseline is questioned – leading to increasingly adversarial relations.
- As we saw with the Treasury, organisational culture will impact on budgetary behaviour. In the National Health Service clinicians may see their role as providing health care, not managing budgets. Managers and staff need to be motivated towards financial management.
- The structure affects budgetary behaviour. Decentralised structures may mean that budget holders are closer to the point of service delivery, but usually they will not be financial specialists. The introduction of local cost centres may result in people identifying with departmental objectives rather than the objectives of the organisation as a whole. Central finance departments may be reluctant to concede power to the periphery by, for example, allowing cost centres to vire money from one budget heading to another. This may reduce the flexibility which decentralisation aims to promote.

However, as public sector organisations are encouraged to become more cost conscious, as competition is introduced through quasi-markets, as contracts become the normal form of relationship between purchasers and providers, then financial management is becoming increasingly important for managers and professionals at all levels.

FURTHER READING

The importance of organisational culture is examined in Heclo and Wildavsky's study of the Treasury (1981). More recent material on the Financial Management Initiative is contained in Gray and Jenkins (1985) and Metcalfe and Richards (1987). There is little substantial work yet published on the Next Steps, though the Treasury and Civil Service Committee (1990) contains a number of useful appendices. The public spending process is covered by Likierman (1988), and Heald (1983) provides an economist's perspective on public expenditure.

In local government finance, work by Tony Travers (1986) is useful as are the case studies on local authority budgeting edited by Elcock and Jordan (1987) and the ensuing more theoretical book by Elcock *et al.* (1989). The Audit Commission publishes management papers (see, for example, 1989b) which highlight the latest developments. On the National Health Service, see Perrin (1988), and Harrison (1988) on general management. The journal *Public Money and Management* contains topical articles covering the whole of the public sector.

CHAPTER 11

The new agenda

INTRODUCTION

If there is unanimity about one thing, it is that the public services are undergoing a period of rapid change. John Major, in a speech to the Audit Commission in 1989, stated that 'the changes in our public services amount to nothing less than a revolution in progress' (1989, p. 3). While it might not amount to a revolution, the current shape of the public services bears little relationship to that of the mid-1970s. This chapter examines the factors that have led to that change and the ways in which that change has manifested itself.

Pollitt (1993a, pp. 110–46) argues that the managerial approach which dominated the 1980s, typified by target setting, efficiency savings and rewards for individual performance, was neo-Taylorist in nature. In other words he sees Taylor's concept of scientific management which we discussed in Chapter 4 being resurrected as a generic model of management and applied to the public services. In this chapter we assess this proposition.

Also, in this and the following chapter we are going to follow a model developed by Pettigrew (1988) for the analysis of strategic change. He identified three classes of variables – context, content and process (see Fig. 11.1) – which are involved in the process of strategic change. Taking this approach, attending to the internal and external environments, the complexities of organisational change can be captured.

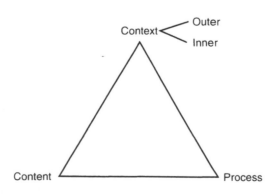

Fig. 11.1 Pettigrew's Model of Strategic Change
(*Source* : Pettigrew, 1988, p. 5)

By the outer context Pettigrew is referring to the broad environment, containing social, economic and political factors, in which organisations must operate. By the inner environment he is referring to organisational structure, organisational culture and politics. These, he argues, set the broad organisational context within which change occurs and can offer reasons as to *why* such change occurs. Content is concerned with *what* change occurs and process deals with *how* change occurs.

This chapter deals primarily with questions relating to the context while the following chapter deals with issues relating to content and processes.

STIMULI FOR THE NEW AGENDA

All organisations exist in a changing environment which has economic, political, social and legal aspects to it. The economy continues to experience periodic booms and slumps generating changes in demand for goods and services. The political environment changes with new parties coming into power and new ideas permeating the political scene. The legal context changes as a result of legislation passed down from the European Union to central government and from central government to local government and courts making judgements. Demographic changes in society in terms of birth rates, death rates or the mobility of the workforce will have an effect upon the services that government is responsible for providing.

Change then is a *constant* in that it will always occur. What is not constant, however, is the *pace* and *direction* of change. Uncertainty makes it so difficult to predict and to deal with. Witness the tremendous changes that have occurred throughout Eastern Europe since 1989 and the problems that this change has brought with it. Certainly the pace of change during the 1980s was rapid and so far in the 1990s it shows little sign of letting up. We need, however, to explore the direction that this change has taken.

In order to appreciate the changes that have taken place we need to appreciate its context. As we saw when we examined systems theory, no organisation exists in a vacuum. Rather, organisations exist in a broad environment which makes demands upon those organisations. In a competitive environment, organisations need to adapt in order to survive and prosper – indeed one of the pressures that many public service organisations have faced in recent years has been to become more competitive.

Johnson and Scholes (1993, p. 82) identify four aspects of the environment which can influence organisations.

- **Political and legal.** These are factors that may give rise to conflict between people or groups of people. This may manifest itself in party politics and its formal products such as legislation and other requirements of government as well as interest group politics which involve power struggles between groups.

- **Socio-cultural**. These may include factors such as changes in population patterns – for example, an increase in the number of elderly people or movement from one geographic area to another – the expectations of people, attitudes to change, cultural expectations and values, etc.
- **Economic**. These issues include the availability and distribution of resources (including land, labour and capital), its price and quality as well as the availability of financial resources.
- **Technological**. This refers to the potential of technology and techniques for an organisation to make efficiency savings and thus improve performance. Organisations that fail to develop may be at a disadvantage compared with organisations that use the potential of technological factors.

Hood's megatrends

It is all too easy to adopt a parochial view and see the changes that we are witnessing in the public services as a curiously British phenomenon. Christopher Hood performs a useful service by placing these changes in an international context by identifying four administrative 'megatrends' which are associated with the rise in what he terms the 'new public management'.

(i) attempts to *slow down or reverse government growth* in terms of overt public spending and staffing;
(ii) the shift toward *privatisation and quasi-privatisation* and away from core government institutions, with renewed emphasis on 'subsidiarity' in service provision;
(iii) the development of *automation*, particularly in information technology, in the production and distribution of public services; and
(iv) the development of a more *international* agenda, increasingly focused on general issues of public management, policy design, decision styles and inter-governmental cooperation, on top of the older tradition of individual country specialisms in public administration. (Hood, 1991, p. 3.)

It is worth noting at this point that different solutions have been applied in different countries. The Organisation for Economic Co-operation and Development (OECD) have identified two contrasting approaches to organisational and structural change.

Two predominant types of broad restructuring emerge: . . . those concerned to distribute responsibilities between different levels of government; and those seeking to create more market-orientated operating conditions for specific government bodies. (OECD, 1992, p. 10.)

This serves to illustrate the point that, while the reform of public services is a major agenda item for governments throughout the developed world, there is no consensus on the solution to the problem, as demonstrated in Table 11.1.

Table 11.1 **Approaches to organisational and structural change**

Country	Approach
Decentralisers	
Finland	Increasing self-governance and economic responsibility of municipalities.
Japan	Devolution of authority to local governments.
The Netherlands	Devolution of central government tasks to subsidiary tiers of government.
Sweden	New powers for local government to adapt structures to meet local conditions.
Market orientators	
Austria	Transfer of tasks to the private sector.
United Kingdom	Privatisation of 46 major businesses.
Decentralisers and market orientators	
Belgium	Transfer of powers including conditions of service to Communities and Regions; greater financial freedom for public enterprises.
France	New forms of co-operation between regional and local authorities; transformation of post and telecommunications.

Source : Adapted from OECD (1992).

Demographic and social change

Changing population structures mean that demands placed on public services will change. As we have already discussed, public service organisations need to respond to articulated needs from certain groups in society. For example, the increasing number of elderly people will need certain types of health and social care. Population projections show that the public services are likely to experience serious problems in recruiting and retaining labour in the near future (Callender and Pearson, 1989).

Similarly, knowledge about the birth rate enables policy makers to make projections about the future demand for school places. On this, estimates of demand for school places can be made.

In addition, Hood refers to the increasing expectations that the public has of public services. Thus, a better educated society is no longer prepared to accept poor and uniform levels of service (Hood, 1991, p. 7).

Political and economic aspects

Throughout this book we have examined the proposition that public service organisations are distinctive. One of the major reasons for this proposition is the political dimension that makes up such an important part of their environment. Any examination of this environment in the United Kingdom in the 1990s needs to take full account of the influence of the Thatcher and Major governments that have provided the principal political backdrop since 1979.

Many commentators have undertaken a fruitless search for complete internal consistency in the Thatcherite ideology and practice. For example, the term privatisation did not appear in the 1979 manifesto and it was only in the early 1980s that they stumbled on one of the central platforms of their agenda for the public services. Political pragmatism can often override ideology as it did when the politically unpopular community charge was reduced and compensated by an increase in a central government tax, value added tax (VAT). We can, however, identify a number of core themes and assumptions that have, to a greater or lesser extent, underpinned their approach to the public services:

- the objective of a flourishing private sector;
- the need to reduce the size of the Public Sector Borrowing Requirement;
- the need to reduce the overall size of the public sector;
- the assumption that monopolistic public services are inherently inefficient;
- the wish to create a mixed economy of welfare with a range of providers of services from both the public and private sectors;
- the wish to create competition inside the public sector.

A major part of this programme was based on the view that within the public services there were groups of people who dominated and controlled service provision with a view to serving their own interests rather than the consumers of services. Initially attention was directed at public service trade unions through a legislative programme of reform breaking up closed shops, abolishing secondary picketing, introducing compulsory strike ballots and introducing competition.

More recently attention has been devoted to attacking monopolies of professional groups such as doctors in the National Health Service and local authority professionals and the police (see, for example, Sheehy, 1993).

This went hand in hand with a series of measures aimed at curbing local government spending in order to comply with policy requirements to reduce overall public expenditure. Hogwood notes, nevertheless, that between 1979 and 1990 the Thatcher governments managed to reduce overall public expenditure in only one year, 1988 (Hogwood, 1992, pp. 41–2).

Taken together these can be seen as part of an attempt to reform what economists call the supply side of the economy – in other words, to ease up those factors such as wage rates and restrictive practices which inhibit the supply of labour.

Technological aspects

New technology offers both threats and opportunities for public service organisations. For example, new systems of data storage, transfer and retrieval offer the possibility of developing and changing organisation structures by either centralising or decentralising. Organisations which have to compete to deliver services may be able to gain an advantage over competitors if they invest in new technology systems in order to become more efficient and flexible.

ECONOMY, EFFICIENCY AND EFFECTIVENESS

Using Pettigrew's model of strategic change, a consideration of economy, efficiency and effectiveness needs to be situated under all three of his headings: context, content and process. In this section we will consider it as part of the outer context of public service organisations since the pursuit of the three Es has been paramount in government policy for well over a decade and no public service manager can have escaped its influence.

Improving economy, efficiency and effectiveness

The desire to improve organisational performance has focused attention on the pursuit of greater efficiency and effectiveness. This pursuit, which dominated government thinking in the 1980s and continues in the 1990s, merits detailed scrutiny. First we will define the terms, secondly we will look at how these concepts have been applied in the public sector, and thirdly we will look at how they are measured.

Economy, efficiency and effectiveness defined

While we recognise there is debate about the various definitions of the terms we use, we follow the most commonly used ones in order that the reader can refer to further material with ease. If we take a variant of the systems approach (see Fig. 11.2), we can see an organisation as having inputs, processes and outputs. Take, for instance, a production process such as the manufacture of a motor car. Physical inputs such as metals, plastics and glass will be combined with designs, labour and energy and put through the production process in order to produce the output – the motor car.

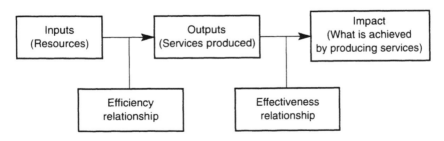

Fig. 11.2 The three Es
(*Source* : Audit Commission, 1988)

Box 11.1 Economy defined

An economy measure describes the extent to which the cost of inputs is minimised. Economy is usually measured in terms of money saved by switching to cheaper inputs. (Treasury, 1992, p. 31.)

The concept of economy relates to the inputs to the process (see Box 11.1). Jackson and Palmer add the important caveat 'having regard to the quality of the inputs' (1989, p. 50). For the manufacture of our motor car, this will involve minimising the cost of physical inputs, labour and so on but at the same time maintaining their quality. For public services, economy may mean, for example, purchasing goods and services at the lowest price or using competitive tendering to lower labour costs.

Box 11.2 Efficiency defined

Given the objectives and the means to pursue the objectives the minimising of inputs to the programme in relation to the outputs from it. (Treasury and Civil Service Committee, 1982, para. 52.)

Efficiency is concerned with the relationship between the inputs and the outputs (see Box 11.2). Therefore an efficient programme is 'one where the target is being achieved with the least possible use of resources. Similarly, on the way to achieving the target, the actual output should be secured with the least use of resources' (Treasury and Civil Service Committee, 1982, para. 52).

Thus, efficiency is about getting more for less. It can be achieved by minimising inputs in relation to outputs or, alternatively, maximising outputs in relation to inputs or both. The determinant of this relationship will be the process that transforms the inputs into the outputs. In the case of the car company, it will be about making the best use of manufacturing processes, technology and staff in order to add value to the raw materials when making the car. For the public services, the emphasis has been on managerial reform and the introduction of new working practices. Advocates of competitive tendering argue that the process of preparing a tender encourages the in-house organisation to ask fundamental questions about what needs doing and how it should be done.

Box 11.3 Effectiveness defined

An effectiveness measure reveals the extent to which objectives have been met: it makes no reference to cost. (Treasury, 1992, p. 33.)

Effectiveness is about achieving what we want to achieve (see Box 11.3). It is about the relationship between intended outputs and actual outputs.

The car company will have set a target. It might be to produce quality saloon cars and achieve a 10 per cent share of the market for such cars. It will then be able to compare how it actually performed against that target. As we shall see, effectiveness in the public services is a more problematic concept.

Economy, efficiency and effectiveness in the public sector

So far, we have illustrated the concepts using the example of the motor company. It is a commercial operation aiming to maximise its profits (though some theories of the firm contest this assumption (see Cyert and March, 1963). It has to compete in the market-place against a number of competitors who are equally keen to maximise profits. The spur to improve performance is that, if the customer considers the price too high or quality too low, there are alternative cars to choose from. It has been argued that it is much more difficult to apply these concepts to the public sector. Some of the reasons offered are as follows.

- Many public sector organisations are monopoly suppliers of a good or service. For example, there is only one Department of Social Security. If the claimant is not satisfied with the service, he or she cannot go elsewhere for payment. In a competitive environment there is an incentive to be efficient. Inefficiency will lead to reduced profits, lower dividends for shareholders and ultimately closure. A monopolist does not have that incentive.
- The car company has a clearly identifiable product – the car. This is not always the case in the public sector. For example, what does a university produce? Is it lectures and seminars, or research, or ideas, or educated citizens or personnel for business?
- The car company has a clearly identifiable customer who will enter into a financial exchange with the company. In the public sector it is not always easy to identify the customer. For example, the civil servant in one of the executive agencies established under the Next Steps initiative could see several people as customers. Firstly, the customer could be the member of the public with whom he or she is dealing, secondly it could be the minister in charge of the service, or thirdly it could be Parliament which is elected by and represents the electorate, or fourthly it could be the taxpayer. Ministers may be anxious to reduce the overall expenditure on services while the public want more services.
- The motor company has an explicitly stated objective – the maximisation of profits. Savings achieved through greater efficiency will contribute to greater profitability. Public sector organisations may not be able to produce such explicit statements. The values that underpin the public sector include a demand for equity. Would it be acceptable for a police force to concentrate its resources on preventing crime in an affluent middle class area with articulate and vociferous residents at the expense of a run-down inner city estate?

These problems make the pursuit of economy, efficiency and effectiveness in the public sector more difficult. Various initiatives have been undertaken to improve performance. Study of strategies to improve public sector performance must be seen in the context of the Conservative approach to the public sector. The early 1980s were dominated by the government's efficiency strategy. The Rayner scrutinies were aimed at making lasting savings in the civil service which were to be achieved through cultural change. Critics of the strategy argued that it was not so much about efficiency as about economy. They believed the strategy was aimed at reducing the inputs to the process rather than improving the ratio between inputs and outputs. This reflected the policy of reducing the level of public spending (see Metcalfe and Richards, 1987). They point out that such strategies cannot be seen as neutral: political decisions have to be made about what options to pursue and these will reflect the values of the decision makers.

The Audit Commission promotes economy, efficiency and effectiveness in local authorities and the National Health Service in England and Wales (the Accounts Commission has the same responsibility in Scotland). It aims to do this by encouraging local authorities to improve their management practices. Hence their approach concentrates on improving the process which transforms inputs into outputs. This process is not as easy as it may seem. It requires authorities to consider what demands are made on the organisation – establishing what is wanted, by whom, how and when. They need to reconsider traditional practices. The Local Government Management Board has pointed, in its various publications, to the need to change structures in order to provide a service that is closer to the public. Traditional working patterns based on the 'Purple Book' conditions of service may restrict the opening hours of amenities such as swimming baths. Demarcation disputes may mean that it takes six specialists to do a job that could be done by one generalist. Hence improved efficiency may require structural, cultural and attitudinal change. Evidence that practices have changed is provided by both the Audit Commission (1989b) and the Local Government Training Board (1985).

However, the efficiency strategy cannot be value free. As Metcalfe and Richards note:

> Efficiency, portrayed as a purely technical instrumental means to politically approved ends, is often presented as an unqualified good like apple pie or motherhood. Political opponents are easily wrong-footed and put on the defensive when efficiency is portrayed as a neutral concept. (Metcalfe and Richards, 1990, p. 29.)

As we consider in Chapter 13, management in the public services involves analysing and balancing a range of values. As Stewart argues:

> In the public domain collective values can be realised: equity, justice, citizenship, democracy are all involved in the provision of public service. Management cannot merely be concerned with the three Es – economy, efficiency and effectiveness, it must be concerned with the fourth E of equality. Public service management must confront these value issues underlying service provision. (Stewart, 1989a, p. 14.)

Emphasis on outputs and outcomes

One of the major criticisms of the efficiency strategy has been that it paid too much attention to inputs, particularly costs and their reduction, and insufficient attention to outputs and outcomes. This criticism was acknowledged in the Efficiency Unit report which led to the creation of executive agencies in the civil service. The report stated:

. . . pressures on departments are mainly on expenditure and activities; there is still too little attention paid to the results to be achieved with the resources. (Efficiency Unit, 1988, p. 4.)

Banks makes a useful distinction between public management and policy analysis which explains why perhaps insufficient attention had been paid to outcomes:

In the public sector, intermediate outputs can include regulations which impose costs on others, in order to produce final outputs such as a better environment. Management is concerned with buying resources economically and using them efficiently to produce intermediate outputs: cars, hip replacements. Policy analysis, including appraisal before implementation and evaluation afterwards, is concerned with deciding what intermediate outputs will be effective in achieving final outputs. (Banks, 1990, p. 47.)

Targets have become a primary lever in the strategy to improve management in British public services. Executive Agencies in the civil service are set a number of individual targets by ministers. There are four types of targets. These are set out with examples of key targets for the Benefits Agency for 1992–3:

- **Quality targets** (85 per cent of customers to regard the service they receive from the agency as satisfactory or better);
- **Financial targets** (£460m saved through the detection and prevention of fraud);
- **Efficiency targets** (achieve at least £57.3m from new efficiency savings);
- **Throughput targets** (Social Fund crisis loans applications cleared on the day the need arises). (Office of Public Service and Science, 1992, pp. 80 and 96–7.)

THE CHANGING LOCUS OF PUBLIC SERVICES

In the introduction we raise the problem of defining the scope, scale and boundaries of the public sector. Changes that have taken place over the last decade have made the possibility of making a satisfactory distinction even more remote. Thus it is perhaps more helpful to refer to the public services rather than the public sector. By doing this we avoid making the assumption that those

Table 11.2 Examples of the commissioner/deliverer split

	Policy area		
	Housing	Health	Social security
Service commissioners	Local authorities	DHA	DSS
Service deliverers	Housing associations	NHS hospitals NHS trusts Private hospitals	Benefits Agency

responsible for providing the service are employed as 'public servants'. This is important as those who provide services may be employed in the private sector or the voluntary (third) sector.

A major reason for this is the increasingly common distinction that is being made between those responsible for commissioning the service and those responsible for providing the service. This split is made in central government, local government and the National Health Service (see Table 11.2).

A major stimulus for this distinction comes from the New Right critique of public services, with its attack on bureaucratic growth, producer dominated services with powerful professions and trade unions and failure to deliver. The late Lord Ridley demonstrated the New Right view in this area:

> The root cause of rotten local services lies in the grip which local government unions have over those services in many parts of the country . . . Our competitive tendering provisions will smash that grip once and for all. The consumer will get better quality services at lower costs. (Ridley, 1989.)

The competitive tendering provisions in local government seek to make an explicit division between those responsible for commissioning the service and those responsible for providing it. In Chapter 2 we discussed the distinction between policy and management. Osborne and Gaebler pursue this distinction using the analogy of steering and rowing. Steering is the equivalent of policy making while rowing is the actual delivery of services. They argue for a clear distinction between the two activities as they require different competences:

> Steering requires people who see the entire universe of issues and possibilities and can balance competing demands for resources. Rowing requires people who focus intently on one mission and perform it well. Steering organisations need to find the best methods to achieve their goals. Rowing organisations tend to defend 'their' method at all costs. (Osborne and Gaebler, 1992, p. 35.)

This distinction does not make any assumptions about who provides the service. For Osborne and Gaebler, for example, this depends on the nature of the activity to be performed. They identify 36 approaches to service delivery which can be categorised as traditional, innovative or avant-garde. Traditional techniques include creating legal rules, licensing, grants and contracting. Innovative techniques include franchising, providing technical assistance and vouchers. Avant-garde techniques include using seed money, demand management and restructuring the market (Osborne and Gaebler, 1992. p. 31). They argue that government should consider which is the best way of providing a particular service. They recognise that government may have a strength in some areas while the private sector may be stronger in others. For example, government is better at policy management and ensuring equity while the private sector is better at performing complex tasks and delivering services which become obsolete quickly (p. 345). Above all, Osborne and Gaebler believe that government at all levels should be more entrepreneurial:

Most entrepreneurial governments promote *competition* between service providers. They *empower* citizens by pushing control out of the bureaucracy, into the community. They measure the performance of their agencies, focusing not on inputs but on outcomes. They are driven by their goals – their *missions* – not by their rules and regulations. They redefine their clients as *customers* and offer them choices . . . They *prevent* problems before they emerge, rather than simply offering services afterward. They put their energies into *earning* money, not simply spending it. They *decentralize* authority, embracing participatory management. They prefer *market* mechanisms to bureaucratic mechanisms. And they focus not simply on providing public services, but on *catalysing* all sectors – public, private and voluntary – into action to solve their community's problems. (1992, pp. 19–20.)

We will consider a number of public management approaches that have been adopted in Britain. We start by looking at an approach which involves service delivery within the public sector and proceed to examine a number of more radical alternatives.

Agency models

One of the major tools of public service managerial reform in the 1980s and 1990s has been the creation of agencies *within* organisations. The best example – and the one which we will concentrate on – is in the civil service. However, it is also worth noting that this tool has been used extensively in local government (especially as a consequence of competitive tendering legislation) and the National Health Service.

The agency model has its roots in economic theories of organisations. It involves a distinction between a principal and agent, similar to the accountability relationship discussed in Chapter 2. Thus 'in a large corporation, shareholders can be regarded as principals in a contract engaging managers as agents to control the company' (Clarke and McGuinness, 1987, p. 4). In the civil service model, ministers act as principals with the responsibility for delivering services entrusted to managers working in agencies. During the last century and the early years of this century systems of internal contracting developed inside private sector organisations. Thus, economic transactions would take place inside organisations:

individual sub-contractors would negotiate a lump sum payment with the capitalist in a contract in which they would agree to provide a specific number of goods, by a specified date or on a specified basis, by hiring labour to work within the organisation, using its technology, raw materials and so on to produce commodities only for the organisation. (Clegg, 1993, p. 128.)

This is worth citing at length as it illustrates an alternative form of organisation to the bureaucratic model discussed in Chapter 3. Clegg (1993, pp. 129–30) argues that it offers several advantages to the capitalist, particularly flexibility and the opportunity for innovation.

The creation of executive agencies in the civil service has been described as 'the most ambitious attempt at Civil Service reform in the twentieth century' (Treasury and Civil Service Select Committee, 1990). The stimulus for change in the civil service came from an Efficiency Unit scrutiny, *Improving Management in Government: The Next Steps*, published in February 1988. This proposed that the executive responsibilities of the civil service should be discharged in agencies which would be headed by a chief executive directly accountable to the minister. It is worth noting that this idea was not a new one – its origins can be traced back to the Fulton Report (1968) though little action followed at the time, perhaps a testament to the conservatism inherent in the civil service.

The case of social security operations

Advocates of the agency model envisage up to 95 per cent of civil service work being carried out by or for agencies. However, this does not mean that the decision to move executive work from the core department to agencies is an automatic one. The Department of Social Security presents a special case because of its unique characteristics. Firstly, both in budgetary and establishment terms, it is the largest department. Secondly, the sensitive nature of the social security operations means that it is subject to close scrutiny by politicians, employers and the public.

In July 1988, the Secretary of State for Health and Social Security set up a team to consider whether social security operations could be run as along Next Steps lines. The team considered four options. These were

● privatisation;
● contractorisation;
● public corporation;
● abolition. (Department of Social Security, 1989, p. 12.)

Privatisation was dismissed as social security operations are not trading activities capable of being self-financing. Abolition was also rejected. However, contractorisation was considered in detail. Under contractorisation, the Department of Social Security:

> . . . would enter into a contract with an **outside** organisation or organisations to deliver the service in accordance with statutory requirements and to specified standards. The department would pay a fee, from which the contractor would expect to cover his costs and to make a profit. To ensure that the fee was not artificially high, a competitive tendering exercise would be held. (Department of Social Security, 1989, p. 12.)

In 1987 the Department of Health and Social Security accepted an efficiency scrutiny which rejected the contracting out of the core services of handling of benefits claims and collecting National Insurance contributions. Since then, and notwithstanding the move to agencies, there has been a shift towards greater market testing (see below) and contracting out of work.

It was argued that this would have the advantages of being cheaper, would avoid the need for direct government management, would lead to the tighter specification of objectives, 'tighter monitoring of outputs and greater internal drive and incentives to rationalise and innovate' (Department of Social Security, 1989, p. 12).

The agency study concluded that contractorisation was compatible with but not an alternative to agency status. According to the report, agency status offered two key advantages:

- clarification of activities as being primarily policy or executive in nature and, in addition, clarification of the responsibility for monitoring standards. The 'what services' questions should be answered at the centre, the 'how' questions would be settled at an operational level;
- control through outputs rather than through processes.

While social security operations had been subjected to greater scrutiny through target setting and performance measurement (through the Financial Management Initiative), it was argued that agencies would provide an 'in-built dynamic for better performance' through:

- clarification of roles and responsibilities;
- the discipline of contracts, by having specific and meaningful objectives and more accountability;
- incentives for good performance – stronger carrots and sticks, rewarding efficiency and effectiveness, and competition;
- management flexibility;
- strengthened commitment from the top. (Department of Social Security, 1989, p. 18)

However, the report also identified a number of potential risks:

- that the move to agency status could be seen as a cost cutting exercise or could even increase costs;
- it could widen the gap between policy and operations instead of developing much needed close links;
- it may result in a lack of effective control and the agency could become too powerful;
- it may lead to worse terms and conditions of service for staff;
- the move to agency status becomes an end in itself rather than a means to the end of improving management in government;
- any changes could be cosmetic rather than dealing with the substance of the problem.

Three agencies were created to deal with social security operations: the Benefits Agency, the Contributions Agency and the Information Technology Services Agency. You will recall that we looked at the target approach to management in the Benefits Agency earlier in this chapter. We will return to the Benefits Agency in the next chapter when we look at organisational culture.

Competitive tendering and contracting out

Contracting services is neither new nor peculiarly British. Britain has now adopted the most systematic approach to competitive services as well as being the only country to add compulsion to the tendering process. France has a long history of private partnerships with local authorities to provide a range of services and French firms have expressed an interest in providing services for English local authorities (Walsh, 1991, pp. 7–8).

It is important to distinguish between competitive tendering and contracting out. Competitive tendering is a process whereby an activity is exposed to a test in order to allocate responsibility for delivering the activity. For many local government activities this process is required by law. Contracting out is the provision of a service or good by an outside organisation and does not necessarily require a competitive test to allocate the task.

Traditionally, private sector organisations have supplied goods and services for the public sector, such as building work for local authorities, military equipment for the armed services and drugs for the National Health Service. Equally, much work has been provided by the service delivering organisation, for example cleaning, refuse collection, drawing of plans and so on. This state of affairs has been under challenge since the 1980s. The critique of large public service organisations argues that they are inefficient and that traditional bureaucratic command structures do not provide sufficient focus on the task to be completed and the cost of completing that task.

Virtually all large public organisations have at least considered the possibility of contracting work out to private sector organisations. Local government faces legislative requirements to put work out to compulsory competitive tendering. Initially in 1980 the Local Government (Planning and Land) Act required local authorities to put a limited range of services including construction and the maintenance of buildings and highways out to tender. More recently the 1988 Local Government Act added further services to this list including refuse collection, building and street cleaning, catering, grounds maintenance and leisure management. Government policy is to extend this list to cover a range of white collar professionalised and managerial activities.

Privatisation

Perhaps the most widely known of the Thatcher strategies for public service reform was privatisation. We define privatisation as the transfer of public sector assets out of the public sector. This can involve the sale of nationalised industries, council houses and management buy-outs of public sector enterprises.

The privatisation programme took off in the early 1980s with the sale of British Aerospace (partly in 1981) and Britoil (partly in 1982). The programme took on increased pace after the Conservative's re-election in 1983 with further sales of shares in British Aerospace and Britoil together with British Telecom (1984),

British Gas (1985) and British Airways (1987). Several water and electricity companies were added to that list in 1989 and 1990 respectively. More recently British Rail and British Coal have been under active consideration for privatisation.

The explicit rationale behind privatisation follows the free market ideas that such activities are better run in the marketplace where the forces of competition will increase organisational efficiency resulting in a better service or product for the consumer and the elimination of a liability on the taxpayer. Critics of privatisation argue that, in many cases, the newly privatised organisations have not faced genuine competition in the market-place. Instead, all that has happened is that a state monopoly has become a private monopoly and that the consumer has not realised the intended benefits that privatisation was intended to produce. They argue that the attraction for government has been the money raised from the sale of these companies which has been used to subsidise income tax cuts. As Maloney and Richardson (1992) point out, privatisation in Britain was introduced just as much for pragmatic reasons as for ideological reasons, producing over £27 billion in revenues for the Treasury by the end of the 1980s.

The privatisation of the major public utilities has been accompanied by the creation of regulatory agencies intended to protect the consumer. For example, Oftel has a statutory duty to protect British Telecom's users while the Ofwat has a duty to regulate the water industry.

Deregulation

One of the New Right criticisms of the public sector of the 1970s was the overuse of regulation and planning as a method of organising services. This, it was argued, results in inefficiency and a supply of goods and services which the consumer did not want. The solution offered was greater freedom for potential suppliers of goods and services to meet the needs of the public. A prime example was the deregulation of buses (through the Transport Act 1985) which allowed private operators to seek licences to run services.

Transfer payments and vouchers

Transfer payments or vouchers represent a more radical step than compulsory competition. As Kristensen (1987) argues, while the state remains responsible for financing the service, the choice is exercised by the public. The possible gains are increased efficiency, the consumers getting the service they want, and the worse off benefiting more than the affluent. Child benefit involves making a payment to, usually, the mother of the child who can them make a decision on how best to use the money. A criticism of this benefit is that it may be paid to people who may not need it. This could be solved by targeting the benefit at those who need it, but this would inevitably mean that many deserving cases would not get the benefit.

Another example is the case of education vouchers. Instead of the local education authority telling the parent which school their child should attend, the parents would be issued with a voucher which they could 'spend' at a school of their choice. The parents could also choose an independent school with an additional payment by them. While this proposal is controversial with critics saying that it is unworkable, we should bear in mind that a similar system already operates with mandatory grants and fees paid to students who choose which college or university they go to.

Charging for services and targeting services

A further alternative is charging for services. The cost of National Health Service prescriptions has risen dramatically since 1979, charges have been introduced for eye tests and dental charges have been increased. This method can be used to encourage more efficient use of a service but it may mean that people who need a service do not take advantage of it. The ring fencing of local authority housing revenue accounts has meant that tenants are now paying more or less the full cost of the service instead of benefiting from a subsidy.

For some time there has been an intensive debate on targeting of services, for example child benefit which is available to all those responsible for rearing children irrespective of their means. An alternative policy would be to target certain groups who are able to demonstrate need. This would increase the allocative efficiency of available resources but may result in low take-up because of lack of information or stigmatisation attached to claiming what may be perceived as 'handouts'.

Withdrawal and let the market decide

One alternative is for the public sector to refuse to provide a good or service and allow the market-place to provide it instead. Given the Conservatives' belief in market mechanisms as the most efficient allocator of resources and decision making, this would appear to be an attractive proposition. For example, the Channel Tunnel is being constructed using private sector resources only based on assumptions by Eurotunnel that it is a financially viable proposition.

At the heart of the New Right critique of public services is the proposition that bureaucracies are inherently inefficient allocators and managers of resources. The New Right has argued that the market mechanism is a much more efficient system for making decisions. Thus one of the principal ways of reforming public services has been to either transfer activities to the market-place or introduce the disciplines of the market-place. Markets are said to improve efficiency and effectiveness by introducing competition. Thus, for example, where schools have to compete for pupils the standard of service offered, it is argued, will be improved. The assumption is that by opening up activities to competition a host of organisations will spring up ready to compete for public sector work. Of course, in practice, organisations have a vested interest in limiting competition, creating monopolies and cornering the market. There is no reason to suppose that monopolies will not develop in the provision of public services. Competition is also based upon the notion that the purchaser has perfect information concerning the products on offer and can 'shop around' for the best deal. In practice, the consumer of, say, health services may not have the necessary information and knowledge to decide what the best deal is. A further dilution of the 'perfect' market is the entry barriers for new providers. Capital costs to build a new private hospital will be high; the acquisition of appropriate skills and expertise may be lengthy; the market itself may not be very attractive. Thus, for example, private sector organisations may not be keen to provide community care for those who require constant care and attention. Other markets may be more attractive. A further problem for government is who picks up the pieces if the market fails? A local authority may have many of its services contracted out to the private sector and may not have the in-house capacity to take over if, say, the firm that has won the contract to manage the local community leisure centre goes bust.

Internal markets, such as those proposed for the National Health Service, aim to make the allocation of decisions more efficient by enabling doctors, for example, to make decisions about how to spend their budgets. Hospitals will become profit centres competing against each other and the new self-governing hospitals will trade on their own account. Large GP practices can apply for their own budgets and can shop around between hospitals for services for their patients. GPs can now contract with private providers, or provide minor surgery themselves. However, the advantages of allowing GPs greater choice in their purchasing decisions and allowing the market to determine where resources flow may mean that the health authority loses control over any strategic direction it has for the health of the community as a whole. A final problem is that of cream-skimming where purchasers and providers may discriminate against expensive or dependent patients or clients. Commercial considerations replace needs as the basis of resource allocations (see Le Grand and Bartlett, 1993).

Changing structures and patterns of control

Since 1979 the Conservatives have passed a number of Acts of Parliament which have challenged the power of the trade unions. Closed shop agreements, restrictive practices and picketing arrangements have all been subject to reform. Trade unions have been banned at Government Communications Headquarters (GCHQ) and school teachers lost their pay negotiating rights. There have also been a number of industrial disputes which have led to structural change in the public sector, for example the miners' strike, disputes in the civil service, and the strike at British Steel.

Stewart (1992) points to the increasing use of new institutions to bypass elected local authorities. For example, we have witnessed the creation of urban development corporations, grant maintained schools, Housing Action Trusts and

Training and Enterprise Councils. Chapter 2 examines these developments from the point of view of accountability. The local control exercised by elected politicians from the local area is being replaced by appointees of the Secretary of State with little or no accountability to the local community.

Market testing

During the 1980s the government was been keen to introduce compulsory competitive tendering in local government while the civil service was isolated from this exposure to competition. This, however, was to change with the introduction of *market testing* as part of the Citizen's Charter initiative. The Department of Social Security defines market testing as

> the process by which services currently provided in-house are compared to services offered by the private sector to ensure that Managers obtain best value for money and that the efficiency of in-house operations is maximised. (Department of Social Security, 1992, p. 2.)

Market testing is to cover a range of services including accountancy, building services, catering, forms design, information technology, legal work, office services, personnel, printing and training. One possible threat to market testing, along with compulsory competitive tendering in local government, comes from the Transfer of Undertakings (Protection of Employment) Regulations 1981 which were introduced by the government to comply with the European Union Directive on acquired rights. These regulations afford workers some protection if their employer changes following a merger or takeover (see Chapter 2).

THE CITIZEN'S CHARTER

What is the Citizen's Charter?

The Citizen's Charter has become closely identified with John Major who wants it to be 'one of the central themes of public life in the 1990s' (Prime Minister, 1991, p. i). However, it is worth noting that several local councils, including Labour-controlled York City Council, had previously developed their own charters and, as long ago as 1980, central government promulgated the Tenants' Charter.

In 1991 the government set out their proposals in a White Paper, *The Citizen's Charter*. It represents perhaps the most systematic attempt to date to make explicit what users of services can expect from them. The French government is currently developing a Public Service Charter (OECD, 1992, p. 41).

Principles of public service

Based on four themes – quality, choice, standards and value – the Charter introduces a set of 'principles of public service'. These are displayed in Box 11.4.

Box 11.4 Principles of public service

Standards
Setting, monitoring and publication of explicit standards for the services that individual users can reasonably expect. Publication of actual performance against these standards.

Information and openness
Full, accurate information readily available in plain language about how services are run, what they cost, how well they perform and who is in charge.

Choice and consultation
The public sector should provide choice wherever practicable. There should be regular and systematic consultation with those who use services. Users' views about services, and their priorities for improving them, to be taken into account in final decisions on standards.

Courtesy and helpfulness
Courteous and helpful service from public servants who will normally wear name badges. Services available equally to all who are entitled to them and run to suit their convenience.

Putting things right
If things go wrong, an apology, a full explanation and a swift and effective remedy. Well publicised and easy to use complaints procedures with independent review wherever possible.

Value for money
Efficient and economical delivery of public services within the resources the nation can afford. An independent validation of performance against standards.

(*Citizen's Charter*, First report, 1992, Cm 2101.)

These principles differ from those set out in the original charter. Originally there were seven principles – the most noteworthy changes are the deletion of the principle of non-discrimination on the grounds of race or sex and the addition of value for money.

Implementation of the Charter

In many ways the Charter can be seen as an umbrella for many of the reforms of public services which government wishes to implement. A special Citizen's Charter Unit has been created and is now part of the Office of Public Service and Science (which also has units dealing with efficiency, the implementation of executive agencies and market testing in the civil service). While the principles of public service may inspire little dissent (though little is said about public participation), the mechanisms by which those principles are delivered arise from the government's widely debated agenda for the reform of the public services. These mechanisms include:

- more privatisation;
- wider competition;
- further contracting out;
- more performance-related pay;
- published performance targets – local and national;
- comprehensive publication of information on standards achieved;
- more effective complaints procedures;
- tougher and more independent inspectorates;
- better redress for the citizen when things go wrong.

(Prime Minister, 1991, p. 5.)

The Charter covers all public services including central government, local government, the National Health Service, nationalised industries, and the key utilities in the private sector.

Service-related charters

One of key features of the initiative has been the publication of service-related charters. By April 1993, 32 of these had been published. including:

- the Council Tenant's Charter (first published in Scotland in December 1991);
- the Jobseeker's Charter (December 1991);
- a National Insurance Contributors' Charter (July 1991);
- a National Insurance Employers' Charter (July 1991);
- the Northern Ireland Child Support Agency Charter (April 1993).

Citizen's Charter Indicators for local government

Earlier in this chapter we looked at the possible uses to which information on performance can be put. One of the major elements of the Citizen's Charter initiative has been a plan to publish comparative information about the performance of local authorities. Already government publishes so-called 'league table' of examination performance by schools. The Local Government Act 1992 requires the Audit Commission to determine a set of indicators for each local authority-run service with information published in a local newspaper. For example, local authorities are required to collect the following information in relation to crime:

- The number of items issued by the authority's libraries
  (a) books
  (b) other items
- The number of libraries
  (a) open 45 hours per week or more
  (b) open 30–44 hours per week
  (c) open 10–29 hours per week
  (d) mobile libraries
- The number of visits by members of the public to public libraries

- The amount spent per head of population on books and other materials
- The net expenditure per head of population on libraries

(Audit Commission, 1992, pp. 24–5.)

In developing this set of indicators, the Audit Commission has been forced to address a number of criticisms. Perhaps the most frequently articulated one is that measures such as examination pass rates may tell us more about the qualities and circumstances of the pupils attending the school than the quality of the school itself.

The government awards *Chartermarks* to organisations that meet the standards of the Charter. It has also piloted a telephone service, *Charterline*, which will provide service users with information about who to complain to. They also intend to set up a *Complaints Taskforce* which will investigate complaints procedures in the public services.

Citizen's Charter assessed

The Citizen's Charter can be seen as a response to the rising expectations that people have of public services and may enhance accountability by making service standards more explicit and visible. However, as Doern (1993) argues, the success of the Citizen's Charter will be judged against John Major's success in changing the political landscape and the way in which it is implemented. Lovell raises a key issue which will be explored in the next chapter:

> If the improvements in the customer service required by the Citizen's Charter are to be effective and long lasting, changes in structures and systems will need to be accompanied by change in culture and management style. (Lovell, 1992, p. 395.)

Many of the long-standing criticisms of performance measures apply to Charter-based initiatives. The Audit Commission recognise the criticisms that interested parties have levelled at the legislation on indicators:

> There were too many indicators to be of interest to citizens, yet too few to reflect complex services adequately. In particular, there were insufficient indicators of effectiveness, quality and efficiency. (Audit Commission, 1992, p. 3.)

In addition they recognise the following points:

- Nationally determined indicators may skew local policies. Commenting on the Commission's proposals, Rodrigues argues that:

> Unless there is complete agreement between the policy priorities implicit in the Commission's measures and those of each local authority the new indicators will in effect cut across the latter. This will have a distorting effect on local priorities and local rationing decisions, skewing organisational processes to a centrally determined perspective. Messages to staff will be confusing. Just whose priorities are they supposed to be working to? (Rodrigues, 1992, p. 13.)

- Figures may be misused or misunderstood.
- The cost of collecting information may outweigh the benefits.

However, on the benefit side, such indicators may:

- lead to increased visibility and accountability of public services, thus strengthening local democracy;
- lead to an informed debate about the quality of public services, leading to improved services.

However, a more fundamental criticism of the Citizen's Charter is that it is based on a flawed understanding of the concept of citizenship. Instead of seeing citizenship as membership of the community, citizenship is seen in terms of individual rights.

CONCLUSION

In this chapter we have concentrated on the context in which public service organisations operate. In so doing, we have raised a number of issues about the distinctiveness of the public services and the appropriateness of importing private sector management techniques. Before we can draw any conclusions we need to consider how organisations have responded to the demands that have been placed upon them.

FURTHER READING

Since this chapter discusses recent developments in the public services, detailed analysis of the issues raised has, in many cases, yet to appear in book form. Examinations of recent initiatives such as the Citizen's Charter are beginning to appear in the public policy and public management journals. Recently published texts which cover material discussed in this chapter include Isaac-Henry *et al.* (1993) and Wilson and Hinton (1993). Osborne and Gaebler (1993) set out a model for change that has influenced the Clinton administration in the United States. Pettigrew (1988) sets out the model of strategic change upon which we based the framework for Chapters 11 and 12.

CHAPTER 12

Responding to the new agenda

INTRODUCTION

This chapter deals with the internal organisation and management of public service organisations. We will deal with the content and process of change in the public services. Following Pettigrew's model of strategic change, we will examine how organisations have changed given the context that we have already examined. We begin by looking at theories of organisational change and then proceed to examine what has changed and how it has changed.

ORGANISATIONAL CHANGE

In Chapter 4 we distinguished between open and closed systems. Similarly, organisations vary in their openness to the environment. Relatively closed organisations tend to comprise formal rules, stress routine and predictability and adopt an inward-looking orientation. In contrast to this, open organisations are characterised by flexibility, responsiveness and the ability to adapt to the environment (Burns and Stalker, 1961).

A number of writers have contended that the end of bureaucracy is in sight (Bennis, 1966) and have heralded the coming adhocracy (Toffler, 1970). They argue that the bureaucratic form of organisation is no longer viable since it cannot cope with:

- rapid and unpredictable change since it relies on hierarchical organisational structures which inhibit responsiveness. Problems tend to be referred up the hierarchical chain of command for approval, resulting in delay and insensitive decisions;
- the complexity of modern society. New organisational structures and patterns of behaviour are required in order to address the increasingly varied tasks and conditions that modern government face;
- changing management thinking with its emphasis on more participative management styles whereby senior managers give up some control to those lower down the organisation. Indeed, public authorities can all too easily wrap themselves with the cloak of the electoral mandate in order to avoid responding to competing demands made by multiple stakeholders.

Hence, the modern organisation requires people with new and diverse skills and competences. The traditional division of labour and professional demarcation lines are inappropriate.

ORGANISATIONAL LEARNING

There are forces that seek to drive change and those that seek to restrain it. Lewin's force-field analysis describes this process (see Fig. 12.1). In the previous chapter we examined some of the driving forces, such as new values, legislation and economic factors. We also noted that some commentators pointed to restraining factors such as bureaucracy, trade unions and restrictive professional practices.

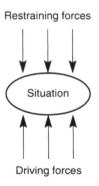

Restraining forces

Situation

Driving forces

Fig. 12.1 Lewin's force field analysis
(*Source* : Lewin, 1947)

    The conundrum remains that change is being demanded of a set of institutions that have, according to the overwhelming evidence from research, demonstrated, above all, a capacity to resist change. Indeed, if organisations are to adapt to the current turbulent environment, improve performance and become more responsive then they need to focus on the possibilities that alternative modes of organisation offer (see Lawrence and Lorsch, 1967). In order to do this, organisations need to develop a learning capability. Morgan points to a number of barriers to organisational learning which are particularly common in bureaucratic organisations. First, fragmented organisational structures lead to poor flows of information and knowledge and people in those organisations taking departmental views. Second, systems of bureaucratic accountability tend to reward success and punish failure. This encourages a defensive culture in the organisation where issues are obscured and problems are hidden (Morgan, 1986, p. 90).

    Additionally, we need to recognise the legacy that the public sector has inherited. In the National Health Service, clinicians have asserted power. In the civil service the generalist or 'gifted amateur' distilled policy advice and delivered it to ministers with the emphasis very much on managing the relationship with the politician rather than responsibility for managing services. Local government's history is, to a large extent, that of the dominance of the professional officer. As Stewart observes, these factors mitigated against the organisation developing a capacity to learn:

> Organisational tendencies to restrict learning are reinforced in the traditional management of local government. Professionalism is a powerful force restricting learning to established professional patterns. Local authorities do not hear easily of, or accept, information or knowledge that challenges accepted professional knowledge or practice. (Stewart, 1985, p. 52.)

Morgan makes the distinction between the process *of* learning and the process of learning *to* learn. Learning to learn involves systems which:

> . . . are often able to detect and correct errors in operating norms and thus influence the standards that guide their detailed operations. It is this kind of self-questioning ability that underpins the activities of systems that are able to learn to learn and self-organise. (Morgan, 1986, p. 87.)

He suggests the following guidelines for the development of a learning-oriented approach. Following this approach, organisations should be open and reflective, and accept that uncertainty and errors are inevitable features in complex and turbulent environments. Problem-solving approaches should recognise the importance of exploring different approaches. Decision makers should avoid the imposition of predetermined goals and objectives on organisations (Morgan, 1986, p. 92).

While Morgan writes about the factors that inhibit learning in bureaucratic organisations generally, Willcocks and Harrow's research considers the problems that public sector organisations in particular face in developing such a capacity. Among the factors they identify are:

- ambiguity over the common purpose of the organisation;
- lack of political support;
- poor communication structures to disseminate findings;
- management concerns about budgetary savings;
- organisations adopting a crisis management approach. (Willcocks and Harrow, 1992, pp. 72–3.)

As public service organisations respond to the new agenda, new organisational forms will, as we shall see later in this chapter, develop. Harrison argues that:

> the introduction of contracts and competition to the British public sector during the 1990s represents a massive programme of learning by doing. (Harrison, 1993, p. 188.)

This, however, raises a fundamental question about the capacity of organisations to learn. First, it is not enough for organisations to face pressure for change, they need to perceive that pressure:

Organisational change is stimulated not by *pressures* from the environment, resulting in a build-up of problems triggering an automatic response, but by the *perceptions* of that environment and those pressures held by key actors. (Kanter, 1983, p. 281.)

Argyris (1990) makes the distinction between single-loop learning and double-loop learning. Single-loop learning involves solving problems that currently face the organisation (see Fig. 12.2). For example, an organisation may detect that it has a high error rate in payments made to the public. Once this becomes apparent, the organisation takes corrective action in order to reduce the error rate.

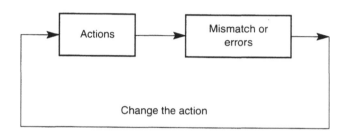

Fig. 12.2 Single-loop learning
(*Source:* Argyris, 1990, p. 92)

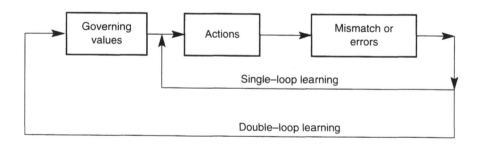

Fig 12.3 Double-loop learning
(*Source:* Argyris, 1990, p. 94)

Double-loop learning requires the ability to question operating norms (see Fig. 12.3). Such questioning may reveal contextual constraints such as policies, culture and attitudes which lead to errors or unintended outcomes. Only when such fundamental weaknesses are corrected can the organisation expect lasting improvement in performance (see Morgan, 1986, pp. 91–5). This implies a profound change in organisational culture which, as Handy argues, can generate ongoing benefits:

Organisations which encourage the wheel of learning, which relish curiosity, questions and ideas, which allow space for experiment and for reflection, which forgive mistakes and promote self confidence, these are learning organisations, and theirs is a competitive advantage which no-one can steal from them. (Handy, 1990, p. 199.)

The changing demands that the environment places on public service organisations are offering opportunities for learning. The pressures to move away from bureaucratic structures to more responsive ones offer the possibility of a virtuous circle of improvement. However, the extent to which this opportunity is seized is dependent upon the attitudes of people in those organisations. Willcocks and Harrow's research shows that people vary in their views about the capacity of public sector organisations to learn from private sector practice. They identify four categories of response

- resisters;
- doubters;
- inevitable acceptors;
- welcomers. (Willcocks and Harrow, 1992, p. 74.)

AGENTS OF AND OBSTACLES TO CHANGE

The impetus for change may come from outside or inside the organisation. In the last chapter we examined a number of external agents of change. We need also to consider the role that factors inside the organisation can play in stimulating change.

Just as bringing new blood from outside the organisation is a way of bringing about change, then promoting people or transferring them from one task to another is likely to have an effect. Indeed, some individuals, when promoted, will immediately attempt to effect change to justify their promotion and demonstrate their individual dynamism. Education and training, whether through short courses or more extended periods such as a Masters in Business Administration, can play an important role in challenging people's assumptions and introducing new ideas. On the other hand, continued rotation of staff from one task to another, which is common in the civil service, may develop a well-trained staff who may become disaffected unless tangible rewards are offered.

Changing from a service dominated by the centre to a decentralised service can have profound implications for the morale of employees and the responsiveness of the service to the public if decentralisation involves the transfer of power from the centre downwards. However, such changes in organisational structure will have profound effects on existing power relations within the organisation and, as we argued in Chapter 6, there may be many vested interests to be overcome and much bargaining to take place. As Elizabeth Mellon comments in relation to the Next Steps initiative:

Unsurprisingly, this decentralisation initiative is difficult. It attempts to change deep-seated ways of working and cultural norms. It threatens power relationships and questions not just how work is done, but what work *should* be done. (Mellon, 1993, p. 30.)

It is essential to appreciate the numerous stakeholders that have an interest in politically sensitive areas of government work such as employment policy. For example, one of the principal areas of concern for many commentators has been that the injection of more rigorous managerial accountability has been accompanied by a decline in political accountability to Parliament. If agencies are to be more responsive to customers and clients then the Treasury will need to be much less interventionist than it has been in the past (see Davies and Willman, 1991; Jordan, 1992).

If change involves challenging existing power arrangements then resistance to change is almost inevitable. Obstacles to change may include:

- the self-interest of individuals and groups who fear that it may encroach on their territory and challenge existing power bases and practices;
- the fear, insecurity, and resentment of individuals who may perceive change as a threat. For example, the introduction of a new computer system may mean that their existing skills will become redundant or a structural reorganisation may threaten job security;
- the lack of trust that may follow if change is imposed from above and without consultation. Individuals may question the motives behind the change.

People see change in different ways. A new manager may not understand why others resent his or her dynamic reorganisation and how work may be more rewarding as a result. At the same time a clerical officer may be quite happy with existing work patterns and relations even though they may appear to be inefficient. More widely, different groups may disagree about what change agent is required. Professional groups in the National Health Service may believe that an injection of funds will improve health care treatment. The government may argue that improved resource management will solve problems. A crucial element is the way in which change is brought about. For example, does it involve full consultation and communication with all those that change will affect and is full account taken of the views of the workforce and their representatives? Are there proper mechanisms for consultation? Is consultation effective and meaningful or is it just going through the motions? Unless these questions are addressed by management then those affected by change may well feel that it is just imposed from above and resent it.

We can ask ourselves, then, a number of general questions concerning change:

- **Who brings about change?** Is it internally or externally driven and is it best brought about by outsiders?
- **What changes?** Is it the structure, the people, the processes, the tasks or the culture? We suggest that all these are interdependent upon each other within

the organisation. Thus encouraging individuals to be more dynamic, flexible and responsive will not work if the same old hierarchical, top-down structure still exists.

- **Who does it affect?** And hence who is likely to obstruct it? Change may affect all the staff or just certain groups of it. The person bringing about change will have to identify and overcome entrenched interests.
- **Are there appropriate mechanisms for change?** Change requires implementation. If the necessary process or techniques are not employed then the status quo may prevail.
- **How much will it cost?** Change is expensive not just in terms of financial cost but also in terms of goodwill with staff and clients. However, a more important question may well be 'can the organisation afford not to change?' If an organisation in a competitive environment does not respond effectively to new markets and products it will go out of business. Similarly, if central government is prepared to bypass local government and encourage non-elected bodies such as urban development corporations or training and enterprise councils then local government has to respond to the challenge and show that it can do the job just as well.
- **Is it crisis management or is change under control?** It is difficult for public service organisations to plan ahead given the short timespan with which politicians operate but flexible organisations may find it easier to deal with unexpected change.

MANAGEMENT CONSULTANTS AND CHANGE

Reform of the public services has often tended to focus on changing structures. For example, the ongoing initiative to reform local government led by the Local Government Commission focuses on reviewing boundaries for local authorities. Similarly, the creation of agencies in the civil service has focused on the structural aspects of organisation theory. Elcock counsels caution about structural change, concluding that it is 'expensive, disruptive, addictive and its effectiveness is uncertain' (1991, p. 63). However, despite the lure of structural change, reform has not been one dimensional. Improving management has focused on what are referred to as the 'soft' as well as the 'hard' aspects of organisations. McKinsey consultants advanced a generic seven S framework as a toolkit for organisations strategists which is set out in Box 12.1.

Peters and Waterman in their book *In Search of Excellence* (1982) made the distinction between hard Ss (structure and strategy) and soft Ss (systems, staff, skills, style and shared values). They argued that corporate strategists had devoted insufficient attention to the soft Ss. Peters and Waterman studied the attributes of a number of companies, including Boeing, IBM and McDonald's, which they identified as being excellent and suggested that excellent companies had a number of characteristics:

Box 12.1 The McKinsey seven Ss

---

1 **Structure**. Those attributes of the organisation which can be expressed through an organisational chart (span of control, centralisation vs decentralisation, etc.).
2 **Strategy**. Actions the organisation plans or undertakes in response to or in anticipation of the external environment.
3 **Systems**. Procedures and processes regularly followed by the organisation.
4 **Staff**. The kinds of specialities or professions represented in an organisation ('engineering types', 'MBAs', and 'computer jocks').
5 **Skills**. Distinctive attributes and capabilities of the organisation and its key people in comparison with its competition.
6 **Style**. Patterns of behaviour and managerial style of senior managers.
7 **Shared values**. Spiritual or philosophical principles and concepts that an organisation is able to instil in its members. (*Source* : Sharplin, 1985, p. 69.)

- **A bias for action**. The effective organisation gets on with the job, unlike in government where the official analyses and consults but does not take a decision unless forced to do so. Organisations must become more flexible and be prepared to experiment. They must get away from the traditional patterns of formal communication and rigid and fixed organisational structures that stifle action.
- **Get close to the customer**. The successful organisation hears what the customer is saying and responds to customer requirements. If not they go out of business. Most public sector organisations have, in the past, never faced the possibility of going out of business. Local authorities, for example, have traditionally been monopoly providers of services without the monopoly being challenged.
- **Autonomy and entrepreneurship**. Individuals should be encouraged to take responsibility for their actions and show initiative rather than merely follow routine and allow themselves to be governed by the rulebook.
- **Productivity through people**. Everybody within the organisation is encouraged to innovate in order to improve the product or service. It is based on a culture where people have high expectations of each other. Too often public services have emphasised reducing costs rather than improving the quality of the service. Staff training has tended to be a victim of budgetary cuts.
- **Hands on, value driven**. Individuals within the organisation share a set of common values and are motivated by organisational goals. We know politicians have values and that these change over time. If public officials are to subscribe to a particular set of values determined by politicians then are they in a position to serve another party elected with a different set of values? This may call for a dramatic cultural change.
- **Stick to the knitting**. Organisations must identify what they are good at and stick to it. In the public sector, statutes require public sector organisations to

provide specific services whereas in the private sector companies can withdraw from one business and concentrate on another. However, increasingly public service organisations have the ability to define *how* they provide a service. One solution may be to concentrate on core activities and contract out other activities.

- **Simple form and lean staff**. The successful organisation has a lean structure with few hierarchical tiers. Of course, one of the features of classic public sector organisations such as civil service and local authority departments has been hierarchical organisation.
- **Simultaneous tight-loose properties**. Core values are controlled at the centre but autonomy is located lower down the organisation to enable action based upon core values. A balance is there to be struck between central direction and local discretion.

In Search of Excellence was an important influence on organisations in both the public and private sectors – for several years it was a 'bible' for aspiring executives. The Benefits Agency, the largest of the civil service executive agencies and one with a long history of bureaucratic organisation, adopted *Bias for Action* as one of its four core values. For the Benefits Agency, *Bias for Action* is defined as:

- fostering innovation at all levels;
- producing a clear sense of direction throughout the organisation;
- building on our reward and recognition system by acknowledging achievement;
- empowering all those in the Agency to take responsibility for dealing with problems and to make improvements when and where opportunities occur;
- developing confident visible leadership throughout the organisation;
- using setbacks and mistakes as a basis for learning and improvement, not recrimination;
- focusing the activities for Agency Central Services on support for those delivering services in the field.

(Benefits Agency, 1992, p. 30.)

Perhaps the most detailed application of the Peters and Waterman prescription to public services in Britain has been at East Sussex Social Services (Hadley and Young, 1990). The authors develop the theme of responsive management. Box 12.2 sets out the characteristics of responsive public services and a comparison with the Peters and Waterman values will demonstrate the similarities in their thinking.

There are also links to be made with the Osborne and Gaebler model which we examined in the previous chapter. Similar to Osborne and Gaebler, Hadley and Young advocate that public services should be entrepreneurial and responsive to the customer and client. By entrepreneurship they mean maximising the utility obtained from available resources and recognising that there may be many ways to provide a service other than the traditional local authority approach of in-house provision. Responsiveness for Hadley and Young means involving users in the

---

Box 12.2 Characteristics of a responsive public service

---

1 **Leadership and values**
   - Clarity of the organisation's values and goals
   - Values shared by leadership
2 **Action**
   - An orientation to action, achievement and change
3 **Customer and client**
   - Obtaining and maintaining a political mandate
   - Involving the users and responding to their influence
4 **Autonomy and enterprise**
   - Delegation of authority to the front line
   - Creating sustaining local autonomy
   - Encouraging enterprise and risk-taking
5 **Involving staff**
   - Creating a synergic work environment
6 **Control**
   - Clear definition of scope and boundaries of local action
   - Clear system of evaluation.

(Adapted from Hadley and Young, 1990, p. 223.)

---

evolution and provision of policy. In doing so, they encounter two major problems. First, they define customers as government as opposed to users who may often receive the service against their will, for example those taken into care. Second, the influence of some users may, because of the inequalities of access to power, be greater than others.

EXCELLENCE FOR THE PUBLIC SERVICES?

It cannot be denied that the ideas of Peters and Waterman have been influential, but questions have been raised about the validity of their prescription. In January 1993, one of the so-called excellent companies, IBM, recorded a loss of $4.97 billion, the largest annual loss in corporate history (*Financial Times*, 1993) We are concerned with the relevance of the excellence model for public service organisations and for this purpose we will draw on a paper by Salaman (1992). He raises a number of relevant criticisms:

- Peters and Waterman's methodology is questionable. Particularly, they chose to examine successful companies and did not show that unsuccessful organisations (including those delivering public services) did not have those attributes.
- They did not examine the characteristics needed to turn unsuccessful companies into successful ones – an approach that may be more useful when considering reform of the public services.

- The identified attributes relate to the internal organisation rather than the environment in which the organisation finds itself. This may be especially important for public service organisations with less scope for the determination of their core activities, or to use the Peters and Waterman vocabulary, the knitting they should stick to.
- Since the publication of *In Search of Excellence*, one of the co-authors, Tom Peters, has since changed the emphasis that he places on the various attributes to the point where he wrote in 1988 'There are no excellent companies.' (See Salaman, 1992, pp. 8–12; see also Peters and Austin, 1985; Peters, 1988.)

CHANGING ORGANISATIONAL FORMS

So far we have looked at a range of solutions which have focused on cultural change and entrepreneurial solutions to problems. The remainder of this chapter examines what has changed and how it has changed. We begin this by examining changing organisational forms.

As we saw in the previous chapter, initiatives such as the purchaser–provider split in the National Health Service and the client–contractor split in local government have led to new organisational structures. The distinction between policy formulation and service delivery draws heavily on a trend of fragmentation and extensive use of outside suppliers which is being followed in many large private sector organisations.

Shamrock organisations

According to Handy (1990, pp. 202–9) many business organisations facing an increasingly competitive environment are taking on a shamrock shape with three components to the workforce:

- core employees who are essential to the organisation;
- specialist contractors who carry out tasks that can be done just as well outside the organisation;
- flexible labour which is bought in as required.

The example is interesting as this trend can be identified throughout the public services. The moves towards contracting peripheral (and sometimes core) services is paralleled by the increasing use of part-time labour. This increases an organisation's flexibility but also raises questions of managerial skills and employment practice. As Handy points out, the shamrock shape places much greater emphasis on the role of the purchaser and the monitoring of outputs from contractors. In addition, local authorities that have placed objectives of urban regeneration, anti-poverty strategies and full employment at a premium may find that new flexible practices offer little or nothing to those members of the community who they seek to serve.

The client–contractor split in local government

Competitive tendering has important implications for organisational structures and patterns of behaviour. If an in-house 'direct service organisation' manages to win the contract, we have two sets of actors. Firstly, there is the client department, for example social services, who put the contract out to tender, and secondly, there is the contractor who provides the service. The basis of the relationship is the contract. In many cases, authorities are specifying the task to be completed and standards of work for the first time and are now aware of the true cost of activity. This sharpens the process of management and financial accountability – the contract becomes the focus – as the contractor is responsible for delivering the service as specified in the contract and will be judged by the client on that basis.

In his review of the initial experiences of compulsory competitive tendering, Walsh identified three advantages of the new organisational form:

- it clarifies responsibilities;
- it ensures that the client side has responsibilities for determination of standards of service and their monitoring;
- it made the need for management clearer and the fact that there had often been too little management in the past.

However, he also noted a number of disadvantages. These included:

- increased costs, particularly on the client side, particularly in the preparation of quality systems;
- the organisation increases in complexity;
- the lack of experience on the client side, especially in negotiating contracts;
- the possibility that profit comes before service and consequent antagonism in the client–contractor split;
- antagonistic clients can make life difficult for contractors, especially internal ones. (Walsh, 1991, pp. 82–4.)

Painter sets out the stages that the client side of a local authority will have to carry out:

- prepare service profile;
- prepare specification;
- advertise for interested contractors;
- issue invitations to tender;
- evaluate bids and award the contract;
- monitor contract. (Painter, J., 1991, pp. 196–7.)

Given that approximately three-quarters of local government costs are paid in wages and salaries, it would seem reasonable to assume that the major area for savings for a contractor would be in reducing labour costs. To date there has been too little research from which to draw conclusions as to whether contracting out has produced the lasting savings which were intended. A study by Szymanksi and Wilkins shows that 'most of the cost savings have been associated with improvements in labour productivity rather than through wage cuts' (1992, p. 112).

Under the Citizen's Charter, the government has announced that local authorities will be required to expose certain percentages of administrative and professional work to competitive tender. For example, 33 per cent of legal services and 80 per cent of computing will be subject to a bidding process (Prime Minister, 1991, p. 65).

Technology and change

The introduction of new technologies will have an impact upon the organisation in a number of different ways and will affect the structure, the decision making, the organisational politics and the people and their skills within the organisation.

Structure

The increasing use of information technology could lead either to a more centralised or to a more decentralised structure. It may mean that more information is controlled by the centre thereby reducing the scope for individual discretion. At the same time terminals at local offices will allow information to flow down the organisation much more quickly to the operational level. It may also mean a reduction in the tiers of middle management since many of the tasks of communication and co-ordination can be performed through the use of networked systems.

An example of information technology influencing the structure of the organisation is in the Department of Social Security where drastic changes are occurring in its London offices. Much of the work that was previously done in the local offices has been transferred to new centres in the provinces, linked to London by computer. The advantage of this is cheaper rents outside London and the easier recruitment and retention of staff. The technology will allow a reduction in the size of local offices and it is anticipated that local branches in London will become more accessible and more responsive to the local community.

Decision making

More information will be available and the quality of that information may be improved upon. The information will allow quicker decisions to be made and will allow decisions to be taken lower down the organisation. It may also reduce risk and uncertainty since modelling and simulation exercises can be carried out. LAMSAC developed a number of packages that act as aids to management decision making in local authorities. It has also developed databases which hold information about contractors and contracts awarded by local authorities.

Increasingly, moves are being made towards a common computer intelligence network linking police forces throughout Europe. Information will be pooled and will be widely available. At present photographs, fingerprints and documents are available to European anti-terrorist squads.

Organisational politics

There is evidence that information technology is used in the public services as a solution to a crisis rather than as the product of a rational decision-making process. The successful introduction of IT requires commitment from senior management. In organisations where there are powerful internal stakeholders, such as clinicians in the National Health Service, the introduction of IT required the support of those stakeholders (Willcocks, 1992, pp. 181–3).

If knowledge is power then information technology and access to it is a powerful tool for those who control it. It may also lead to a new breed of specialists or professionals within the organisation.

People and skills

The big fear is that it may lead to job losses and to the loss of traditional skills. While this may be true in a particular organisation it is argued that by improving output and efficiency the economy as a whole will benefit. It may also rejuvenate the workforce and liberate the individual from the routine work that is a part of administration. There is also a certain status associated with new skills and it may lead to job enrichment. Evidence from the Audit Commission (1988) on the police revealed large savings in administrative time through the use of computers (see Table 12.1).

Table 12.1 Percentage time spent on administration

	Pre-computerisation	Post-computerisation
Inspectors	58	22
Sergeants	50	20
Constables	21	4

Adapted from Audit Commission (1988).

An extra dimension to the increased use of information technology is the concern for confidentiality, particularly given the sensitive nature of much of the work of the public sector. The Data Protection Act 1984 was introduced to protect the rights of citizens concerning information about them held by organisations on computer files. This applies to all organisations but is particularly relevant to the public sector where the holding of for example, police records, social services records, medical records gives cause for concern. It has implications for the concept of open government that we examined earlier and the ethical dimension within which the public sector operates.

INFLUENCE OF BUSINESS MANAGEMENT TECHNIQUES

As we have seen, the influence of business management techniques is not new. Earlier in this chapter we examined the thinking of management consultants, such as Peters and Waterman. However, this is not a new phenomenon; indeed it is possible to cite many long-standing examples of business influence on the public services. For example, the Plowden Committee on Control of Public Expenditure (Plowden, 1961) used business consultants. In local government, the Bains Report urged the newly created local authorities to adopt corporate management techniques in the early 1970s (Bains, 1972; see also Alexander, 1982) and the Griffiths Report argued the case for the application of general management principles in the National Health Service (Griffiths, 1983; Strong and Robinson, 1990).

More recently, reconstituted health authorities and trusts and police authorities contain people appointed by the relevant secretary of state often for their business experience to replace local authority nominees. The rationale for their inclusion on such bodies is that they will be able to contribute their business experience which will lead to improved performance.

The new executive agencies in the civil service have drawn extensively on business planning techniques. Taking the case of HM Prison Service, an executive agency of the Home Office established in April 1993, we can see how they have approached planning. It takes place at three levels. Firstly, like all executive agencies, its relationship with the Home Office is set out in a Framework Document. This sets out the role and task of the agency. This is then followed by a corporate plan which covers the period 1993–6 and a short-term business plan for 1993–4 (see Table 12.2).

QUALITY

Recently, a further private sector initiative, this time developed in Japan (but drawing on American writers), has begun to impinge on management thinking in the public sector – the quality approach. The literature on quality emphasises that in an increasingly competitive environment, organisations need to improve organisational performance in order to gain an edge over rivals. Peter Drucker argues that the success of the Japanese economy is not based on its advantage in product design but in the leadership qualities of their managers. Faced with competition from Japan, British companies have sought to emulate their management philosophy. As with corporate management, systems analysis and other approaches, quality has hit the public sector management agenda.

Table 12.2 The principal contents of the Prison Service's planning documents

	Main contents
Framework Document	Role and task Accountability Planning, finance and support services Personnel matters Review and variation of the framework. (HM Prison Service, 1993a.)
Corporate Plan	Sets out a three-year plan for the service taking into account the six goals of the service. Considers how the service is to be improved. (HM Prison Service, 1993b.)
Business Plan	Within the context of the Corporate Plan, to implement various policy initiatives including 'making recommendations to Ministers later in 1993 on the extent, form and timing of increased private sector involvement in the management of prison establishments'. (HM Prison Service, 1993c, p. 3.)

A variety of approaches can be adopted. These vary from obtaining certification from the British Standards Institution that the process conforms to British Standard 5750 Quality Systems to the attitudinal approach of Total Quality Management. Writers on quality see it as a managerial philosophy which should permeate thinking on all issues at all levels in the organisation (see Deming, 1986). The quality approach is based on the assumptions of the human relations school, particularly McGregor (1960) whose Theory Y argued that people actively seek responsibility and given the right environment have a positive contribution to make to the effectiveness of the organisation. According to Crosby, an organisation has the capacity to develop from uncertainty (where problems are dealt with as and when they occur) through a number of stages to certainty (where the organisation has a prevention system to ensure that few significant problems occur) (see English, 1990).

The Local Government Training Board defined quality as 'that which gives the customer satisfaction. Quality assurance is about setting up systems that ensure that a service or product consistently achieves customer satisfaction' (1989, p. 42). We have argued in previous chapters that the management of organisation is contingent on the nature and task of the organisation. Hence there cannot be one simple formula for quality – each organisation has to develop its own approach. However, we can look at some issues of general concern and then look at how these may be applicable to the public sector.

Bone and Griggs lists their three Cs of quality (1989):

- **commitment**: to customers, organisational goal, personal quality, etc.;
- **competence**: in organising, solving problems, communicating, designing, etc.;
- **communication**: by both word and mouth with particular emphasis on feedback.

Most approaches to quality emphasise:

- change in the culture of the organisation and attitudes of staff;
- commitment of management to quality;
- the education and training of staff at all levels in the organisation;
- quality written into the objectives of the organisation;
- error-free work – 'get it right first time, on time, every time' thus moving from 100 per cent inspection to the use of control mechanisms.

The Local Government Training Board summarise the steps necessary to ensure quality:

1 Know the customers needs
2 Design a product or service to meet the needs
3 Guarantee performance
4 Provide clear instructions
5 Deliver punctually
6 Provide a back-up service
7 Use feedback.
(Local Government Training Board, 1989, p. 42.)

Thus, the Local Government Training Board approach sees quality as an extension of customer orientation. This makes the important assumption that the member of the public who consumes the service or the taxpayer is the customer. As we have already discussed, this assumption is a problematic one. In large organisations, people are encouraged to see the first user of their service as the customer. For example, if an officer's task is to supply budgetary information to the central treasurer's department then that department is the customer.

An initial reading of BS5750 shows how it can easily be applied to a repetitive manufacturing process or routine activities such as the payment of benefits where there is an easily identifiable output. Many of the features of the public sector require us to consider how applicable quality approaches are to the public sector. Some of the possible benefits that a quality orientation may produce include the following:

- Agencies which compete with others for contracts (for example, direct service organisations in local authorities or Her Majesty's Stationary Office) can develop a competitive edge over commercial rivals and could use BS5750 as a marketing tool.

- Advocates of quality argue that after the initial investment, quality saves money. For example, getting it right first time eliminates the need to do jobs again or the need for 100 per cent inspection. Much quality can be achieved by better organisation and management. Building properties to a high standard may mean spending more at the construction stage but will incur lower maintenance costs in the long run (English, 1990). According to the former project manager for the Next Steps executive agencies, Sir Peter Kemp, under the new arrangements, departments must move towards light-handed monitoring after the event thus relying on the agency to ensure quality (Public Accounts Committee, 1989).
- Better relationships with clients because they are more satisfied with the service.

However, such a strategy generates a number of problems. These include the following:

- A quality policy requires long-term planning. To take the example of building properties, local authorities may be reluctant to commit large amounts of scarce resources to the construction of high quality accommodation when there are other priorities which are high on the agenda.
- As we have noted in previous chapters, the only certainty that public sector organisations face is uncertainty. This inevitably means that they will continue to face strategic problems.
- The absence of the profit motive may mean that the incentive to achieve quality may not be as high as if there was a balance sheet demonstrating what has been achieved.
- Where an organisation is a monopoly provider of a service there is less incentive to improve quality.
- Politicians who determine policy are not elected by virtue of their management expertise and may not be sympathetic to quality policies. However, there is evidence to show that politicians can and do demonstrate a concern for these issues (see examples demonstrated by the Local Government Training Board (1985) and the Treasury and Civil Service Committee (1990)).
- As the Local Government Training Board pointed out (1989, p. 43), other values need to be assured: equity, effectiveness and efficiency. Whereas a private sector organisation can target its services towards a particular market, an environmental health department may prioritise equity in service provision. Often services that are appreciated by customers may not be meeting with the objectives set by political masters. For example, what customers (or claimants) want from the benefits service may be very different from what the secretary of state wants.
- If customers are highly satisfied with a quality service they may demand more. As we have noted in previous chapters, a problem in the public sector is the need to limit demand to avoid budgetary expansion. This may cease to be a problem if customers are paying the full cost.

- The possibility that the required cultural change may not extend to those at the street level in the organisation – those who deal with the public on a day-to-day basis and are therefore crucial to the projection of a quality image.
- Sceptics say that quality management is not applicable to service organisations. Advocates of quality such as Crosby (1984) argue that at the heart of most services is a production process using machinery – whether it is ovens in a kitchen or office machinery in a government department. Hence it is not appropriate to make the distinction between the two types of organisation.

Though relatively few public sector organisations have been awarded the British Standards Institute kite many organisations have made moves towards quality. These moves include assessment of consumer needs and satisfaction, better complaints procedures which not only process the complaint but seek to amend procedures in the light of the complaint, and improved staff development programmes including customer care training. Thus, for example, Wrekin Council has attempted to create a corporate culture based upon 'Quality, Caring and Fairness' (Hancox *et al.*, 1989).

CONCLUSION

In conclusion, it is worthwhile to cite two conflicting opinions about change in the public services. In an assessment of these reforms Stewart and Walsh counsel caution:

> The mistake is to assume that there is one approach to management applicable to public services based on an over-simplified model of the private sector. The language of consumerism, the development of government by contract and of contractual accountability, the form of performance management, the use of quasi-markets and a stress on private sector values create problems if the limits to their application in the public domain is not recognised. (Stewart and Walsh, 1992, p. 517.)

On the other hand, Pettigrew *et al.* (1992, p. 13) are sceptical about the case for a distinctive public service. They identify three sources of commonality between the public and private sectors:

- sets of generic issues such as human resource management that are common to both sectors;
- a common political and economic context that has forced similar issues on to the agenda in both sectors;
- common sets of managerial issues, such as the need for competences and political skills which are required in both sectors.

Perhaps this divergence of opinion can, in part, be explained by the diverse nature of the public services. If we borrow Stewart and Ranson's framework (1988), we can argue that within the public services there exists a variety of purposes, conditions and tasks. These will be contingent on value systems, the organisational setting, organisational culture and the nature of the task to be accomplished.

FURTHER READING

Chapter 3 of Wilson and Hinton (1993) and Pollitt (1990) discuss the new managerial culture in the public services. Mullins (1989) and Morgan (1986) both provide a detailed analysis of organisational development and the techniques used to bring it about. Reports by the National Audit Office and the Audit Commission give useful accounts of the changes demanded of and made by organisations in central government, local government and the health service.

CHAPTER 13

The management task

INTRODUCTION

In Chapter 1 we offered a working definition of how management may be perceived to be different from administration and may be characterised as dynamic, entrepreneurial, innovative, flexible and so on. In recent years there has been a growing interest in the development of skills and knowledge for managers working in the public services. All political parties currently recognise the need for public services to be delivered in an efficient and effective manner and to respond to the needs of the users of the services. Improving the performance of managers is recognised as one way of achieving this. In this chapter we focus on the increasing interest in management education, the distinctiveness of managing in the public services and the tasks that managers perform at different levels.

We are as much concerned with identifying what management does as prescribing what management ought to do. A common failing in the management literature is the desire to offer prescription before description.

MANAGEMENT EDUCATION

The concern with improving the performance of management is not confined to the public sector. The Constable and McCormick (1987) report and the Handy (1987) report both argued that British managers lacked management skills in comparison with managers abroad. Both reports advocated improved management education and training. The ensuing debate led to the Management Charter Initiative (MCI) as the operating arm of the National Forum for Management Education. Part of MCI's function is to provide standards and guidelines for management development and training. Underpinning MCI is the provision of a set of generic management competences. At Level 1 for first-line managers, for example, these are constructed around four key roles: managing operations, managing finance, managing people and managing information.

The approach adopted is based upon competences which can be defined as:

> The ability to perform effectively a series of work activities. It can include skills, knowledge, understanding and values.

Table 13.1 describes the key roles and their associated units of competence.

Table 13.1 Key roles and associated competences

Manage operations
1 Maintain and improve service and product operations.
2 Contribute to the implementation of change in services, products and systems.

Manage finance
3 Recommend, monitor and control the use of resources.

Manage people
4 Contribute to the recruitment and selection of personnel.
5 Develop teams, individuals and self to enhance performance.
6 Plan, allocate and evaluate work carried out by teams, individuals and self.
7 Create, maintain and enhance effective working relationships.

Manage information
8 Seek, evaluate and organise information for action.
9 Exchange information to solve problems and make decisions.

Apart from the units of competence and the elements of competence, the MCI standards also require performance criteria that distinguish satisfactory from unsatisfactory performance and range statements which give indications of the range of circumstances to which the elements apply.

Supporters of the MCI approach argue that it is important because:

- it focuses on management competences;
- it offers a list of generic competences, supporting the belief that there are general management skills which can be applied across different types of organisation;
- it supports management development and training;
- it is grounded in the workplace such that management is about doing not theorising;
- it recognises the need for management training.

However, the competency approach to management development has been criticised. Burgoyne (1989) argues that although such approaches have an important role to play in management development there are difficulties:

- Managing is of a holistic nature and managing is not the exercise of discrete competences.
- There is no agreed method for measuring competence.
- A universal list of competences may not be appropriate for specific circumstances.
- A competence-based approach concentrates on the technical and has little to say about the moral, political and ideological aspects of management.
- Management is never static and new competences may be required.
- There is more than one 'right way' to manage.

- A competence-based approach concentrates on the individual and yet much of management involves working in teams.

We return to MCI later when we discuss the notion of generic competences and offer an example of its suitability for the public services.

GENERIC AND DIFFERENTIALIST APPROACHES

In recent years the debate about public services management has had a number of strands. Hood describes the key elements of New Public Management (1991). These include:

- hands-on professional management in the public sector;
- explicit standards and measures of performance;
- greater emphasis on output controls;
- a shift to disaggregation of units in the public sector;
- a shift to greater competition in the public sector;
- stress on private sector styles of management practice;
- stress on greater discipline and parsimony in resource use.

As Hood indicates, one approach has been underpinned by an assumption that private sector management styles and techniques can be applied to the public sector. In other words, management is generic and can be applied across different organisations in different sectors. This view has not been universally accepted. At one extreme is the argument that the public sector is different from the private sector and hence managing in the public sector is intrinsically different from the private sector. At the other extreme is the argument that managing in the two sectors is very similar. This is the genericist position: that management comprises common tasks and competences irrespective of the sector within which an individual is working. A dimension to this debate that is often neglected is the third (voluntary and not-for-profit) sector where similar debates are held concerning the application of general management competences. For example, Paton and Cornforth (1992) argue that such differences will focus on resource acquisition, different stakeholders and governance, and a culture that encourages participative decision-making and operation through small, informal units.

The debate concerning the public sector and the application of general models of management centres on a number of different areas. Stewart and Ranson (1988) examine the purposes, condition and tasks of the public sector and argue that the public sector is distinct and that management in the public sector requires a different basis from that of private sector management. Using Stewart and Ranson's framework we can examine some of the arguments that have been applied to the genericist/differentialist positions.

Purpose (what are their goals)

Private sector:
- promote individual choice in the market
- pursue profit
- promote competition
- increase market share
- clear objectives.

Public sector:
- multiple and fuzzy objectives
- arena for the pursuit of collective values
- expressed through collective choice
- need to serve clients and citizens, not just customers
- driven by needs and availability of resources rather than the market.

In practice such clear differences are rarely found. Any organisation should be concerned with efficiency and effectiveness; businesses do not always seek to make profits at the expense of everything else; many private sector organisations are not interested in promoting competition but rather in driving it away and creating monopoly positions for themselves; some multinational companies have fuzzy objectives (this is particularly apparent during periods of takeover mania when companies seek to buy other companies without thinking through how such acquisitions can contribute to the strategic direction of the purchasing company); private sector organisations can be concerned with corporate social responsibility and be aware of their contribution to the local community.

Conditions (the context in which they carry out their operations)

Private sector:
- through competition
- operate in markets
- free from constraints (political and legal)
- accountable to shareholders
- secrecy in terms of business confidentiality
- can take long-term view on investment
- resourced from operational returns and borrowing
- raise capital
- measurable outputs in terms of a product or service.

Public sector:
- multiple stakeholders (managers, politicians, users, citizens, media, etc.)
- constrained by politics and the law
- public accountability
- short-termism of politicians
- funds raised through taxation

- complex and debated performance indicators
- complexity of policy implementation.

The reality may be different. All organisations operate within a legal and political framework. Thus political decisions to raise interest rates have an impact upon businesses as does legislation requiring anti-pollution controls; shareholders may be just as interested in short-term advantages as politicians; increasingly parts of the public sector, as we have seen, operate under market or quasi-market conditions.

Tasks (what do they do)

Private sector:
- managers have the freedom to manage, to take risks
- flexibility and discretion to take decisions
- responsiveness to the customer
- driven by clear goals and responsibilities.

Public sector:
- pursue collective goals
- bound by regulations
- balance competing interests rather than pursue one interest
- operate under the gaze of the public eye
- little scope for negotiation of inputs – these are determined by politicians
- cannot measure outcomes
- not involved in policy formulation.

To a large extent differences in tasks will depend upon the particular function concerned and where the manager is located in the organisation. Processing invoices, maintaining records, managing residential homes or educating children may be the same whether carried out in the public or the private sector. Stewart and Ranson do argue that some activities may be the same but that the purposes and conditions of the public domain are distinct.

We have addressed, to some extent, purposes and conditions in the previous two chapters and have indicated the ways in which the boundaries between different sectors are becoming more blurred. For the rest of this chapter we shall concentrate on the management task.

THE MANAGEMENT TASK

The first difficulty is in defining precisely the management task. There is much theorising about what the manager should be doing, both in private and public sector organisations, but little empirical evidence to demonstrate, or agreement on, what managers actually do. Hales (1986) argues that:

- Managers seem to perform work of both a generalist nature and work of a specialist nature.
- The generalist work is sufficiently ill-defined for managers to determine their own boundaries.
- Within these boundaries a number of common strands occur. These strands are:
  - acting as figurehead and leader of an organisational unit;
  - forming and maintaining contacts;
  - monitoring, filtering and disseminating information;
  - allocating resources;
  - handling disturbances and maintaining work flows;
  - negotiating;
  - innovating;
  - planning;
  - controlling and directing subordinates.
  (See Hales, 1986, p. 95.)

Hales argues that the evidence seems to indicate that the manager as strategist, planner and thinker is a myth and that even senior managers allow themselves to be diverted by interruption and informal personal contacts. Hales indicates that managerial work tends to focus upon the day-to-day rather than the strategic. He suggests that between two-thirds and four-fifths of a manager's time is spent in imparting or receiving information through face-to-face contact with others. Much of the communication is lateral with other managers of a similar status and managers tend to respond to the requests of others rather than initiating matters. According to Hales many managerial interactions appear to be wide-ranging in topic, often only tenuously connected with business and informal in character. In terms of the informal nature of the job, evidence seems to suggest that much 'political activity' goes on with managers anxious to secure their own personal territories.

A number of key themes emerge from the literature in terms of what the manager does. Variation and contingency are key themes with managerial work being contingent upon function, level in the hierarchy, the type, structure and size of the organisation, and the environment.

However, as Mintzberg (1975, p. 49) sums it up:

> If you ask a manager what he [sic] does, he will most likely tell you that he plans, organises, co-ordinates and controls. Then watch what he does. Don't be surprised if you can't relate what you see to those four words.

As we indicated earlier, what we think managers should be doing may not bear much relation to what they actually do! Are our expectations of managers realistic?

The study of the role of chief executives in local government, carried out by the Audit Commission (1989), revealed that chief executives appear to carry out a wide variety of tasks:

Strategic role:
1 The corporate manager managing the central processes of the authority
2 The political manager managing the relationships with politicians.

Co-ordinating role:
3 The administrative role
4 The communicator
5 The troubleshooter
6 The umpire-broker arbitrating between departments and between officers and politicians.

Operational role:
7 The departmental manager
8 The specialist
9 The project manager.

Representative role:
10 The dignitary
11 The salesperson 'selling' the authority to those outside
12 The figurehead.

In other words the chief executive plays the role of 12 people. The report argues that most chief executives will have to attend to all four types of role and that they will be torn between all of these roles.

Stewart offers us a prescription of management competences in the public services (1986). He suggests that the manager needs to be aware of:

- political sensitivity, awareness and understanding;
- the management of public pressure and protest;
- fulfilling the conditions of public accountability;
- marketing for equity and other purposes;
- strategic management;
- the management of rationing;
- assessing a multi-faceted performance.

The exercise of the management task takes place within an organisational environment that is changing as we have indicated in the previous two chapters. The organisational context will provide a framework for the management task and will involve constraints as well as opportunities.

Hoggett (1991) has termed the organisational context of public services management as post-bureaucratic control and argues that the 'freedom to manage' takes place within boundaries; the public services manager operates within a 'regulated autonomy'. Hoggett considers that even though organisations may have adopted decentralised structures or pushed responsibility for operations lower down the organisational hierarchy, strategic control still operates and indeed may be reinforced and enhanced by, for example, tighter controls over expenditure by those lower down the organisation. Control is also exercised through the use of contracts regulating internal and external relations and through target setting. Control through specifying results has replaced control of processes by hierarchies. Devolved management may not necessarily mean less control by senior managers or those at the centre. Instead it is just a different kind of control.

MANAGING IN THE PERSONAL SOCIAL SERVICES

The period since 1979 has seen many major pieces of legislation affecting local government. Both the National Health Service and Community Care Act 1990 and the Children Act 1989 require a new framework for the provision of care. Both the quantity and substance of legislation has meant that the ability to manage in a turbulent environment has become a key requirement.

A particular feature of government legislation in a wide range of policy areas has been the requirement to work with and through other organisations, both statutory and independent. One of the underlying themes has been the emphasis on the citizen as the consumer of services offered a choice of service deliverers. Local authorities have been encouraged by central government to move away from direct provision and to become enablers. Local authorities have interpreted the enabling role in different ways. The speed of response to such encouragement may vary from authority to authority depending upon such factors as political control, geographical location, the existence of alternative providers and the prevailing organisational culture.

The changing environment has resulted in changes in both the content of what is done by public services organisations and how it is done. Local authorities have moved, to a greater or lesser degree, towards purchaser and provider roles and the contracting out of services. Accompanying this has been the focus on the customer/user/consumer of services. Managers have increasingly had to focus on value for money, on meeting targets and on assuring the quality of services provided by others. Not only that but targets and quality have often been set by politicians or senior managers and middle and front-line managers may have no sense of ownership (see McKevitt and Lawton, 1993).

In the personal social services, the requirements of a mixed economy of care are centred upon the needs of the individual and the need to develop packages of care in co-operation with health authorities that are designed to allow client choice, participation and personal achievement. Many social workers have become care managers. Care managers are responsible for assessing clients against standardised criteria, and the client's entitlement to services is then based on a points rating. It is then the care managers who are responsible for purchasing an appropriate package for their clients. Purchasing services from other organisations has meant that such managers need contract specification, monitoring and assessment skills. Awareness and knowledge of quality assurance is also required. Changing organisational structures has been one response to organisational change with devolved budgeting through cost centres. Working with other organisations has meant that managers require the development of skills of negotiation, networking and managing across organisational boundaries.

MCI generic competences do not seem to account for the particular competences required for managing personal social services. Bell (in Clode, 1992) has argued that managers in personal social services have to attend to the right of individuals, to respect the dignity and privacy of individuals and to provide services on the basis of equity. The value base of personal social services needs to be considered with its concerns for the client or user, anti-oppressive practices and public accountability. There is also a need to satisfy the needs of different stakeholders which will include users and carers, the health authority, the private sector, the voluntary and not-for-profit sector, social services departments, and local and national politicians.

To complement the MCI competences that we described above further competences for managers working in this field will include:

● managing professionals;
● managing ambiguity;
● managing in small units and non-formally appraised settings;
● managing in a contract culture;
● managing networks;
● creating and maintaining client/user involvement;
● managing change;
● coping with legislation;
● coping with ethical dilemmas;
● working with politicians;
● managing in a multi-cultural environment.

First-line managers have to possess the knowledge base that could be provided by professional training. At its starkest: 'Do you want the manager of the local supermarket to run a residential home for those with learning disabilities?'

Alastair Macnish (a deputy director of Strathclyde regional authority) recognises this tension between generic management and professional skills:

> I believe a good manager is a good manager, whatever discipline they come from. But there is an important element in managing social services that involves caring, and I would always want to see that mixture is there. I would prefer to have a social work practitioner, and provide the financial tools to play the part. (Mitchell, 1992, p. 24.)

MANAGEMENT AND PROFESSIONALS

Historically, the role of professionals within the public services has been a very important one. Certainly within the NHS doctors and consultants have played a major, if not the major, role. In local government, social workers, teachers, surveyors, lawyers and accountants have all been well represented. In local government, for example, chief executives have come up through the professional route rather than the general managerial one. The Audit Commission study of chief executives referred to above revealed that the majority of local authority chief executives were lawyers with accountants making up much of the remainder. In central government the tradition has been the specialist 'on tap' with the generalist 'on top' yet the agency initiative provides an opportunity to break with this tradition.

However, the 1980s saw an attack upon what many perceived to be the power of the professionals. It was argued, particularly by the Thatcher governments and Kenneth Clarke specifically, that the consumer or user of services should have a greater voice in deciding what services should be provided. Indeed as Fowler (1992) points out, professionalism almost became a term of abuse. The power of the professionals was perceived to be in terms of accountability to each other, effective performance decided by their peers and limited consumer choice. The producer rather than the consumer made the decisions over what services to provide. Apart from seeking to dilute the power of the professionals it was argued that in order for services to be delivered more efficiently and effectively then professionals should acquire management skills such as managing resources. There has thus been a push for clinicians or head teachers to manage their own budgets. Such developments mean new challenges for professionals but also for managers who have to work out new relationships with professionals.

The arguments of the differentialist that we discussed above, i.e. that there is something distinctive about managing in the public services, would maintain that managing in the public services has to take account of professionalism. Fowler reminds us of the value of retaining a high level of professional expertise across all functions:

> A combination of professional expertise and managerial competence is needed. It is an insult to many first class professionals to assume they are unable to think and act corporately or display the necessary management skills because of their professional identities. (Fowler, 1992, p. 12.)

The power of the professionals has been in no greater evidence than in the NHS and there are a number of problems involved in doctors taking on management roles:

- The concept of clinical freedom has to be reconciled with managing scarce resources. The doctor may have to make a decision based on financial rather than medical considerations. This goes against the grain of their medical training.
- Separate cultures and often years of mistrust will also have to be reconciled.
- Where will the parameters be set between the clinical and the management roles?
- What roles are the clinical directors being asked to perform? According to Fitzgerald (1992, p. 141) clinicians are now being asked to perform:

- **managerial roles** involving the selection of staff, assigning work and resources and appraising performance;
- **co-ordinating/liaison roles** such as proposing actions, communicating to groups and overcoming problems;
- **representative roles** including the presentation of views and advocating positions;
- **monitoring roles** to ensure standards of quality, control of expenditure and checking of output;
- **development roles in service relationships** with other collaborating agencies.

The role of clinical director as a decision maker will, according to Fitzgerald (1992, p. 142), be concerned with:

- learning to operate from a non-expert position (at least initially);
- developing a strategic approach and vision;
- learning a new language and understanding new orientations and ideologies;
- being critically dependent on others such as a business manager and staff manager;
- managing nursing and paramedics as an integral part of medical care;
- developing skills in team building and team work;
- maintaining credibility with clinical colleagues (to overcome the view that 'only poor doctors become managers').

The context, content and processes of managing in the NHS appear to be changing. Thus the changes that we discussed in the previous two chapters in terms of the creation of trusts, purchaser/provider roles and internal markets will have an impact upon the management task as the provision of health care seeks to become more efficient and effective. The task is to ground the management role in the professional role. This is a particular challenge for local government and for the NHS.

MANAGING ACROSS ORGANISATIONAL BOUNDARIES

According to Metcalfe and Richards: 'Public management is getting things done through other organizations' (1987, p. 220). Increasingly, as the boundaries between the public, private and voluntary sectors become more blurred managers will have to manage across these boundaries. Joint working is becoming increasingly important such as a local authority and the voluntary sector jointly managing a community centre. Such joint arrangements mean new forms of relationships and contracts and quasi-contracts increase in importance as the form through which such relationships are managed. The new organisational reality is made up of organisations working with each other to provide a range of services, involving for example:

- the European Commission if such funding is relevant;
- the private sector in economic development or in the provision of services such as leisure or homes for the elderly;
- the voluntary sector in terms of social services, education or care in the community.

The National Council for Voluntary Organisations (NCVO) (1993) gives examples of local authorities working with the voluntary sector in rural development, inner city regeneration, and the development of funding forums and consultative processes. Partnerships can be forged between organisations that are very diverse in terms of financial resources, size, scale of activities, purposes and so on. According to NCVO partnerships that work they have certain things in common including:

- an emphasis on quality;
- the promotion of equality of opportunity;
- a focus on a clearly defined goal;
- sensitivity to creating the right environment which will allow good communications, the creation of trust and understanding, and respect for other partners' views and roles.

The challenge of managing across different organisational boundaries also applies within the same organisation as we find more examples of purchaser–provider, customer–contractor, strategic–operational, centre–periphery splits. One problem for management is that of ensuring co-ordination as different organisations pursue different goals and have different structures and cultures. There are problems of strategic and operational/implementation fit.

One form of interacting across boundaries is through networks which contain the following characteristics:

- reciprocity and bargaining rather than hierarchy;
- recognition of the interests of different stakeholders;
- recognition of the different relationships;
- recognition of different resources in terms of power, people and time;
- mutual advantages involving complementary skills, resources, products and services;
- linkage together by technology;
- the bringing together of a group of people whether with similar interests or living in the same geographical area.

Entering a network raises some interesting questions. These are discussed in detail below.

Why enter into them in the first place?

One answer may be that political impetus and legislation encourages public sector organisations to use other organisations to deliver the actual services, as occurs with community care. Similarly, where the concept of the enabling or empowering authority is adopted, this means allowing other individuals or groups to become involved in activities that were originally the remit of the statutory sector. In so doing common goals may be recognised and the resources of other organisations utilised.

What resources are available?

Such resources may not necessarily be financial but might include expertise and information. Entering into relationships with other groups allows their expertise to be tapped.

What is the position within the network?

In some networks all the partners may be equal; in others one organisation may be dominant at the centre even though it must rely on other organisations. In Wales, for example, the role of the Welsh Office is pivotal in the workings of local government in Wales (see Boyne *et al.*, 1991). We could use the network analysis to describe the relationship between the parent department and its agencies in central government in England. The parent department plays the role of the strategic decision maker and the agencies are its operating arms. A network requires that information and power flows two ways.

How easy is access?

It is all very well to encourage different organisations to be involved in the formulation and implementation of public policy but not all groups are equal. Information and ease of access are sometimes scarce commodities. In community care users and carers may have difficulty in getting themselves organised compared to the statutory sector.

What is to be gained?

In entering a network, then, an organisation may acquire legitimacy and its views become recognised as being important. However, some groups may believe that their most important contribution can be made as autonomous bodies agitating on behalf of their members. This is a problem for some voluntary organisations who perceive that developing closer links with the statutory sector could compromise their campaigning role. There will be a tension between acting as a pressure group and providing a service.

As the public services are delivered through a range of different organisations then managers have to manage the relationships formed through these networks.

Managing across jurisdictions

Members of the network will have separate jurisdictions and will be legitimate in their own right. In community care, health care and social services come together. It may not always be clear who is responsible for what. Similarly in child care the separate concerns of the police, medical profession, social services, parents and children all with their legitimate interests will have to be managed.

Managing different stakeholders

In many areas of the public services many different groups of individuals may have an interest in a particular service. In education, for example, local and national politicians, the local education authority, the Department for Education, pupils, parents, school governors, teachers, school staff and local business men and women may have an interest in a particular education policy. The head teacher may have to balance conflicting interests of different stakeholders. Indeed, one of the distinguishing features of the public services is said to be the multiplicity of stakeholders.

Managing implementation

Managers need to bring together different specialisms to overcome the problems associated with planning and delivery. There is a need for common information, common standards, common structures and common reporting and monitoring mechanisms. There must be agreed objectives. Hogwood and Gunn (1984) indicate the conditions for 'perfect' implementation which include the notion that dependency relations are minimal. They argue that if implemenation of a policy requires that a number of different agencies be involved then the chances of success are reduced. As relationships increase the problems of managing them multiply (see pp. 128–9).

Managing collaboration

This is achieved through open exchanges of information, and through creating trust and respecting confidences. These are not easy to bring about and in the first instance may require agreements such as formal contracts to specify the rights and obligations of the different parties.

Managing across organisations is concerned with bargaining and negotiation in which different parties are seeking to maximise their gains through negotiation and mutual accommodation and avoid mutually damaging behaviour.

The challenges for managers can be summarised as follows:

- reconciling competing values and definitions;
- reconciling competing jurisdictions, both organisational and professional;
- seeking agreement in values, principles and responsibilities;
- compensating for loss of autonomy;
- solving operational problems – changing structure may be necessary but not sufficient;
- creating commitment;
- creating a currency of trust, openness and co-operation;
- developing competences of negotiation, bargaining and communication;
- opening up access, particularly for groups that have traditionally been disadvantaged;
- finding an appropriate form or mode of interaction either through flexible arrangements or through tight contract specification.

Commenting upon the implications for management arising from the community care proposals Sir Roy Griffiths argued that:

> The changes in approach are very substantial. The enabling role to my mind requires in some ways a higher degree of management skill than a providing role because it calls for a real concentration on the precise content of contracts or arrangement with third parties. It requires clarification of the outputs expected from the contract in the sense of clarity as to the quality to be achieved, standards to be attained, as well as the financial aspects. It calls for real management understanding as to how to devolve responsibility effectively and to set local budgets. (1990, p. 20.)

As we move further down the road to a contract culture then management skills need to be developed. Box 13.1 outlines advice offered by the Treasury.

Box 13.1 Guidelines offered by HM Treasury (1991) *Guide to Good Buying*

Managers must:

1 ensure that the contractor has the necessary capacity to deliver the required quality of services at the price set;
2 negotiate tough and appropriate contracts which ensure control;
3 pick contractors with adequate financial resources and technical expertise;
4 develop quality in-house expertise which can draw up specifications, frame contracts and choose and supervise contractors;
5 avoid monopoly providers;
6 make sure that security, confidentiality and privacy are not affected;
7 define properly the task that is to be bought;
8 where in-house provision make sure that appropriate service level agreements between purchasers and providers are in place.

In an ideal world then the advice given by the Treasury will be appropriate. However, there may not be providers willing or able to enter the market, thereby leading to a lack of competition. For example, the private sector may not be willing to provide those aspects of community care which require heavy expenditure on special equipment or specialised staff. Where a service is being contracted out for the first time the purchasers may not have the necessary information concerning the 'adequate financial resources and technical expertise' of new providers. Other stakeholders such as politicians or unions might also wish to influence the terms of the contract.

Management by contracts may not always be the most appropriate relationship between and within organisations. Tightly specified contracts will be inappropriate where there is a lack of perfect information or where the environment is uncertain. At the same time, to replace an informal relationship that has worked well with a tightly specified contract may undermine existing trust. Large-scale contracts may lead to a lack of flexibility and offer less choice.

De Hoog has argued that there are a number of conditions which affect the ideal contracting model:

> These conditions include (a) *the characteristics of the external environment* – especially the number of service suppliers; (b) *the level of organizational resources* (e.g. personnel, funds, time, and expertise) necessary to cover the many transaction costs involved in the contracting process; and (c) *the degree of uncertainty* about funding, future events, service technologies, and causal relationships between service outputs and desired outcomes. (1990, pp. 318–19.)

MANAGEMENT OF CHANGE

As we have seen in previous chapters management in the public services takes place within a turbulent environment and managers have to respond to this environment. In Chapter 8 we also introduced human resource strategy and the links between motivation and performance. Organisational change may be required in a number of different areas:

- changing individuals in organisations in terms of their skills, value, attitudes and behaviour. One solution is to recruit new staff altogether if the retraining of existing staff appears to be too difficult. Mellon (1993) makes the point that where the chief executives of the new Next Steps agencies are recruited from within the civil service, as most of them are, then a lifetime of civil service culture and managing through hierarchical relationships may not be sufficient to encourage a commitment to decentralisation and pushing authority and responsibility downwards;
- changing structures and systems as with decentralisation or in terms of purchaser–provider splits;
- changing processes of decision-making and resource allocation.

According to Lewin (1947) the first step of any change process is to unfreeze the present pattern of behaviour as a way of managing resistance to change. This can be achieved through promotion, terminating employment or changing structures. The second stage is to move change through alterations in behaviour, managing more participatively, and developing trust and openness. The third stage is refreezing the changes into place so that the new behaviour becomes the operating norm.

In order to achieve this Pugh (1993) argues that there are six rules for managing change effectively:

1 Work hard at establishing the need for change and make sure that any change is acceptable to all the different stakeholders.
2 Think through the change as well as think out the change, i.e. what will be the costs and benefits to all the individuals or groups who will be affected by change.
3 Initiate change through informal discussions to allow participation and to get feedback on the proposals.
4 Encourage those affected to voice their objections – do not force change on people.
5 Be prepared to change yourself. Accept that others may have good ideas about change and accept that change can start from the bottom up.
6 Monitor the change and reinforce it. Check to see if change is working and if the benefits are flowing as expected.

The Local Government Management Board has addressed the factors involved in bringing about change in local government in *Challenge and Change* (1993). They argue that change will occur as a result of the pressure of external forces such as legislation, the existence of change agents or a key event such as a change of party after an election. According to LGMB the change process will require a recognition of the need to introduce radical change, a capacity to adjust to major change whilst maintaining continuity of organisational values and culture, a clear sense of direction, a capacity to understand the changing world, and strong leadership from the centre. Strong leadership has to involve both officers and members.

Fogden (1993) describes how change was brought about in the Employment Service and suggests that change activities should:

- Be flexible enough to adapt to different labour markets and different political administrations.
- Relate directly to the changes required.
- Be coherent and co-ordinated.
- Be practicable and affordable.
- Be manageable, measurable and in prioritized steps.
- Be undertaken to reflect the new vision and values.
- Demonstrate senior management's commitment to change.
  (1993, p. 11.)

As the previous two chapters have indicated, the manager working in the public services has to manage within a turbulent environment. This requires the development of new skills which will include:

- developing a sensitivity to the diverse demands of different stakeholders, both internal and external;
- developing strategic management skills which analyse the external environment and assess internal capabilities;
- developing negotiation skills as contracts become the norm as a means of doing business;
- developing monitoring, inspection and regulatory skills for the contracts;
- becoming output rather than input driven;
- developing change management skills.

In its report, *Managing Tomorrow* (1993), the LGMB panel of inquiry into management in local government found a number of trends including:

- fewer layers of management;
- functional management replacing profession-based structures;
- core tasks becoming clearer such as continuous updating of strategy and an outwards-looking role.

The report also stressed the governance role of managers in local government:

Management will help give voice to public grievance and suggestion, and enhance the ability of citizens to acquire leverage not only in their dealings with the authority itself but with other public service providers operating in the locality. (1993, pp. 11–12.)

MANAGEMENT DEVELOPMENT

It is important to recognise that change is messy, that it will affect most people within the organisation and that a strategy for change is essential. It is also important that the change process is attended to through organisational development (OD) as we indicated in Chapter 8.

Organisational development recognises that in order to bring about change individuals have to be involved in the process of change. It is based upon the assumption that individuals respond to responsibility (remember McGregor's Theory Y in Chapter 8). It recognises the importance of groups and is concerned to increase effectiveness through team-building approaches. For organisational development to be effective it requires a learning organisation where communication is valued and where skills development is encouraged. Increasingly public sector organisations are looking to develop as learning organisations to facilitate organisational change.

Graham indicates some of the techniques that have been used in the public sector:

- customer care training;
- the encouragement of personal responsibility through:
  - career planning,
  - appraisal systems,
  - human resource strategy;

- self-managed learning;
- the integration of politicians/managers through, for example, joint training;
- the use of troubleshooting teams;
- networking;
- coaching;
- mentoring;
- lateral moves to gain experience of other departments. (Graham urges some caution here since 'in some parts of central government . . . [lateral moves] . . . resemble a game of musical chairs run by a demented pianist' (1989, p. 27).)

Kemp (1990) gives the example of organisational development in the Employment Service where job shadowing and 'buddy' schemes are used to ensure that managers who work in different offices can understand the work of other parts of the organisation.

As managers increasingly network and manage across organisational boundaries then integration of management development becomes more important. Fitzgerald (1990) illustrates the importance of overcoming professional boundaries within the NHS. With so many members of the medical profession having to develop management skills, Fitzgerald argues that joint learning is crucial. A common language needs to be developed where managers and professionals can learn from each other.

CONCLUSION

This chapter has tried to indicate some of the issues that are on the agenda as public services managers are encouraged to be more effective. We have also indicated how the concern to become better managers pervades all levels and all parts of the public services including professionals within those services. The discussion of generic management skills points up the difficulties of adopting private sector techniques without thinking through the appropriateness of those techniques for particular parts of the public services. This chapter has focused on managers. In the conclusion we return to the role of management in the wider democratic process.

FURTHER READING

In the past three or four years a number of books and articles have been published which focus on public sector management. Pollitt (1993a) offers one view of managerialism and contrasts the UK and American experiences. Willcocks and Harrow (1992) provide an edited collection of readings on public service management in a number of functional areas. The Local Government Management Board have published a growing collection of books and pamphlets on public sector management.

CHAPTER 14

Conclusion

INTRODUCTION

In previous chapters we have discussed the changing environment that public sector organisations have been forced to address. We have also examined how they have faced up to this change by focusing on their internal structures, policies and practices. Part of the response has been the emergence of an increasingly diverse public sector. In local government, for example. there are new patterns of service delivery and the all-purpose, self-sufficient authority is being replaced by local authorities characterised by diversity in terms of structure, roles and relations with other bodies. We now find:

- decentralised administration;
- the creation of cost centres;
- management buy-outs;
- direct-service organisations operating as contractors to the council as client;
- private sector firms providing services as a result of competitive tendering;
- locally managed schools.

The key phrases now being used as a way forward for public sector organisations are:

- the learning organisation;
- the innovative organisation;
- the responsive organisation;
- the adaptable organisation.

It is argued that the government of uncertainty is best done by these types of organisation rather than the traditional bureaucratic organisation (see Stewart, 1986).

THE CHANGING ENVIRONMENT

Throughout the book we have constantly emphasised that organisations operate within a changing environment and we would expect any changes within society to have an impact upon public sector organisations. Such changes may result from the following:

Demography

The projected decline in the number of young people coming on to the labour market after 1993 and the projected greater share of that market taken by women means that employers have had to rethink their employment policies. The civil service, for example, will be competing for increasingly valued groups of people, and its ability to attract them will be dependent upon how its employment packages compare with those in other public sector organisations as well as those in the private sector. As we argued in Chapter 6, the possession of a scarce resource, such as the individual's own labour, may give that individual increased bargaining power in the market-place. Similarly, the demand for more professionals with computing skills and financial and management skills may mean a higher cost labour market.

Organisations will have to recruit from those groups that are presently under-represented in the workforce – such as members of ethnic minority groups and the disabled. Organisations will have to rethink their traditional employment practices and come to more flexible arrangements. We would expect to see, therefore:

- increased use of part-time workers;
- rethinking retirement policies;
- increase in job sharing;
- increased use of short-term contracts;
- more working from home;
- improved child care facilities (see RIPA, 1988).

Social changes – post Fordism

The term 'Fordism' is derived from Henry Ford's mass production approach to the manufacture of standardised motor cars using automation and a semi-skilled workforce. The concept extends well beyond Ford's car factories. It led to the development of a society oriented towards the mass consumption of mass produced goods. Large producers produced goods to a uniform specification, and this was accompanied by mass regulation of the workforce and wage rates. It is argued that we no longer live in such a society. Instead, society has become more fragmented with numerous cleavages. Different groups of people want more customised products and production has changed to reflect this demand. The public sector does not stand in isolation from this trend. The Thatcher governments actively promoted this by encouraging competition and contracting out of services and thus creating alternatives to what were monopoly suppliers of services. We now have the enabling authority, customer orientation and the end of the 'captive user'. The idea of a local authority having one meeting a year to hand out contracts does not seem as remote as it did ten years ago.

Changing ideas

Part of the changing environment has been the debate concerning the appropriate scale, scope and size of the public sector. Old assumptions are being challenged and arguments advanced that, in theory, no part of the public sector cannot be subject to market forces. We now have prisons managed by the private sector. To what extent, therefore, does a core public service exist? Traditional arguments for state provision have included:

- the state will have to intervene when the market fails and when individuals have to be protected;
- there are certain goods, such as defence, that are public goods which benefit everybody and could not be provided by the private sector;
- it is in society's interest to have a healthy and well-educated citizenry and the state should provide health, welfare and education.

We do not intend discussing the relative merits of these and similar arguments but rather point out that such theoretical debates do have an impact upon the public services manager, particularly as the public sector is required to justify its reason for being.

At a less abstract level, traditional notions such as accountability, responsiveness or effectiveness are being challenged by competing definitions. A new language is entering the debate, that of entrepreneurialism, innovation, risk-taking and empowerment. Such developments are not without their critics. Stewart (1992), for example, argues that market and contract accountability cannot replace public accountability.

Regulation

Despite the rhetoric of devolved decision making, public services managers still operate within constraints. Under, for example, local management of schools, strategic control is still exercised by central government in curricula developments. Financial control is exercised through watchdogs such as the National Audit Office and the Audit Commission. Not only that but such bodies are seeking to exercise a greater influence and widen their brief to include value-for-money exercises. The Audit Commission, for example, is seeking to present itself as the guardian of quality public services (see *Local Government Chronicle*, 18 June 1993, p. 1).

A CHANGE IN CULTURE

All of these changes presuppose that there is a culture that can accommodate a dynamic environment. The expectations put on staff to be entrepreneurial, responsive and dynamic will not happen merely by changing the structure. If people are a major organisational resource then their perceptions will also have to change. In local government, for example, the responsive organisation requires a change in philosophy and in the core values of the organisation. It will also require a change in the values of both politicians and officials.

THE SCEPTIC'S RESPONSE

Critics question the extent to which this new agenda has taken hold and indicate the difficulties that such change brings. Thus, in a reader poll carried out by the *Municipal Review* in conjunction with the Institute of Local Government Studies in 1989, survival was ranked top of the list when asked about the policy priorities for local authorities over the next two years. Sceptical responses may also be expressed concerning the following:

Culture

As indicated above, requirements to be more responsive will have an effect upon both councillors and officers, and we wonder to what extent it will be welcomed by officers who may see their traditional power bases of professionalism and departmentalism being undermined by the increasing power of consumers.

The requirements to be more responsive has implications for the decision-making processes of the organisation and for the management task. It will mean directly involving citizens in decisions that affect them. The concept of empowering the citizen means increasing the ability of individuals and groups to take effective action on their own behalf (see Skelcher, 1993). Managers may have to give up some of their own control of the agenda. At the same time managers and professionals should not lose sight of their own professional ethos and judgement, particularly when trying to allocate scarce resources. At the same time, councillors may perceive that their authority is being undermined as the electorate have more channels open to them to express their views. Consumers will be able to express their satisfaction or dissatisfaction more directly in terms of consumer forums, customer surveys, tenant participation and so on.

Perhaps the ease of change has been overestimated. Metcalfe and Richards argue that there is a cultural lag before new ideas are put into practice so that:

> . . . the ruling ideas appropriate to an earlier age persist and continue to exert an influence on administrative behaviour and organisational structure long after the conditions in which they developed have disappeared. (1987, p. 16.)

They suggest that there is a 'disbelief' system in Whitehall that refuses to take management ideas seriously and is sceptical of reform. Perhaps also there is a wish to retain elements of the old culture or values. As Tyson argues:

> At the heart of the difficulty of developing public servants as leaders is the question of public policy objectives. The Civil Service is trying to develop managers in different

organisational cultures or climates in order to achieve diverse objectives. Most of these objectives are political and change as priorities change. An ideology of managerialism based on efficiency is not enough in motivational terms. (1990, p. 30.)

From administration to management

Although the *language* of the public sector is now concerned with performance, productivity, rationalisation, efficiency and so on, there may well still be a reluctance to embrace these ideas. Haigh and Morris argue that in large parts of the National Health Service there is a reluctance to speak this new language and that the shift from administration to management has been greeted with less than enthusiasm. They give three reasons for this:

- There is no consensus on the state of the National Health Service and hence no agreed solution to its problems.
- The groundwork necessary for the introduction of a new ethos has not been systematically undertaken.
- The move from administration to management has been lost amongst a host of other changes in funding, technology, government involvement and so on. (Haigh and Morris, 1990.)

There is also the danger that, as managers are encouraged to be more efficient and economic and desire greater 'freedom to manage', some of the traditional values associated with administration such as probity, equity and impartiality will be lost. There is still something to be said for the concept of public officials acting in the public interest. As Tyson puts it: 'There must also be a commitment to the public good, because unless there is a moral purpose to public policy, it has no intrinsic worth.' (1990, p. 30.) As we have seen in Chapter 13, management is more than the mechanical application of a set of competences which take no account of the context within which organisations operate and the values that they espouse.

Changing people

We suggested in Chapter 11 that changing people inside an organisation is one way of bringing about organisational change. However, proponents of management or human resource development may have underestimated the difficulties inherent in this:

- if power is the organisational currency then to expect senior managers to give up power to those lower down or to break up departmental empires into decentralised units is too optimistic;
- according to contingency theory the style of management should be appropriate to the context and hence it may not always be possible, or appropriate, to adopt the participative style of management that human resource development requires;

- an investment in individuals is time consuming and costly and, therefore, organisations may not feel certain that employees will stay with them long enough for the organisation to benefit;
- if efficiency and cost cutting are organisational goals then a people-centred approach may prove too expensive – training budgets are often hit first when resources are scarce;
- the commitment to a common goal is a prerequisite of human resource development, but too often a public sector organisation does not have a mission statement or a clearly defined set of core values.

ROUND AND ROUND AGAIN?

In assessing the impact of the so-called public management movement it is important to reflect on the past to examine whether these are new concerns at all. The most important examination of the civil service this century was the Fulton Report. Published in 1968, the Fulton picture of the service was one of an outdated organisation which was in need of major reform. Consider the following quotation relating to the structure of departments and the promotion of efficiency:

> Accountable management means holding individuals and units responsible for performance measured as objectively as possible. Its achievement depends upon identifying or establishing accountable units within government departments – units where output can be measured against costs or other criteria, and where individuals can be held personally responsible for their performance. (Fulton, 1968, p. 51.)

Here, it appears, is much of the public management philosophy: ideas of accountable management, performance measurement, individual responsibility for performance, etc. – also, perhaps, the seeds of the Financial Management Initiative. The Fulton committee considered the option of hiving off – the Next Steps style – and proposed an early and thorough review of the whole question (Fulton, 1968, p. 62). Many of the ideas of the new agenda are not new. Indeed Fulton was followed by attempts to implement rational techniques such as Programme Analysis and Review in the 1970s, but the resurgence of rationalism in the 1980s under the guise of managerialism has seen at least some of Fulton's aspirations realised. (See Greenwood and Wilson, 1989.)

In local government, the Bains Report provided a stimulus for performance review – what happened and why is the Local Government Management Board still encouraging it? Perhaps the answer lies in a shift in values. Under the old value systems, the possibility of the change advocated by, for example, Fulton and Bains, was limited. With a shift towards the values emphasised by, for example, Peters and Waterman these ideas can be taken on board.

THE QUALITY ORIENTATION

Despite doubts about the impact of the new managerialism upon organisations it does seem that the concept of quality as we described in Chapter 12 is firmly on the agenda. It is not only private sector organisations that are taking an interest in the quality approach: local government, the National Health Service and central government are also actively considering how they can improve the quality of their services. The stimulus of BS5750 and similar international standards, the requirements of the European Union and more demanding customers serve to place quality firmly on the agenda. The Audit Commission has set up a Quality Exchange which will enable local authorities to exchange ideas on how to improve quality, initially in a limited number of services including refuse collection, waste disposal and street cleaning. The Labour Party has promised to replace the Audit Commission with a Quality Commission to promote the quality of local government services irrespective of who provides them (Labour Party, 1989). The question remains: How can quality be delivered in a consistent and comprehensive way in an austere financial environment?

Not only that, but there are real issues concerning which stakeholders actually define quality. If organisations are to be more responsive then the user of the service will have to be involved in defining what is to count as a quality service. We still appear to be some way from this. Pollitt (1993b), for example, argues that in the NHS quality is defined by the medical profession with minimal influence from patients.

THE EUROPEAN DIMENSION

The creation of a single market for goods, services, capital and labour in Europe after 1992 has increased the impact of the European dimension on Britain's public sector organisations. Some authorities already have European liaisons and information offices and some services such as the police have close links with their European counterparts. We would expect funds from the European Union to continue to flow into Britain in the form of regional aid and development grants. Within Europe notions of harmonisation, internationalisation and liberalisation are taking hold. According to one commentator:

> Changes in perspective and in organisation will be essential for managerial success in the public sector. The worldwide trends of internationalisation, liberalisation and harmonisation will continue to require constant re-appraisal and review of the role, the functions and procedures of public sector organisations. (Phillip, 1989, p. 45.)

Europe will continue to affect the public sector in Britain in terms of the following:

- **Legislation**. As major employers, public sector organisations will be affected by legislation on health, safety and conditions of work. Trading standards and consumer protection will need to be systematised on a European basis.

- **Training**. This will have to take account of the European dimension and language training will need to be included in training programmes. A number of colleges and universities already have staff and student exchanges with similar institutions in Europe through, for example, Erasmus programmes, and there is a move to 'Europeanise' courses in business studies and public administration.
- **Public procurement**. This is one area that will have a significant impact upon the public sector. The Public Works Directive, which has been in force since 1973, requires contracts in excess of £5 million to be advertised in the European Union's Official Journal Supplement (OJS), opening up work to competition from the whole Union. Similar directives on utilities (in force since 1990) and on the supply of goods (in force in 1992) involve contracts for smaller amounts. European legislation specifies the procedures that must be followed and time limits, with clauses on contract splitting, lease backs and loan agreements. Public sector purchasing costs could fall dramatically as contracts for public works and supplies are exposed to competition from the Community.
- **Management practices**. As there are more and more managers with knowledge of, and experience in, the management practices in other countries, good practices will be shared and managers will learn from each other.

SUMMARY

The agenda will continue to be set, in part, by the wider context within which public sector organisations operate as we have indicated in this final chapter. We cannot predict how public organisations will react to change in the future and to what extent they will be instrumental in setting their own agenda. While prediction is a dangerous business, we venture to suggest that the theme of quality will continue its rise up the public sector agenda as it serves to motivate staff and develop public enthusiasm for the services offered. The challenge of the single market within Europe is one that the public sector has yet to reveal that it is capable of rising to.

Finding out more about public sector organisations

A persistent theme of this book has been change. If we look back to the mid-1970s, we find a public sector which had never heard of compulsory competitive tendering, contracting out, internal markets, customer orientation and so on. This book has covered, described and analysed these developments which dominated the debates of the 1980s and early 1990s. The student of public sector organisations studies in interesting and challenging times where the pace of change is seemingly unrelenting. The first problem that the student faces is trying to find out what is happening. This section points the reader in the direction of potential sources of information.

Each chapter of the book concludes with a guide to further reading on the topics examined in that chapter. This together with the references included in the text will enable the reader further to explore particular issues. This section will assist the reader in researching specific issues which will unfold in the 1990s. Sources of information can be listed under a number of headings.

Reference books

Basic statistical information and reference information on many public bodies is contained in *Whitaker's Almanac* (published annually); *The Statesman Yearbook* (annual) performs a similar purpose but is more international in its focus. *Public Domain: a yearbook for the public sector* (annual since 1986) reviews development in the public sector on a sector by sector basis. *Great Britain – a handbook* (annual) is aimed primarily at giving overseas readers the official line on what Britain is like. Perhaps it is more noteworthy for what is missing rather than what is included.

There are various specialist dictionaries available including *The Fontana Dictionary of Modern Thought* (1977) which, though dated, is an excellent guide to major topics in modern thinking.

Newspapers

Quality newspapers (*Daily Telegraph*, the *Guardian*, *The Financial Times*, *The Independent* and *The Times*) are an essential resource for students of the public sector. All cover major political, governmental and economic affairs in detail and will provide commentaries which reflect the political line of the paper. *The Guardian* is particularly strong on social policy issues and *The Independent* currently carries an informative column entitled 'Public Services Management' on Thursdays.

HMSO publications

Despite cutbacks in their statistical output, HMSO publications remain a rich resource for students of the public sector. Good institutional libraries will hold most important HMSO publications and many will employ specialist staff who can advise on how the collection is organised. Among the potential sources of information are:

- Annual publications including *Civil Service Statistics*, *The Civil Service Yearbook*, the *Guide to Official Statistics*, the *Guide to Public Sector Financial Information*, *Public Bodies*;
- Parliamentary debates;
- Select Committee Reports;
- Green and White Papers. Bills and Acts of Parliament;
- publications by government departments including departmental annual reports.

European documents

As the impact of the European Union takes on increasing importance, students will have to make increasing reference to European documentation. At present there are 48 European Documentation Centres in the United Kingdom which act as depositories for all documents published by EU institutions. These documents include periodicals, annual reports, monographs, bibliographies and non-published material such as commission documents and the *Official Journal*.

Weekly and monthly publications

Throughout the public sector there is a range of weekly and monthly publications (for example by professional bodies and collaborative organisations such as the local authorities associations) which are aimed at specialist subject areas. These are useful because they will inform the reader of developments in their area, summarise and discuss legislative proposals, and debate key issues.

Academic journals

Academic journals provide the reader with informed analysis based on the latest research. Because they can publish more quickly than books, they are often a fruitful source of the latest thinking in a given area. Most academic journals will ensure quality by referring articles to suitably qualified experts in the area for comments and approval. Most journals include book reviews. In this area, the major journals include *Public Administration* (quarterly), *Public Policy and Administration* (published quarterly by the Public Administration Committee) and *Local Government Studies* (published quarterly by the Institute of Local Government Studies). *Public Money and Management* (quarterly) contains short articles by academics, practitioners and consultants on many issues that were raised in the later chapters in this book.

Textbooks

At the introduction to most courses of study, the teacher will recommend a textbook. Textbooks aim to introduce the subject area and will normally refer the reader to further reading in particular areas. Normally they do not aim to present a particular view but because of the very nature of topics in the social and political sciences, the choice about what to include and what to exclude, and how the material is presented, will reflect what the authors consider to be the main issues. The major texts relating to public sector organisations are referenced at the end of the relevant chapters in this book.

Readers

Readers can take many forms. For example, they may be collections of essays demonstrating approaches or presenting case studies on a particular subject. Alternatively, they may take the form of a book reflecting the approach of the author.

Research books

The most specialised form of book is the research book. This will be highly specific and located within a particular subject area and an approach to study. Often research books will review the existing literature on the subject and then present the findings of the actual research. Conclusions from the research will be presented and can be constructively criticised by examining how the research was conducted and whether the conclusions are valid ones. It is usually inappropriate to read research books until you are familiar with the general subject area.

In-house documents

Local authorities are required by law to place much information, including annual reports, plans, minutes of meetings and reports, in the public domain. You may be able to get access to other documents, for example organisational charts, if inquiries are made. These can be particularly useful as they will indicate the latest practice.

People

The oft repeated maxim that 'an organisation's most important asset is its people' usually holds true for the inquiring mind. The researcher can consult teachers, librarians and practitioners.

Good teachers will provide detailed reading lists together with advice on how to use them. Such lists can only summarise the available work on a topic – if you require more specific references then ask. If you have specific inquiries about the work of a particular author. you will usually find that details of their employing organisation are mentioned in the work.

Each library will organise its collection in a specific way. Make use of organised tours of libraries with which you are unfamiliar. Many libraries employ subject specialists who are qualified in a subject area as well as librarianship and are worth their weight in gold. Get to know them and the services they offer. You may find that they keep indexes on topics of frequent interest and may offer special facilities for those studying on a part-time basis. If you are undertaking a major project, you will need to conduct a literature search. This is a major undertaking on which librarians will advise you.

Inside large organisations there will be people specialising in collecting data, managing, studying the environment, evaluating policies, etc. Usually specialists are more than willing to discuss their work if they are asked politely. Make sure that you prepare properly: read around the subject, prepare a set of questions, and approach your interviewee politely.

As well as public sector organisations, there are other organisations which are among the so-called policy communities which can provide useful information. For example, local authorities belong to local authority associations and regional networks who may assist you by providing information. The Local Government Management Board and the Institute of Health Service Management publish management papers and specialist academic bodies such as the Institute of Local Government Studies (University of Birmingham) and the School for Advanced Urban Studies (University of Bristol) publish influential papers.

Exercises

DECISION-MAKING EXERCISE

This exercise is designed to develop an understanding of the different approaches to decision making within society and within organisations.

Read the statements below quickly and register an immediate response. You have a choice of five responses:

(a) I strongly agree with this.
(b) In general I agree with this.
(c) I am unsure.
(d) In general terms I disagree with this.
(e) I strongly disagree with this.

Responses

1 2 3 4 5 6 7 8 9 10 11 12 13 14 15 16

1 At one time decisions are made in one way but at other times in a different way. It all depends upon the issue.
2 In order to understand how decisions are made it is necessary to recognise that the power of the organisation is divided between a number of different groups and individuals.
3 The decision-making process in your organisation is dominated by a small group of individuals with little access to this group for anybody else.
4 Your boss consults you on all decisions.
5 Your boss never consults you on any decision.
6 You feel like a small cog in a large machine.
7 Civil service mandarins really run the country.
8 In local government chief officers have all the power.
9 Power in Britain is in the hands of the people.
10 Those with positions of authority within organisations should make all the decisions.
11 Decision making in your organisation is made by a few cronies behind closed doors.
12 The decisions made in your organisation are the result of careful deliberation of all the issues and involvement of all the people that have an interest in the issue.

13 Central government always decides.
14 The elected representatives of the people should make decisions.
15 It should be experts that make all the decisions in public sector organisations in Britain.
16 There should be more discretion in your organisation.

What to do now

Take the statements and group them according to your responses to them. Ask yourself the following questions:

1   What is it that the statements I agree with have in common?
2   What is it that makes the statements I agree with similar and yet different from those that I disagree with?
3   Are the explanations offered by the pluralists or the élitists any use here?

BUREAUCRACY EXERCISE

Consider each of the following scales. Indicate on the scale (where 1 = very closely and 5 = not at all closely) how closely your organisation approximates to the end of each scale.

formal rules	1	2	3	4	5	informal rules
job descriptions	1	2	3	4	5	unspecified duties
written communication	1	2	3	4	5	oral communication
specialised functions	1	2	3	4	5	workers are generalists
clear hierarchy	1	2	3	4	5	fluid organisational form
criteria for promotion	1	2	3	4	5	no criteria for promotion
permanent appointments	1	2	3	4	5	temporary appointments

Low scores indicate that the organisation approximates closely to the bureaucratic form: high scores indicate the lack of bureaucratic structures. Compare and contrast your answers with someone from a different organisation and establish what differences there are and what you have found in common.

Bureaucracy may be a suitable form of organisation for the completion of many tasks: however it may be inappropriate for the completion of others. Ask yourself the following questions in relation to your organisation:

1   Are clear rules which are not open to ambiguity good for the organisation, or would greater flexibility and discretion assist effectiveness?
2   Do explicit job descriptions assist the organisation in setting out who is responsible for what, or do they hamper efficiency by requiring specific tasks to be done by specific people, thus slowing the process down?

3 Does written communication and record keeping lead to precision and accuracy, or does it just generate huge amounts of paper that is never read?

4 Would the organisation benefit from specialists, for example in housing, lettings officers, repairs clerks, etc., or would it benefit from staff having training in a wide range of tasks and could answer public queries more quickly?

5 Is it beneficial for the organisation to have clear chains of command so that decisions can be referred up the hierarchy to the appropriate person, or would it benefit from a more flexible form where structures are based on the particular task in hand?

6 Would the organisation benefit from having clearly established criteria for promotion, such as having attained certain qualifications or having performed certain tasks, or would this mean that young and talented people cannot get promotion because experienced but less able staff are above them in the queue?

7 Is a system of appointments on a permanent basis good for the organisation in that it assists in the provision of a permanent expertise, or would short-term appointment motivate staff and see a continuing flow of ideas into the organisation?

The answers that you give will depend upon a number of factors, including the type of organisation that you work in, the culture of the organisation, the perspective from which you view the organisation – you may find that colleagues in similar positions give different answers. It is important to remember that different *forms* of organisation may be appropriate to different *types* of organisation.

ECONOMY, EFFICIENCY AND EFFECTIVENESS EXERCISE

This exercise will assist you to understand how your organisation is using the three E's: economy, efficiency and effectiveness. Before you do the exercise you should have read Chapter 12. As most public sector organisations undertake a large number of complex tasks, it is important that you select one activity for your study.

Task 1

By referring to published documents, for example policy plans or annual reports, establish the aims and objectives of the activity that you have chosen. Summarise these in Box 4 in Figure B.1 with a number of statements which indicate what the organisation intends to achieve.

Task 2

Using the systems approach that we discussed in Chapter 4, consider the inputs to the process, the process whereby inputs are transformed into outputs, and the outputs from the process. Prepare these in the form of simple lists of inputs, activities and outputs and note these in Boxes 1, 2 and 3 respectively in Figure B.1.

Task 3

You now need to collect information on performance measurement. Prepare a list of activities that are measured. Identify which of the following categories each of the measures falls into:

1 Measures of inputs.
2 Measures of inputs in relation to outputs.
3 Measures of outputs in relation to objectives.

Enter these into the appropriate boxes.

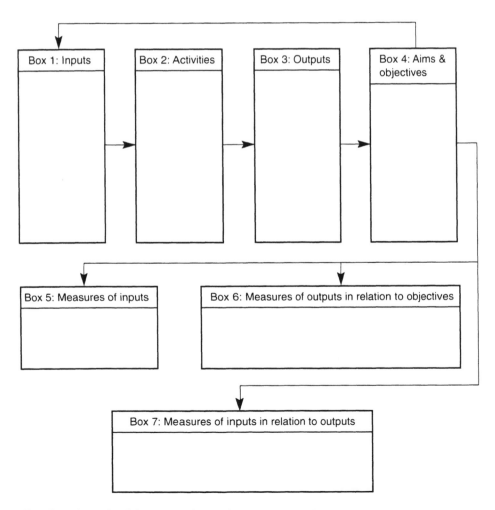

Fig. B.1 A method for considering improvement

Task 4

You now have a picture of how your organisation measures its performance of the task that you have chosen. Examine Figure B.1 and consider whether it emphasises the pursuit of economy, efficiency or effectiveness. You will need to consider *who* uses the information and *how* they use it. All such information should be used to improve performance. Some questions you might ask are:

- are the opinions of employees and customers solicited?
- is the information used to compare performance over time or with other organisations?
- does your organisation formulate action plans to set targets for improved performance?

Task 5

Consider how your organisation could improve its performance measurement. How could it improve its effectiveness? How could it improve the quality of the service?

LEADERSHIP EXERCISE

Below are a number of statements for you to consider. Your response should be from 1–5 where:

1 = agree strongly
5 = disagree strongly.

When you have made your choice, circle the appropriate number

Questions

		Agree strongly				Disagree strongly
1	Managers should manage and not delegate responsibility.	1	2	3	4	5
2	The participative style of leadership is not appropriate for your organisation.	1	2	3	4	5
3	Most employees are at work only for the money.	1	2	3	4	5
4	The manager should set a good example.	1	2	3	4	5
5	The manager should provide a vision for the organisation.	1	2	3	4	5
6	It is the role of the politician to provide the goals of the organisation.	1	2	3	4	5

7	The manager should always consult her staff.	1	2	3	4	5
8	Junior staff should be encouraged to use their own judgement.	1	2	3	4	5
9	Anyone not pulling their own weight should be sacked immediately.	1	2	3	4	5
10	Any personal differences between staff should be sorted out between themselves.	1	2	3	4	5
11	The manager should defend his staff to his colleagues.	1	2	3	4	5
12	Those with knowledge should be deferred to whatever their position within the organisation.	1	2	3	4	5
13	The manager should try out new ideas with staff.	1	2	3	4	5
14	Poor work should be criticised.	1	2	3	4	5
15	All members of the department should be treated as equals.	1	2	3	4	5

Once you have responded to the statements, give your boss a copy and ask him or her to respond to them. Then compare the two sets of responses and answer the following questions:

1 Are your perceptions of the manager's role the same as your managers? If not, why not?
2 What is your preferred style of leadership, judging by your responses? Is it autocratic or participative? Is it the same as your manager's perception?
3 Would the modern theory of leadership discussed in Chapter 7 work in your organisation? If not, why not?

BIBLIOGRAPHY

Aberach, J.D. and Rockman, B.A. (1988). 'Image IV Revisited: Executive and Political Roles', *Governance*, Vol. 1, No. 1, pp. 1–25.

Aberach, J.D., Putman, R.D. and Rockman, B.A. (1981). *Bureaucrats and Politicians in Western Democracies*, Cambridge, Mass.: Harvard University Press.

Ackerman, L. (1985). 'Leadership vs. Management', *Leadership and Organization Development Journal*, Vol. 6, No. 2, pp. 17–19.

Adams, J.S. (1965). 'Injustice in Social Exchange', in Berkowitz, L. (ed.), *Advances in Experimental Social Psychology*, London: Academic Press.

Adler, M. and Asquith, S. (eds) (1981). *Discretion and Welfare*, London: Heinemann Educational Books.

Albrow, M. (1970). *Bureaucracy*, London: Macmillan.

Alexander, A. (1982). *Local Government in Britain since Reorganisation*, London: Allen & Unwin.

Argenti, J. (1980). *Practical Corporate Planning*, London: Allen & Unwin.

Argyris, C. (1957). *Personality and Organization*, New York: Harper & Row.

Argyris, C. (1990). *Overcoming Organizational Defenses: Facilitating Organizational Learning*, Boston: Allyn & Bacon.

Armstrong, R. (1985). 'Ministers, Politicians and Public Servants', *Public Money*, September, pp. 39–43.

Audit Commission (1985). *Good Management in Local Government: successful practice and action*, London: Audit Commission.

Audit Commission (1986). *Performance Review in Local Government: a handbook for auditors and local authorities*, London: HMSO.

Audit Commision (1988). *Administrative Support for Operational Police Officers*, Policy Papers No. 1, May. London: Audit Commission.

Audit Commission (1989a). *Managing Services Effectively – Performance Review*, London: HMSO.

Audit· Commission (1989b). *Management Paper No. 3: Better Financial Management*, London: Audit Commission.

Audit Commission (1989c). *Management Paper No. 2: More Equal Than Others: The Chief Executive in Local Government*, London: Audit Commission.

Audit Commission (1992). *Citizen's Charter indicators: charting a course*, London: HMSO.

Bacharach, S.B. and Lawler, E.J. (1980). *Power and Politics in Organizations: The Social Psychology of Conflict, Coalitions and Bargaining*, San Fransisco: Jossey-Bass.

Bachrach, P. and Baratz, M.S. (1962). 'Two Faces of Power', *American Political Science Review*, Vol. 56(4), pp. 942–52.

Bains Committee (1972). *The New Local Authorities: Management and Structure*, London: Department of the Environment.

Banks, T. (1990). 'Public management: the needs of managers and policy makers,' *Public Money & Management*.

Banner, D.K. and Blasingame, J.W. (1988). 'Towards a Developmental Paradigm of Leadership', *Leadership and Organization Development Journal*, Vol. 9, No. 4, pp. 7–16.

Barratt, J. and Downs, J. (1988). *Organising for Local Government – a local political responsibility*, London: Longman.

Barrett, S. and Fudge, C. (1981). *Policy and Action*, London: Methuen.

Barrett, S. and McMahon, L. (1990). 'Public Management in Uncertainty: a micro-political perspective of the health service in the United Kingdom', *Policy and Politics*, Vol. 18, No. 4, pp. 257–68.

Bartlett, W. (1991). 'Quasi-markets and Contracts: A Markets and Hierarchies Perspective on NHS Reform', *Public Money & Management*, Autumn, pp. 53–61.

Beetham, D. (1987). *Bureaucracy*, Milton Keynes: Open University Press.

Behrens, R. (1989). 'Equality of Opportunity in the Civil Service', *Public Money & Management*, Winter, pp. 43–8.

Bell, L. (1990). 'Social Service Departments: preparing for the 1990s', *Public Money & Management*, Spring, pp. 23–5.

Benefits Agency (1992), *Benefits Agency Business Plan 1992/3*, London: Benefits Agency.

Benn, T. (1980). 'Manifestos and Mandarins', *Policy and Practice: the experience of government*, London: Royal Institute of Public Administration.

Bennis, W. (1966). *Beyond Bureaucracy: Essays in the development and evaluation of human organisations*, New York: McGraw-Hill.

Birkinshaw, P. (1988). 'Open Government – Local Government Style', *Public Policy and Administration*, Vol. 3, No. 1, pp. 46–55.

Blake, R.B. and Mouton, J.S. (1964). *The Managerial Grid*, Houston, Texas: Gulf Publishing.

Blau, P.M. (1963). *The Dynamics of Bureaucracy: a study of interpersonal relations in two government agencies*, Chicago: The University of Chicago Press.

Blau, P.M. and Scott, R.W. (1963). *Formal Organisations: A Comparative Approach*, London: Routledge & Kegan Paul.

Bone, D. and Griggs, R. (1989). *Quality at Work*, London: Kogan Page.

Boyne, G.A., Griffiths, M.P., Lawton, A. and Law, J. (1991). *Local Government in Wales: Its Role and Functions*, York: Joseph Rowntree Foundation.

Bradford, D.L. and Cohen, A.R. (1984). *Managing for Excellence: the guide to developing high performance in contemporary organisations*, London, New York: J.Wiley & Sons.

Braverman, H. (1974). *Labor and Monopoly Capital: the degradation of work in the 20th century*, Monthly Review Press.

Bridges, Sir E. (1950). *Portrait of a Profession*, Cambridge: Cambridge University Press.

Brimelow, E. (1981). 'Women in the Civil Service', *Public Administration*, Vol. 59, Autumn, pp. 313–35.

Brown R.G.S. and Steel D.R. (1979). *The Administrative Process in Britain*, London: Methuen.

Bruce-Gardyne, J. (1986). *Ministers and Mandarins: Inside the Whitehall Village*, Sidgwick & Jackson.

Burch, M. and Wood, B. (1990). *Public Policy in Britain*, Oxford: Martin Robertson.

Burgoyne, J. (1989). 'Creating the Managerial Portfolio: Building on Competency Approaches to Management Development', *Management Education and Development*, Vol. 20, Part 1, pp. 56–61.

Burns, T. and Stalker, G.M. (1961). *The Management of Innovation*, London: Tavistock.

Butcher, T. (1984). 'Public Administration and Policy Studies', in Englefield, D. and

Drewry, G. (eds), *Information Sources in Politics and Political Science: a survey worldwide*, London: Butterworth.

Cabinet Office (1987). 'The Challenge of Change in the Civil Service', *A report on the work of the Management and Personnel Office*, London: HMSO.

Cabinet Office: Office of the Minister for the Civil Service (1988). *Service to the Public*, Occasional Paper, London: HMSO.

Callender, C. and Pearson, R. (1989). 'Managing in the 1990's: the challenge of demographic change', *Public Money & Management*, Autumn, pp. 11–17.

Campbell, C. and Guy Peters, B.G. (1988). 'The Politics/Administration Dichotomy: Death or Merely Change', *Governance*, Vol. 1, No. 1, pp. 79–99.

Carvel, J. (1984). *Citizen Ken*, London: Chatto & Windus.

Cassels, J.S. (1983). 'Civil Servants and Management', *Management in Government*, No. 1, pp. 2–19.

Central Transport Consultative Committee (1990). Annual Report 1989/90, London: Central Transport Consultative Committee.

Chandler, J.A. (1986). *Public Policy-Making for Local Government*, London: Croom Helm.

Chapman, L. (1979). *Your Disobedient Servant: The continuing story of Whitehall's overspending*, Harmondsworth: Penguin.

Chapman, R.A. (1984). *Leadership in the British Civil Service*, Beckenham: Croom Helm.

Chapman, R.A. (1988). 'The Next Steps: A Review', *Public Policy and Administration*, Vol. 3, No. 3, pp. 3–10.

Chapman, R.A. and Greenaway, J.R. (1980). *The Dynamics of Administrative Reform*, London: Croom Helm.

Chapman, R.A. and Hunt, M. (eds) (1987). *Open Government*, London, New York, Sydney: Croom Helm.

Chell, E. (1987). *The Psychology of Behaviour in Organisations*, London: Macmillan.

Child, J. (1977). *Organisation: A Guide to Problems and Practice*, London, New York: Harper & Row.

Citizen's Charter: First report (1992). London: HMSO Cm 2101.

Clarke, M. and Stewart, J. (1988). *Managing Tomorrow*, Luton: Local Government Training Board.

Clarke, R. and McGuinness, T. (1987). 'Introduction', in *The Economics of the Firm*, Oxford: Basil Blackwell.

Clegg, S. (1993). 'Efficiency Rules, OK? Weber and economic enterprise alternatives', in Hill, M. (ed.), *The Policy Process: a reader*, London: Harvester Wheatsheaf, pp. 121–34.

Clode, D. (1992). 'A New Wave Manager', *Community Care*, 15 October, pp. 16–17.

Connolly, W.E. (1974). *The Terms of Political Discourse*, Heath & Co.

Constable, J. and McCormick, R. (1987). *The Making of British Managers*, BIM/CBI.

Cousins, C. (1987). *Controlling Social Welfare*, Brighton: Wheatsheaf.

Cox, A., Furlong, P. and Page, E. (1985). *Power in Capitalist Society: Theory, Explanations and Cases*, Brighton: Wheatsheaf.

Crosby, P. (1984). *Quality without Tears: The art of hassle free management*, New York: McGraw-Hill.

Crossman, R. (1979). *The Crossman Diaries: Selections from the Diaries of a Cabinet Minister 1964–1970*, London: Magnum.

Crozier, M. (1964). *The Bureaucratic Phenomena*, London: Tavistock.

Curwen, P. (1986). *Public Enterprise: A modern approach*, Brighton: Wheatsheaf.

Cyert, R.M. and March, J.G. (1963). *A Behavioural Theory of the Firm*, Englewood Cliffs, New Jersey: Prentice-Hall.

Dahl, R.A. (1961). *Who Governs? Democracy and Power in an American City*, New Haven, Conn.: Yale University Press.

Davies, A. and Willman, J. (1991). *What Next? Agencies, Departments and the Civil Service*, London: Institute of Public Policy Research.

Davies, M.R. (1988). 'Promoting Organisational Change: Organisational Development as an Approach to Training', *Teaching Public Administration*, Vol. VIII, No. 1, pp. 29–42.

Davis, K.C. (1969). *Discretionary Justice*, Louisiana State University Press.

Dawson, S. (1988). *Analysing Organisations*, London: Macmillan.

Day, P. and Klein, R. (1987). *Accountabilities: five public services*, London: Tavistock.

Dearlove, J. (1979). *The Reorganisation of British Local Government: Old orthodoxies and a political perspective*, Cambridge: Cambridge University Press.

De Hoog, R.H. (1990). 'Competition, Negotiations or Cooperation: Three Models for Service Contracting', *Administration and Society*, Vol. 22, No. 3, pp. 317–40.

Deming, W.E. (1986). *Out of Crisis: Quality, Productivity and Competitive Position*, Cambridge: Cambridge University Press.

Department of Education and Science (1989). *Developments in the Appraisal of Teachers*, Report by HM Inspectorate, London: HMSO.

Department of Employment Group. *Developing People in the Employment Department Group: A Human Resource Development Strategy*, London: HMSO.

Department of Social Security (1988). *The Business of Service*, Report of the Regional Organisation Scrutiny, London: HMSO.

Department of Social Security (1989). *Department of Social Security Agency Study*, London: HMSO.

Department of Social Security (1992). *Market Testing*, Issue 1, Leeds: Department of Social Security.

Department of Transport (1983). *Railway Finances*, Report of a Committee chaired by Sir David Serpell, London: HMSO.

Doern, G.B. (1993). 'The UK Citizen's Charter: origins and implementation in three agencies', *Policy and Politics*, Vol. 21, No. 1, pp. 17–29.

Doig, A. (1985). 'Corruption in the Public Service: The Case of the Property Services Agency', *Public Money*, March, pp. 43–7.

Dopson, S. and Stewart, R. (1990). 'Public and Private Sector Management: The case for a wider debate', *Public Money & Management*, Spring, pp. 37–40.

Downs, A. (1967). *Inside Bureaucracy*, Boston: Little, Brown.

Downs, J. (1983). 'Organisational Development: Making Change Happen', *RIPA Report*, Spring, Vol. 4, No. 1.

Dror, Y. (1988). 'Options for Increasing Innovativeness', in Schaefer, G.F. and McInemy, E. (eds), *Strengthening Innovativeness in Public Sector Management*, Maastricht: European Institute of Public Administration.

Dunleavy, P. (1985). 'Bureaucrats, Budgets and the Growth of the State; Reconstructing an Instrumental Model', *British Journal of Political Science*, Vol. 15, pp. 299–328.

Dunleavy, P. (1990). 'Introduction: prospects for British politics in the 1990s', in Dunleavy, P., Gamble, A. and Peele, G. (eds), *Developments in British Politics 3*, London: Macmillan, pp. 1–14.

Dunleavy, P. and Rhodes, R.A.W. (1988). 'Government beyond Whitehall', in *Developments in British Politics 2* (revised edition), London: Macmillan.

Dunsire, A. (1984). 'The levels of politics', in Leftwich, A. (ed.) *What is Politics?*, Oxford: Blackwell, pp. 85–105.

Efficiency Unit (1988). *Improving Management in Government: The Next Steps*, London: HMSO.

Elcock, H. (1986). *Local Government: Politicians, professionals and the public in local authorities*, London: Methuen.

Elcock, H. and Jordan, G. (eds) (1987). *Learning from Local Authority Budgeting*, Aldershot: Avebury.

Elcock, H., Jordan, G. and Midwinter, A. with Boyne, G. (1989). *Budgeting in Local Government: Managing the margins*, Harlow: Longman.

Elcock, H. (1990). *Change and Decay? Public Administration in the 1990s*, London: Longman.

Englefield, D. and Drewry, G. (eds) (1984). *Information Sources in Politics and Political Science: A survey worldwide*, London: Butterworth.

English, G. (1990). 'Total Quality in the Public Services', *Total Quality Management*, June.

Etzioni-Halevy, E. (1985). *Bureaucracy and Democracy: A political dimension*, London: Routledge & Kegan Paul.

Falcon, D. (1989). 'Reflections', *RIPA Report*, Winter, p. 2.

Fayol, H. (1949). *General and Industrial Management*, London: Pitman.

Ferguson, K. and Lapsley, I. (1989). 'Resource Management in the NHS: The information requirements of hospital doctors', *Public Money & Management*, Winter, pp. 21–5.

Fiedler, F.E.A. (1967). *A Theory of Leadership Effectiveness*, New York: McGraw-Hill.

Fisch, R. (1988). 'The Entrepreneurial Senior Official', in Schaefer, G.F. and McInemy, E. (eds), *Strengthening Innovativeness in Public Sector Management*, Maastricht: European Institute of Public Administration.

Fitzgerald, L. (1990). 'Management Development in the NHS: Crossing professional boundaries', *Public Money & Management*, Spring, pp. 31–5.

Fitzgerald, L. (1992). 'Clinicians Into Management: On the Change Agenda or Not?', *Health Services Management Research*, Vol. 5, No. 2, pp. 137–46.

Flynn, N. (1990). *Public Sector Management*, London: Harvester Wheatsheaf.

Fogden, M.E.G. (1993). 'Managing Change in the Employment Service', *Public Money & Management*, April–June, pp. 9–16.

Forster, D. and Hadley, R. (1989). 'The NHS Reforms: Conditions for Successful Change', *Health Services Management*, October, pp. 215–18.

Fowler, A. (1988a). *Human Resource Management in Local Government*, Harlow: Longman.

Fowler, A. (1988b). 'New Directions in Performance Pay', *Personnel Management*, November, pp. 30–4.

Fowler, A. (1992). 'An Officer and a Professional', *Local Government Chronicle*, 23 October, p. 12.

Fraser, D. (1973). *The Evolution of the British Welfare State: A history of social policy since the industrial revolution*, London: Macmillan.

Fry, G., Flynn, A., Gray, A., Jenkins, W. and Rutherford, B. (1988). 'Symposium on Improving Management in Government', *Public Administration*, Vol. 66, No. 4, pp. 429–45.

Fudge, C. and Gustafsson, L. (1989). 'Administrative Reform and Public Management in Sweden and the United Kingdom', *Public Money & Management*, Summer, pp. 29–34.

Fulton, Lord (1968). *The Civil Service*, Vol. 1, Report of the Committee, London: HMSO Cmnd. 3638.

Gamble, A. (1988). *The Free Economy and the Strong State: The politics of Thatcherism*, London: Macmillan.

Garratt, B. (1987). *The Learning Organisation: and the need for directors who think*, Aldershot: Gower.

Garrett, J. (1972). *The Management of Government*, Harmondsworth: Penguin.

Geeson, T. and Haward, J. (1990). 'Devolved Management – The Berkshire Experience', *Local Government Studies*, January/February, pp. 1–9.

Goldsmith, M. and Newton, K. (1986). 'Local Government Abroad', in Widdicombe, D. (ed.), *Committee of Inquiry into the Conduct of Local Authority Business*, Research Volume IV, London: HMSO Cmnd. 9797.

Golembiewski, R.T. (1977). *Public Administration as a Developing Discipline*, New York, Basel: Marcel Dekker.

Gouldner, A.W. (1954). *Patterns of Industrial Bureaucracy*, New York: The Free Press.

Graham, A. (1989). 'Management Development in the Public Sector', *Public Money & Management*, Autumn, pp. 25–33.

Gray, A. and Jenkins, W.I. (1985). *Administrative Politics in British Government*, Brighton: Wheatsheaf.

Greenwood, J. and Wilson, D. (1989). *Public Administration in Britain Today*, London: Unwin Hyman.

Greenwood, R. (1987). 'Managerial Strategies in Local Government', *Public Administration*, Vol. 65, No. 3, pp. 295–312.

Greenwood, R. and Stewart, J. (1985). 'The Key to Excellence? An introduction to Local Government Training Board', *Excellence and Local Government*, Luton: Local Government Training Board.

Greenwood, R. and Stewart, J.D. (1986). 'The Institutional and Organisational Capabilities of Local Government', *Public Administration*, Vol. 64, No. 1, pp. 35–50.

Greenwood, R., Smith, S. and Street, J. (1992). *Deciding Factors in British Politics: a case studies approach*, London: Routledge.

Grey, A. (1983). 'Public Service Ethics', *RIPA Report*, Vol. 4, No. 4, pp. 8–9.

Griffiths, P. (1987). 'Mid-Glamorgan County Council', in Elcock, H. and Jordan, G. (eds), *Learning from Local Authority Budgeting*, Aldershot: Avebury.

Griffiths, Sir R. (1983). *NHS Management Inquiry*, London: Department of Health and Social Security.

Griffiths, Sir R. (1988). *Community Care: Agenda for Action*, London: HMSO.

Gunn, L. (1987). 'Perspectives on Public Management', in Kooiman, J. and Eliassen, K.A. (eds), *Managing Public Organisations: Lessons from Contemporary European Experience*, London: Sage.

Hadley, R. and Young, K. (1990). *Creating a Responsive Public Service*, Brighton: Harvester Wheatsheaf.

Haigh, R.H. and Morris, D.S. (1990). 'The NHS: The Administration-Management Interface, A Test to Destruction?', *Teaching Public Administration*, Vol. X, No. 1, pp. 47–53.

Hales, C.P. (1986). 'What Do Managers Do? A Critical Review of the Evidence', *Journal of Management Studies*, Vol. 23, No. 1, pp. 88–115.

Hall, R.H. (1972). *Organizations: Structure and Process*, Englewood Cliffs, New Jersey: Prentice-Hall.

Hall, R. and Quinn, R.E. (eds) (1983). *Organisational Theory and Public Policy*, Beverly Hills and London: Sage.

Ham, C. and Hill, M. (1984). *The Policy Process in the Modern Capitalist State*, Brighton: Wheatsheaf.

Hambleton, R. (1986). *Rethinking Policy Planning: a study of planning systems linking central and local government*, Bristol: School for Advanced Urban Studies.

Hambleton, R. and Hoggett, P. (eds) (1984). *The Politics of Decentralisation: Theory and Practice of a Radical Local Government Initiative*, Bristol: School for Advanced Urban Studies.

Hancox, A., Worrall, L. and Pay, J. (1989). 'Developing a Customer Orientated Approach to Service Delivery: The Wrekin Approach', *Local Government Studies*, Vol. 15, No. 1, pp. 16–25.

Handy, C. (1985). *Understanding Organisations*, Harmondsworth: Penguin.

Handy, C. (1987). *The Making of Managers*, VISC/NEDO/BIM.

Handy, C. (1990). *Inside Organisations*, London: BBC Books.

Harrison, A. and Gretton, J. (eds) (1987). *Reshaping Central Government*, Berkshire: Policy Journals (Hermitage).

Harrison, A. (1993). *From Hierarchy to Contract*, Hermitage: Policy Journals.

Harrison, S. (1988). *Managing the NHS*, London: Chapman & Hall.

Haynes, R.J. (1980). *Organisation Theory and Local Government*, London: Allen & Unwin.

Haywood, S. and Day, C. *Introduction to Health Services Management*, Birmingham: University of Birmingham Health Services Management Centre.

Heald, D. (1983). *Public Expenditure*, Oxford: Martin Robertson.

Health Care Wales (1989). Issue 5 December.

Heclo, H. and Wildavsky, A. (1981). *The Private Government of Public Money*, London: Macmillan.

Heffron, F. (1989). *Organisation Theory and Public Organisations*, New Jersey: Prentice-Hall.

Henley, Sir D., Holtham, C., Likierman, A. and Perrin, J. (1983). *Public Sector Accounting and Financial Control*, Wokingham: Van Nostrand Reinhold.

Hennessy, P. (1989a). *Whitehall*, London: Secker & Warburg.

Hennessy, P. (1989b). 'The Ethic of the Profession', *FDA GCHQ Lecture*, London: Royal Commonwealth Society.

Herriot, P. (1992). *The Career Management Challenge: balancing individual and organisational needs*, London: Sage.

Herzberg, F. (1966). *Work and the Nature of Man*, Cleveland and New York: World Publishing Co.

Hinings, C.R., Greenwood, R. and Ranson, S. (1975). 'Contingency Theory and the Organisation of Local Authorities: Part II Contingencies and Structure', *Public Administration*, Vol. 53, pp. 169–90.

HM Prison Service (1993a). *Framework Document*, London: Home Office.

HM Prison Service (1993b). *Strategic Plan*, London: Home Office.

HM Prison Service (1993c). *Business Plan*, London: Home Office.

HM Treasury (1991). *Competing for Quality*, London: HMSO.

HM Treasury (1992). *Executive Agencies: A Guide to Setting Targets and Measuring Performance*, London: HMSO.

Hoggett, P. (1991). 'A New Management in the Public Sector?', *Policy and Politics*, Vol. 19, No. 4, pp. 243–56.

Hoggett, P. and Vince, R. (1988). 'Organising for a Change', *Local Government Studies*, Vol. 14, No. 2, pp. 11–17.

Hogwood, B. (1992). *Trends in British Public Policy: do governments make any difference?*, Buckingham: Open University Press.

Hogwood, B.W. (1987). *From Crisis to Complacency? Shaping Public Policy in Britain*, Oxford: Oxford University Press.

Hogwood, B.W. and Gunn, L. (1984). *Policy Analysis for the Real World*, Oxford: Oxford University Press.

Homans, G.C. (1950). *The Human Group*, New York: Harcourt, Brace and World.

Home Office (1989a). *Magistrates' Courts: Report of a Scrutiny 1989*, Volume 1: The Management and Funding of the Magistrates' Courts, London: HMSO.

Home Office (1989b). Report on the Work of the Prison Service, London: HMSO Cm 835.

Hood, C. (1976). *The Limits of Administration*, London: John Wiley & Sons.

Hood, C. (1986). *Administrative Analysis: An introduction to rules, enforcement and organisations*, Brighton: Wheatsheaf.

Hood, C. (1991). 'A Public Management For All Seasons?' *Public Administration*, Vol. 69, Spring, pp. 3–19.

Hood, C. and Jones, G. (1990). 'Progress in the Government's Next Steps Initiative', in Treasury and Civil Service Committee (1990). *Eighth Report: Progress in the Next Steps Initiative*, London: HMSO Appendix 6, pp. 78–83.

Hoskyns, Sir J. (1984). 'Conservatism is not enough', *Political Studies*, Vol. 55, No. 1, pp. 3–16.

Howells, D. (1981). 'Marks & Spencer and the Civil Service: A Comparison of Culture and Methods', *Public Administration*, Vol. 59, Autumn, pp. 337–52.

Humphris, P. (1990). 'Developing a Management Structure', in Fielding, P. and Berman, P.C. (eds), *Surviving in General Management: A Resource for Health Professionals*, Basingstoke: Macmillan.

Institute of Health Services Management (1988). *Report on Alternative Delivery and Funding of Health Services*, London: IHSM.

Isaac-Henry, K. (1987). 'Information Technology: A Case Study of a Local Authority – the City of Birmingham', *Teaching Public Administration*, Vol. VII, No. 2, pp. 10–26.

Isaac-Henry, K., Painter, C. and Barnes, C. (1993). *Management in the Public Sector*, London: Chapman Hall.

Jackson, P. (1982). *The Political Economy of Bureaucracy*, Oxford: Philip Allen.

Jackson, P. and Palmer, B. (1989). *First Steps in Measuring Performance in the Public Sector: A management guide*, London: Public Finance Foundation.

Jaques, E. (1991). 'In Praise of Hierarchy', in Thompson, G., Frances, J., Levacic, R. and Mitchell, J. (eds), *Markets, Hierarchies and Networks*, London: Sage with the Open University.

Jenkins, W.I. (1978). *Policy Analysis*, London: Martin Robertson.

Jenkins, W.I. and Gray, A. (1983). 'Bureaucratic Politics and Power: Developments in the Study of Bureaucracy', *Political Studies*, Vol. XXXI, pp. 177–93.

Johnson, G. and Scholes, K. (1993). *Exploring Corporate Strategy: text and cases*, London: Prentice-Hall.

Joint NHS Privatisation Research Unit (1990). *The NHS Privatisation Experience: Competitive tendering for NHS services*, London: NHSPRU.

Jones, K., Millard, F. and Twigg, L. (1990). 'The "right to know": government and information', in Savage, S.P. and Robins, L. (eds), *Public Policy under Thatcher*, London: Macmillan.

Jones, P.D. (1982). 'Public Services Management – An Elusive Concept', *Management in Government*, No. 3, pp. 154–62.

Jordan, G. (1992). 'Next Steps Agencies: from managing by command to managing by contract', *Aberdeen Papers in Accountancy, Finance and Management*, Aberdeen: Aberdeen University.

Kakabadse, A. (ed.) (1982). *People and Organisations*, Aldershot: Gower.

Kanter, R.M. (1983). *The Change Masters: corporate entrepreneurs at work*, London: Routledge.

Kanter, R.M. (1990). *When Giants Learn To Dance: Mastering the Challenges of Strategy, Management and Careers in the 1990s*, London: Unwin.

Kast, F.E. and Rosenzweig, J.E. (1985). *Organization and Management: A Systems and Contingency Approach*, New York: McGraw-Hill.

Keeling, D. (1972). *Management in Government*, London: Allen & Unwin.

Kemp, P. (1990). 'Can the Civil Service Adapt to Managing by Contract?, *Public Money & Management*, Autumn, pp. 25–31.

King's Fund Institute (1988). *Health Finance: assessing options*, London: King's Fund Institute.

Klein, R. (1989). *The Politics of the NHS* (2nd edition), Harlow: Longman.

Kleiner, B.H. and Corrigan, W.A. (1989). 'Understanding Organisational Change', *Leadership and Organization Development Journal*, Vol. 10, No. 3, pp. 25–31.

Körner, E. (1984). *A Report on the Collection and Use of Financial Information in the NHS* (Sixth report of the Steering Group on Health Services Information), London: DHSS.

Kooiman, J. and Eliassen, K.A. (eds) (1987). *Managing Public Organisations: Lessons from Contemporary European Experience*, London: Sage.

Kossen, S. (1983). *The Human Side of Organisations*, New York: Harper & Row.

Kristensen, O.P. (1987). 'Privatisation', in Kooiman, J. and Eliassen, K.A. (eds), *Managing Public Organisations: Lessons from Contemporary European Experience*, London: Sage.

Labour Party (1989). *Quality Streets*, London: Labour Party.

LAMSAC 86 (1986). *Managing to Compete*, Conference Proceedings.

Lavery, K. and Hume, C. (1991). 'Blending Planning and Pragmatism: Making Strategic Planning Effective in the 1990s', *Public Money & Management*, Winter, pp. 35–41.

Lawrence, P. and Santry, L. (1989). 'Motivating Staff and Raising Productivity in a DTI Division', *RIPA Report*, Summer, pp. 7–9.

Lawrence, P.R. and Lorsch, J.W. (1967). *Organization and Environment*, Harvard: Harvard University Press.

Layfield, Sir F. (1976). *Local Government Finance: Report of the Committee*, London: HMSO Cmnd 6453.

Leach, S. and Stewart, J. (eds) (1982). *Approaches in Public Policy*, London: Allen & Unwin.

Lee, R. and Lawrence, P. (1985). *Organisational Behaviour: Politics at Work*, London: Hutchinson.

Leftwich, A. (1984). Introduction: 'On the politics of Politics in Leftwich', A. (ed.), *What is Politics?* Oxford: Basil Blackwell, pp. 1–18.

Le Grand, J. and Bartlett, W. (eds) (1993), *Quasi Market and Social Policy*, Basingstoke: Macmillan.

Lewin, K. (1947). *Field Theory in Social Service*, New York: Harper.

Likierman, A. (1983). 'Applying Private Sector Techniques to the Public Sector', *London Business School Journal*, Winter, pp. 27–30.

Likierman, A. (1988). *Public Expenditure: Who really controls it and how*, London: Penguin.

Lindblom, C.E. (1959). 'The science of muddling through', *Public Administration Review*, Spring, pp. 79–88.

Lipsky, M. (1979). *Street Level Bureaucracy*, New York: Russell Sage Foundation.

Litterer, J.A. (ed.) (1969). *Organisations: Structure and Behaviour*, Vol. 1, New York: J. Wiley & Sons.

Livingstone, H. and Wilkie, R. (1981). 'Motivation and Performance among Civil Service Managers', *Public Administration*, Vol. 59, Summer, pp. 151–72.

Local Government Management Board (1993). *Managing Tomorrow: a panel of inquiry report*, Luton: Local Government Management Board. .

Local Government Management Board (1993). *Challenge and Change*, Luton: Local Government Management Board.

Local Government Training Board (1984). *Ethics in Local Government*, Luton: Local Government Training Board.

Local Government Training Board (1985). *Good Management in Local Government: Successful Practice and Action*, Luton: Local Government Training Board.

Local Government Training Board (1987a). *Politicians and Professionals: The Changing Management of Local Government*, Luton: Local Government Training Board.

Local Government Training Board (1987b). *The Leadership Audit*, Luton: Local Government Training Board.

Local Government Training Board (1988a). *Competition and Local Authorities: Organising for Competition*, Luton: Local Government Training Board.

Local Government Training Board (1988b). *Managing Tomorrow*, Luton: Local Government Training Board.

Local Government Training Board (1989). *New Management Trends*, Luton: Local Government Training Board.

Lovell, R. (1992). 'Citizen's Charter: the cultural challenge', *Public Administration*, Vol. 7, Autumn, pp. 395–404.

Lukes, S. (1974). *Power: A Radical View*, London: Macmillan.

McCann, J. and Galbraith, J.R. (1981). 'Interdepartmental Relations', in Nystrom, P.C. and Starbuck, W.H. (eds), *Handbook of Organizational Design*, Vol. 2, Oxford: Oxford University Press.

McGregor, D. (1960). *The Human Side of Enterprise*, New York: McGraw-Hill.

McKevitt, D. and Lawton, A. (1993). *The Manager, The Citizen, The Politician and Performance Measures*. Paper presented to 23rd annual PAC Conference, York University.

Major, J. (1989). *The Impact of General Economic Developments on Public Services Management*, Address to the Audit Commission, London: HMSO.

Maloney, W.A. and Richardson, J.J. (1992). 'Post-privatisation Regulation in Britain', *Politics*, Vol. 12, No. 2, pp. 14–20.

Malpass, P. and Murie, A. (1987). *Housing Policy and Practice*, London: Macmillan.

Management Matters (1990). *Next Steps Celebration*, No. 5, London: HMSO.

Manning, T. (1984). 'Management in the Civil Service: A Trainer's Views and Some Research Findings', *Management in Government*, No. 1, pp. 59–68.

Mansfield, R. (1986). *Company Strategy and Organisational Design*, London: Croom Helm.

March, J.G. and Simon, H.A. (1971). 'The Dysfunctions of Bureaucracy', in Pugh D.S. (ed.), *Organisation Theory: Selected Readings*, Harmondsworth: Penguin.

Mascarenhas, R.C. (1993). 'Building an Enterprise Culture in the Public Sector: Reform of the Public Sector in Australia, Britain and New Zealand', *Public Administration Review*, July/August, Vol. 53, No. 4, pp. 319–28.

Maslow, A.H. (1943). 'A Theory of Human Motivation', *Psychological Review*, Vol. 50, pp. 370–96.

Mayo, E. (1971). 'Hawthorne and the Western Electric Company', in Pugh, D.S. (ed.), *Organisation Theory*, Harmondsworth: Penguin.

Mellon, E. (1993). 'Executive Agencies: Leading Change from the Outside-in', *Public Money & Management*, April–June, pp. 25–31.

Merton, R.K. (1940). 'Bureaucratic Structure and Personality', *Social Forces*, No. 18, pp. 560–8.

Metcalfe, L. and Richards, S. (1990). *Improving Public Management*, London: Sage.

Michael, J. (1984/85). 'Confidentiality and the Civil Service', *Policy Studies*, Vol. 5, pp. 66–79.

Miller, W.L. (1986). 'Local Electoral Behaviour' in Widdicombe, D. *The Conduct of Local Authority Business*, Research Volume 3: The Local Government Elector, London: HMSO, pp. 101–72.

Mills, Wright C. (1956). *The Power Elite*, Oxford: Oxford University Press.

Mintzberg, H. (1975). 'The manager's job: folklore and fact', *Harvard Business Review*, Vol. 53, No. 4, pp. 49–61.

Mintzberg, H. (1983). *Structure in Fives: Designing Effective Organisations*, New Jersey: Prentice-Hall.

Mitchell, D. (1992). 'A Model of a Manager', *Community Care*, 26 November, pp. 24–5.

Moore, S.T. (1987). 'The Theory of Street-Level Bureaucracy: A Positive Critique', *Administration and Society*, Vol. 19, No. 1, pp. 74–94.

Morgan, G. (1986). *Images of Organisations*, Beverly Hills, Calif.: Sage.

Morphet, J. (1990). 'Women in Local Government: A case study', *Public Money & Management*, Spring, pp. 57–9.

Mullins, L.J. (1989). *Management and Organisational Behaviour*, London: Pitman.

Murlis, H. (1987). 'Performance-Related Pay in the Public Sector', *Public Money*, March, pp. 29–33.

Muskett, H. (1989). '1992 – The Impact on County Councils', *European Access*, August, pp. 17–19.

Nairne, Sir P. (1982). 'Some Reflections on Change', *Management in Government*, No. 2, pp. 71–82.

National Audit Office (1986). *The Financial Management Initiative*, London: HMSO HC 588 1985–6.

National Audit Office (1991). *Staff Appraisal in the Civil Service: a report by the Comptroller and Auditor General*, London: HMSO HC 174 1990–91.

National Council for Voluntary Action with Local Government Management Board (1993). *Building Effective Local Partnerships*, Luton: Local Government Management Board.

Newton, K. (1976). *Second City Politics*, Oxford: Clarendon Press.

Niskanen, W.A. (1971). *Bureaucracy and Representative Government*, New York: Aldine-Atherton.

Niskanen, W.A. (1973). *Bureaucracy: Servant or Master*, London: The Institute of Economic Affairs.

Northcote–Trevelyan (1854). Report on the Organisation of the Permanent Civil Service, reprinted in Vol. 1, Appendix B to the Fulton Report (1968), *Report of the Committee on the Civil Service*, Cmnd 3638.

Norton, P. (1985). *Parliament in the 1980s*, Oxford: Blackwell.

Office of Public Service and Science (1992). *The Next Steps Agencies: review 1992*, London: HMSO Cm 2111.

Opsahl, R.L. and Dunnette, M.D. (1966). 'The Role of Financial Compensation in Industrial Motivation', in Vroom, V.H. and Deci, E.L. (eds) (1992), *Management and Motivation*, Harmondsworth: Penguin.

Organisation for Economic Co-operation and Development (OECD) (1987). *Managing and Financing Urban Services*, Paris: OECD.

Organisation for Economic Co-operation and Development (OECD) (1992). *Public Management Development: update 1992*, Paris: OECD.

Ormond, D. (1993). 'Improving Government Performance' in *OECD Observer*.

Osborne, D. and Gaebler, T. (1992). *Reinventing Government: How the Entrepreneurial Spirit is Transforming the Public Sector*, Reading, Mass.: Addison-Wesley.

Page, E.C. (1985). *Political Authority and Bureaucratic Power: A Comparative Analysis*, Brighton: Wheatsheaf.

Painter, C. (1989). 'Leadership in the British Civil Service Revisited', *Teaching Public Administration*, Vol. IX, No. 1, pp. 1–9.

Painter, C. (1991). 'The Public Sector and Current Orthodoxies: Revitalisation or Decay?', *The Political Quarterly*, Vol. 62, pp. 75–89.

Painter, J. (1991). 'Compulsory Competitive Tendering in Local Government: the first round', *Public Administration*, Vol. 69, Summer, pp. 191–201.

Parker, R.A., Rose, A.G. and Taylor, J.A. (1986). *The Administration of Standards of Conduct in Local Government*, London: Charles Knight.

Parsons, H.M. (1978). 'What Caused the Hawthorne Effect? A Scientific Detective Story', *Administration and Society*, Vol. 10, No. 3, pp. 259–83.

Paton, R. and Cornforth, C. (1992). 'What is Different about Managing in Voluntary and Non-Profit Organisations' in Batsleer, J., Cornforth, C. and Paton, R. (eds), *Issues in Voluntary and Non-Profit Management*, Wokingham, England: Addison-Wesley.

Perrin, J. (1988). *Resource Management in the NHS*, Wokingham: Van Nostrand Reinhold.

Perrow, C. (1967). *Organizational Analysis: A Sociological View*, London: Tavistock.

Perry, J. and Kraemer, K.L. (eds) (1983). *Public Management: Public and Private Perspectives*, California: Mayfield.

Peters, A.R. (1990). 'West Germany', in Kingdom, J.E. (ed.), *The Civil Service in Liberal Democracies: An Introductory Survey*, London: Routledge.

Peters, T. (1988). *Thriving On Chaos*, London: Macmillan.

Peters, T. and Austin, N. (1986). *A Passion for Excellence: The Leadership Difference*, London: Fontana/Collins.

Peters, T.J. and Waterman, R.H. (1982). *In Search of Excellence*, New York: Harper & Row.

Pettigrew, A. (1988). 'Introduction: Researching Strategic Change', in Pettigrew, A. (ed.), *The Management of Strategic Change*, Oxford: Basil Blackwell.

Pettigrew, A., Ferlie, E. and McKee, L. (1992). *Shaping Strategic Change: Making Change in a Large Organisation – the case of the National Health Service*, London: Sage.

Pfeffer, J. (1981). *Power in Organisations*, Marshfield, Mass.: Pitman.

Phillip, A.B. (1989). 'The Public Sector and European Integration', *Public Money & Management*, Summer, pp. 41–5.

Pitt, D.C. and Smith, B.C. (1981). *Government Departments*, London: Routledge & Kegan Paul.

Pitt, D.C. and Smith, B.C. (eds) (1984). *The Computer Revolution in Public Administration: The impact of information technology on government*, Brighton: Wheatsheaf.

Pliatzky, Sir L. (1982). *Getting and Spending: Public Expenditure Employment and Inflation*, Oxford: Basil Blackwell.

Pliatzky, Sir L. (1988). 'Optimising the role of the Public Sector: Constraints and Remedial Policies', *Public Policy and Administration*, Vol. 3, No. 1, pp. 35–45.

Plowden (1961). *The Control of Expenditure*, London: HMSO.

Pollitt, C. (1985). 'Measuring Performance', *Policy and Politics*, Vol. 13, No. 1, pp. 1–15.

Pollitt, C. (1993a). *Managerialism and The Public Services* (2nd edn), Oxford: Blackwell.

Pollitt, C. (1993b). 'The Struggle For Quality: the case of the National Health Service', *Policy and Politics*, Vol. 21, No. 3, pp. 161–70.

Ponting, C. (1985). *The Right to Know*, London and Sydney: Sphere.

Ponting, C. (1986). *Whitehall: Tragedy and Farce*, Hamish Hamilton.

Porter, L.W. and Lawler, E.E. (1968). *Managerial Attitudes and Performance*, Homewood, Illinois: Irwin Dorsey.

Potter, C. (1989). 'What Is Culture: And Can It Be Useful for Organisational Change Agents?', *Leadership and Organization Development Journal*, Vol. 10, No. 3, pp. 17–24.

Prime Minister (1991). *The Citizen's Charter: Raising the Standard*, London: HMSO Cm 1599.

Public Accounts Committee (1989). *The Next Steps Initiative*, London: HMSO.

Pugh, D.S. (ed.) (1984). *Organisation Theory: Selected Readings*, Harmondsworth: Penguin.

Pugh, D.S. (1993). 'Understanding and Managing Organizational Change', in Mabey, C. and Mayon-White, B. (eds), *Managing Change* (2nd edn), London: Paul Chapman Publishing in association with the Open University.

Rainey, H.G. (1983). 'Public Agencies and Private Firms', *Administration and Society*, Vol. 15, No. 2, pp. 207–42.

Redcliffe-Maud (1974). Prime Minister's Committee on Local Government Rules of Conduct: *Report of the Committee*, London: HMSO Cmnd 5636.

Rhodes, R.A.W. (1981). *Control and Power in Central-Local Relations*, Farnborough: Gower.

Rhodes, R.A.W. (1988). *Beyond Westminster and Whitehall: The Sub-Central Government of Britain*, London: Allen & Unwin.

Rhodes, R.A.W. and Midwinter, A.F. (1980). *Corporate Management: The New Conventional Wisdom in British Local Government*, Glasgow: University of Strathclyde – Studies in Public Policy No. 59.

Richards, S. (1989). 'Managing People in the Civil Service', *Public Money & Management*, Autumn, pp. 29–33.

Ridley, F.F. (1983). 'Career Service: A Comparative Perspective on Civil Service Promotion', *Public Administration*, Vol. 62(2), pp. 179–96.

Ridley, P. (1989). 'Ridley Roughs of Quality Plans' *Local Government Chronicle*, 14 April 1989.

RIPA (1985). 'The Search for Excellence in the Public Sector'. *RIPA Report*, Vol. 6, No. 4, pp. 4–5.

RIPA (1988). 'New Approaches to Public Sector Staffing', *RIPA Report*, Vol. 9, No. 3, pp. 8–9.

Roberts, G. (1989). 'Impact of 1992 Starts to Bite', *Municipal Journal*, 3 February, p. 14.

Rodrigues, J. (1992). 'Curtain up on performance', *Local Government Chronicle*, 20 November.

Roeber, R.J.C. (1973). *The Organisation in a Changing Environment*, Reading, Mass.: Addison-Wesley.

Roethlisberger, F.J. and Dickson, W.J. (1939). *Management and the Worker*, Cambridge, Mass: Harvard University Press.

Rose, R. (1987). *Ministers and Ministries: A Functional Approach*, Oxford: Clarendon Press.

Salaman, G. (1992). 'Right enough to be dangerously wrong: an analysis of the *In Search of Excellence* phenomenon', in Salaman, G., Cameron, S., Hamblin, H., Iles, P., Mabey, C. and Thompson, K. (eds), *Human Resource Strategies*, London: Sage.

Salmon (1976). Royal Commission on Standards of Conduct in Public Life: *Report*, London: HMSO Cmnd 6524.

Savage, S.P. and Robins, L. (eds) (1990). *Public Policy under Thatcher*, London: Macmillan.

Schein, E.H. (1987). *Organisational Culture and Leadership*, San Francisco: Jossey-Bass.

Schmidt, M.G. (1983). 'The growth of the tax state: industrial democracies, 1950–1978', in Taylor, C.L. (ed.), *Why Governments Grow: Measuring public sector size*, London: Sage.

Schmitter, P.S. (1979). 'Modes of interest intermediation and models of societal change in Western Europe', *Comparative Political Studies*, Vol. 10(1), pp. 61–90.

Schumpeter, J. (1976). *Capitalism, Socialism and Democracy*, London: Allen & Unwin.

Sedgemore, B. (1980). *The Secret Constitution*, London: Hodder & Stoughton.

Seebohm, F. (1967). *Report of the Committee on Local Authority and Allied Personal Social Services*, London: HMSO Cmnd 3703.

Self, P. (1975). *Econocrats and the Policy Process: The politics and philosophy of cost-benefit analysis*, London: Macmillan.

Self, P. (1977). *Administrative Theories and Politics: An enquiry into the structure and processes of modern government*, London: Allen & Unwin.

Selznick, P. (1957). *Leadership in Administration*, New York: Harper & Row.

Sharplin, A. (1985). *Strategic Management*, New York: McGraw-Hill.

Sheehy, Sir P. (1993). *Inquiry into Police Responsibilities and Rewards*, Vol. 1, London: HMSO, Cm 2280-I.

Silverman, D. (1970). *The Theory of Organisations*, London: Heinemann.

Simon, H.A. (1976). *Administrative Behaviour: A Study of Decision-Making Processes in Administrative Organisation*, London: Collier Macmillan.

Simon, H.A., Smithburg, D.W. and Thompson, V.A. (1950). *Public Administration*, New York: Alfred A. Knopf.

Sisson, C.H. (1959). *The Spirit of Administration*, London: Faber & Faber.

Skeffington, A.M. (1969). *People and Planning: Report of the Committee on Public Participation in Planning*, London: HMSO.

Sketcher, C. (1993). 'Involvement and Empowerment in Local Public Services', *Public Money and Management*, July–September, pp. 13–20.

Smith, B.C. (1988). *Bureaucracy and Political Power*, Brighton: Wheatsheaf.

Smith, B.C. (1985). *Decentralisation: The Territorial Dimension of the State*, London: Allen and Unwin.

Smith, G. (1981). 'Discretionary Decision-Making in Social Work', in Adler, M. and Asquith, S. (eds), *Discretion and Welfare*, London: Heinemann Educational Books.

Stanyer, J. and Smith, B. (1976). *Administering Britain*, London: Fontana.

Steers, R.M. and Porter, L.W. (1979). *Motivation and Work Behaviour*, New York: McGraw-Hill.

Stephenson, T. (1985). *Management: A Political Activity*, London: Macmillan.

Stewart, D.W. and Carson, G.D. (1983). *Organizational Behavior and Public Management*, New York and Basel: Marcel Dekker.

Stewart, J.D. (1980). 'From growth to standstill', in Wright, M. (ed.), *Public Spending Decisions*, London: Allen & Unwin.

Stewart, J.D. (1986). *The New Management of Local Government*, London: Allen & Unwin.

Stewart, J.D. (1989a). 'Management in the Public Domain', *Local Government Studies*, September/October, pp. 9–15.

Stewart, J.D. (1989b). 'In Search of Curriculum for the Public Sector', *Management Education and Development*, Vol. 20, Part 3, pp. 168–75.

Stewart, J.D. (1990). 'Local Government: new thinking on neglected issues', *Public Money & Management*, Summer, pp. 59–62.

Stewart, J.D. (1992). *Accountability to the Public*, European Policy Forum for British and European Market Studies.

Stewart J.D. (1993). 'The Limitations of Government by Contract', *Public Money & Management*, July–September, pp. 7–12.

Stewart, J.D. and Clarke, M. (1987). 'The Public Service Orientation: Issues and Dilemmas', *Public Administration*, Vol. 65, No. 2, pp. 161–77.

Stewart, J.D. and Ranson, S. (1988). 'Management in the Public Domain', *Public Money & Management*, Spring/Summer, pp. 13–19.

Stewart, J.D. and Walsh, K. (1990). *The Search for Quality*, Luton: Local Government Training Board.

Stewart, J.D. and Walsh, K. (1992). 'Change in the Management of Public Services', *Public Administration*, Winter, pp. 499–518.

Stewart, R. (1985). *The Reality of Organisations*, London: Macmillan.

Stewart, R. (1989). *Leading in the NHS: A Practical Guide*, London: Macmillan.

Stoker, G. (1988). *The Politics of Local Government*, London: Macmillan.

Stoker, G. (1989a). 'Urban Development Corporations: A review', *Regional Studies*, Vol. 23, No. 2, pp. 159–73.

Stoker, G. (1989b). 'Creating a Local Government for a Post-Fordist Society: The Thatcher Project', in Stoker, G. and Stewart, J. (eds), *The Future of Local Government*, London: Macmillan.

Stoker, G. and Wilson, D. (1986). 'Intra-Organisational Politics in Local Authorities: Towards a New Approach', *Public Administration*, Vol. 64, No. 3, pp. 285–302.

Stoker, G., Wedgewood-Oppenheim, F. and Davies, M. (1988). *The Challenge of Change in Local Government: A Study of Organisational and Management Innovation in the 1980s*, Birmingham: INLOGOV.

Storey, J. (1989). 'Human Resource Management in the Public Sector', *Public Money & Management*, Autumn, pp. 19–24.

Storey, J. and Sisson, K. (1990). 'Making Managers in Britain: A progress report', *Public Money & Management*, Spring, pp. 9–15.

Stringer, J. and Richardson, J. (1980). 'Making the Political Agenda', *Parliamentary Affairs*, Vol. 33, pp. 23–39.

Strong, P. and Robinson, J. (1990). *The NHS – under new management*, Milton Keynes: Open University.

Szymanski, S. and Wilkins, S. (1992). 'Competitive Tendering: lessons from the public sector', *Business Strategy Review*, Autumn, pp. 101–13.

Taylor, C.L. (1983). 'Introduction: multiple approaches to measurement and explanation', in Taylor, C.L. (ed.), *Why Governments Grow: Measuring public sector size*, London: Sage.

Taylor, F.W. (1967). *Principles of Scientific Management*, New York and London: W.W. Norton.

Taylor, J. and Rose, A. (1985). 'Debating Ethics in Government', *RIPA Report*, Vol. 6, No. 1, pp. 4–5.

Theakston, K. (1990). 'Labour, Thatcher and the Future of the Civil Service', *Public Policy and Administration*, Vol. 5, No. 1, pp. 44–57.

Thompson, D. (1986). *Coalition and Decision-Making within Health Districts*, University of Birmingham Health Services Management Centre: Research Report 23.

Thompson, D.F. (1983). 'Bureaucracy and Democracy', in Duncan, G. (ed.), *Democratic Theory and Practice*, Cambridge: Cambridge University Press.

Toffler, A. (1970). *Future Shock*, London: Bodley Head.

Tomkins, C. and Colville, I. (1989). 'Managing for Greater Innovation in the Civil Service: Customs & Excise', *Public Money & Management*, Winter, pp. 15–20.

Travers, T. (1986). *The Politics of Local Government Finance*, London: Allen & Unwin.

Travers, T. (1989). 'The Threat to the Autonomy of Elected Local Government', *The Political Quarterly*, pp. 3–20.

Treasury and Civil Service Committee (1982). Third Report: *Efficiency and Effectiveness in the Civil Service*, London: HMSO HC 236-I.

Treasury and Civil Service Committee (1990). Eighth Report: *Progress in the Next Steps Initiative*, London: HMSO HC 481.

Treasury and Civil Service Committee (1993). Sixth Report: *The Role of the Civil Service: Interim Report*, London: HMSO.

Tyson, S. (1990). 'Turning Civil Servants into Managers', *Public Money & Management*, Spring, pp. 27–30.

Vickers, Sir G. (1965). *The Art of Judgement: A Study of Policy-Making*, London: Chapman & Hall.

Vroom, V.H. (1964). *Work and Motivation*, New York: John Wiley.

Vroom, V.H. and Deci, E.L. (eds) (1970). *Management and Motivation*, Harmondsworth: Penguin.

Walsh, K. (1991). *Competitive Tendering for Local Authority Services: initial experiences*, London: HMSO.

Warmington, A. (1983). 'Organisation Theory and Health Service Administration', in Allen, D. and Hughes, J.A. (eds), *Management for Health Service Administrators*, London: Pitman.

Wass, Sir D. (1983). 'The Public Service in Modern Society', *Public Administration*, Vol. 61, No. 1. pp. 7–20.

Watson, T.J. (1987). *Work, Sociology and Industry*, London: Routledge & Kegan Paul.

Weber, M. (1971). 'Legitimate Authority and Bureaucracy', in Pugh, D.S. (ed.), *Organisation Theory: Selected Readings*, Harmondsworth: Penguin.

Wedgewood-Oppenheim, F. (1982). 'Monitoring and the planning cycle', in Leach, S. and Stewart, J. (eds), *Approaches in Public Policy*, London: Allen & Unwin.

Widdicombe, D. (1986). *Committee of Inquiry into the Conduct of Local Authority Business*, London: HMSO Cmnd 9797.

Wigley, D. (1989). 'Performance Review, Motivation and Organisational Culture', *Health Services Management*, December, pp. 252–5.

Wilding, R.W.L. (1979). 'The Professional Ethic of the Administrator', *Management Services in Government*, Vol. 34, No. 4, pp. 181–6.

Willcocks, L. (1992). 'The manager as technologist', in Willcocks, L. and Harrow, J. (eds), *Rediscovering Public Services Management*, Maidenhead: McGraw-Hill.

Willcocks, L. and Harrow, J. (eds) (1992). *Rediscovering Public Services Management*, Maidenhead: McGraw-Hill.

Wilmott, P. (ed.) (1987). *Local Government Decentralisation and Community*, London: Policy Studies Institute.

Wilson, J.Q. (1989). *Bureaucracy: What Government Agencies Do and Why They Do It*, New York: Basic Books.

Wilson, J. and Hinton, P. (1993). *Public Services and the 1990s: Issues in Public Service Finance and Management*, Eastham: Tudor.

Woodward, J. (1958). *Management and Technology*, London: HMSO.

Wright, P. (1987). *Spycatcher: The candid autobiography of a senior intelligence officer*, New York: Viking.

Wright, P.L. and Taylor, D.S. (1984). *Improving Leadership Performance*, London: Prentice-Hall.

Young, H. and Sloman, A. (1984). *But, Chancellor: An inquiry into the Treasury*, London: BBC.

INDEX